THE POWER CODE

ALSO BY

KATTY KAY AND CLAIRE SHIPMAN

Womenomics

The Confidence Code

The Confidence Code for Girls

The Confidence Code for Girls Journal

Living the Confidence Code

THE POWER CODE

MORE JOY
LESS EGO
MAXIMUM IMPACT
FOR WOMEN
(AND EVERYONE)

KATTY KAY &
CLAIRE SHIPMAN

HARPER
BUSINESS
An Imprint of HarperCollins*Publishers*

HarperCollins books may be purchased for educational, business, or sales promotional use. For information, please email the Special Markets Department at SPsales@harpercollins.com.

FIRST EDITION

Designed by Bonni Leon-Berman

Library of Congress Cataloging-in-Publication Data has been applied for.

ISBN 978-0-06-334135-7

BUSINESS & ECONOMICS

ScoutAutomatedPrintCode

2 4 6 8 10 9 7 5 3 1

Printed in India by Thomson Press India Ltd

FSC
www.fsc.org
MIX
Paper from responsible sources
FSC® C010615

This book is produced from independently certified FSC® paper to ensure responsible forest management.

To Tom

With love and excitement for adventures still to come

To Kati Jo

My ultimate source of power

CONTENTS

INTRODUCTION

There's a generally accepted narrative, in our collective minds, that the "progress" of women through the ages looks a lot like that illustrated timeline of the evolution and ascent of man. Gradually we've hit the midway point, Homo Erectus, having straightened up to become less burdened by loads of laundry, toddlers pulling incessantly on every part of our bodies, and the basic, historical oppression of being a woman. With each passing century, so the story goes, our ever-more-modern women begin to look more confident and assured, more, well, like men. Perhaps, as we stretch out along the timeline, rising up, we wield first a plow, then a placard of protest, and then a briefcase. Today's Woman stands triumphantly, just under the glass ceiling, with a sledgehammer in hand. Power virtually radiates off this final female likeness; she is poised to join the pinnacle of the existing hierarchy.

In this telling, women's progress follows a linear path, and the logic is clear: beyond the glass ceiling lies a members-only club we desperately want to join, based on a notion of power that was created by men, for men. The journey isn't portrayed as entirely rosy, of course; it's often acknowledged that much of the trek has been unfair, with some recognition of opportunities lost, slights endured, and barriers forcibly broken. But for too long, this depiction—that path, that goal—has been taken as a universal truth.

Humans love that kind of tale, one of clear aspiration and straightforward triumph. But that power story is false, a fable, and not one, frankly, of such virtue, one containing such an exemplary moral lesson, that its misrepresentations can be overlooked.

As we know, and *you* know, our history is so much more complex. A more realistic depiction would have to account for the many moments when we weren't so stooped or stymied, when we were warriors or queens or priestesses, and it would have to examine in great detail what allowed for that, what brought about that short-lived glory. We'd have to pause, for a long time, at various moments in history, and consider the regressive impact of the many dictates handed down on behalf of a "higher power"; Western women in the Middle Ages, for example, might acknowledge that St. Augustine and his Christian brethren did them no favors. We'd have to take a clear-eyed look at the substantially different and more arduous journey women of color have experienced along that timeline, one that continues today. And we'd have to wonder why, despite our heroic progress in the nineteenth and twentieth centuries, when women decided that the only way in was to openly march and fight, most of us are still gazing out, impatiently, at a sea of glass. Why aren't we there yet? How long should this trip take, really? And if we have to break glass to get in, is this the right destination in the first place?

It's not for lack of trying, by the way. We've made Herculean efforts to squeeze ourselves into the world men built. Some of us just felt lucky to be there at all and didn't want to cause a fuss. Others, more confident that they fully deserved a place in the room, still realized the futility of trying to fundamentally change things. We couldn't expect to overturn centuries of habit in a few decades. So we worked harder than the men, played by their rules, and hid the photos of our kids. We even dressed like them.

Our reward? Minimal impact. The number of women in parliaments, C-suites, and boardrooms has stayed depressingly stagnant. Even as the new century ushered in one well-funded diversity program after another, said diversity has been numerically lackluster and woefully one-dimensional. The women who have benefited have been overwhelmingly white, with little effort made to knock down the particularly stubborn barriers faced by women of color.

All of this puts a fine point on a question that has heavily animated our reporting and research: Is the version of power we've been fighting so hard to acquire even fit for purpose? Fit for *our* purposes?

It's certainly blind to the realities of women's lives and dismissive of the real strengths and values we have always used to, well, get shit done. And getting shit done, shit that keeps society functioning, is how we women use our power, whether we are running the International Monetary Fund or getting legislation passed to support private toilets for girls or hauling a minivan full of kids to after-school activities while juggling a Zoom call at a stoplight.

A man at rest, who seems to have *attained*, is the classic portrait of the power endgame. For women, power more often lives in the blur of our action, in the residue of our value-laden and emotionally attuned decision making, in the cracks of our endless efforts to stitch schedules, families, enterprises, humanity together against life's centrifugal forces.

In these pages you will find an alternative story about power. A new origin story, if you will. Imagine a decidedly different version of the "ascent of woman." One in which mid-timeline, she straightens up and sets off in a different direction, on a winding path, an adventure not constrained by a preexisting ceiling. It can still be a glorious march of progress—why not, after all?—but perhaps our Modern Woman is sporting a slouchy shoulder bag for a while, and then a diaper bag or, even, yes, a grocery bag on occasion. She zigs and zags a bit, trading running shoes for heels, then flats or flip-flops, athletic gear for posh jackets, jeans for a stellar dress. That is all negotiable. But, most critically, she is not marching off alone on her expedition. She is constantly encountering others on her path, reaching out to friends, community members, and children, stopping along the way to consult, advise, laugh, parent, dance even, and, of course, to listen. It's a complicated image, and, yes, we are larding it up just a touch to make it that way. But it also might strike you, as it does us, as a new model of power that feels more hopeful, generative, and realistic—a model that plays to women's strengths rather than against them.

The journey we're envisioning here is impossible to reduce to a simple progression from primate to superhuman. Also, to state the obvious (because we have to start stating the obvious, over and over, loudly, if we want things to change), our instincts have always been assets—they just haven't been accurately valued or quantified before. But with a different language, a dynamic framework, and our collective voices—let's call it a new power code—we can reimagine our lives.

In fact, our version of power isn't new; it's just been largely buried, biding its time. These days, if you look carefully, you find it increasingly on the loose, unfolding all around us. There's the senior European leader who watched her daughter-in-law juggle two infants and had an epiphany about how closely the demands of motherhood track the demands of corporate life. (What working mother doesn't know this?) But get this—she actually changed her hiring requirements to start valuing the time candidates had spent as stay-at-home mothers. There's the finance executive who made it her mission to stamp out yelling and bad behavior from star economists in order to create a more collegial atmosphere. There's the leadership team of a regional bank in Alabama that knew it had to change and spent *a year* just listening and talking to people who weren't only straight white men. And there's the sports boss who gave us a lightbulb moment, arguing that when people bring their whole selves to work—problems, idiosyncrasies, personalities and all—that's an advantage, not a complication. Women already have the makings for a new power code; we just need to tap into it.

This is a good place to note a number of important things. As we have always acknowledged in our writing, research, and presentations, while we speak about "men" and "women," all of us, as humans, fall on a spectrum in terms of tendencies, instincts, and behavior. Some women might feel quite comfortable leading in a way that resembles a "male" style, and vice versa. But the data and studies are clear that much of what we write about and observe breaks broadly along gender lines, and so we believe it's meaningful to think and write in those terms.

Moreover, for the purposes of this book, while we write about "women," we certainly hope that most people will find something that resonates here, especially those who've ever felt themselves to be treated as "other," and excluded from traditional power hierarchies. We appreciate the need for more research to be conducted and more books to be written to address issues particular to all groups, but that's beyond the scope of this one.

We also write, as we mention in the authors' note, from our own lived experience as two white women with decades of work experience, who have benefited from considerable access to traditional power structures. Aware of the privileges and limitations of that point of view, we've relied on our experience and skills as reporters, speaking to dozens of women of all ages, races, and backgrounds, some in the United States, many in other countries, too. We have woven their stories into our research, and attempted to find the threads that connect us as women, while recognizing, where we can, disparate experiences.

Indeed, our experiences can be incredibly, distressingly, distinct: even the phrase "women of color," doesn't fully reflect the range of unique challenges different women face. Just one example: As a group, women are more likely than men to experience all levels of microaggressions. But Black women are more likely to have leaders question their competence at work, whereas Asian and Latina women are more likely to be asked "where are you really from."

It's worth noting, too, that our focus in this book is primarily on power as it is currently manifested at work—power that would give women an equal voice in leading organizations and societies. But we also look at how that is linked to power distribution at home. Obviously, myriad other issues affect the distribution, availability, and appeal of power. The impact that race, discrimination, and socioeconomic status have on workplace power, both historically and in the present tense, needs to be examined in greater detail. Economic wealth, and the ability to create it over generations, clearly matters.

In short, we don't presume to speak for every woman, and yet . . . we hope to point out the commonalities in these lived experiences—yours and ours—so that we can find more joy and create more impact when we raise our voices together.

Why does power seem still so elusive for women? This was our animating question, and, hunting for answers, we interviewed academics who've studied power over the centuries, neuroscientists who examine what power does to our brains, women who have power, and those who don't. We've spoken to psychologists about power dynamics between men and women, and business leaders who are genuinely trying to change the equation. We've looked at the hurdles that block our paths in companies and, just as importantly, at what's holding us back in our home lives. We actually didn't expect to dig into marriages, but as one researcher put it, it turns out that what's keeping many women from power isn't bosses. It's husbands.

We've also interviewed plenty of men who are longing for

change, for a more purposeful blend of work and family, who feel trapped in a box where they have to play by the old power rules and wear the threadbare costume of primary breadwinner.

We've been power tripping, in short, and it's been exhilarating, frustrating, and often confusing, so much so that we've paused en route multiple times to remind ourselves *why*—why undertake this confounding exploration?

That *why* is our North Star, and it always gets us back to work. What is to be gained? Nothing short of a better existence for the world. We won't be coy about our ideology: we are writing this book because we firmly believe the world would flourish with more women in power—more women CEOs, more women generals, more women board directors, and, yes, more women presidents. We need women leading everywhere, in every sphere. Women of all races, religions, backgrounds—millions of women running things. Fifty percent of the world's leaders should be women, if not a heavy majority. We simply can't ignore the mounting evidence that the world works better for everybody when women lead alongside men.[1]

For that to happen, we first need to *want* power, to like it, to own it—indeed to enjoy it. The research suggests that, at the moment, many of us don't. How can we get women comfortable with that desire, while getting those who rule the current hierarchy comfortable with our version of it?

We have spent the past decade and a half reporting on and writing about women and work, women and work-life balance, women and confidence, girls and confidence—all critical to the equation. Initially driven by our own struggle to balance home and work, kids and career, we started to write about workplaces, focusing on changes needed to make them work for women documenting innovations. As writers and speakers, we turned our expertise in women's leadership into a second career. That gave us hope, as we witnessed organizations doing it well, with creative strategies around diversity, equity, and inclusion (DEI), pay equity, quotas, and a more holistic sense of work and life.

But it's not enough. At every rung of our rise, women have stalled. And summoning power—calling out what we need to make our version work instead of folding ourselves into an unfit system—is the next frontier.

Moreover, we need respect and compensation for the power we already have and wield in the world, corporate, kitchen, and otherwise—power that hasn't been historically seen as power at all. The stakes are too high. We need to be at least half of the equation. We won't be satisfied until we reach that goal—nor should you.

What, exactly, is wrong with the current power code? Are we really at a halt, you might wonder, or doing so badly? A superficial look around the world might give you false optimism. Jacinda Ardern, until recently the prime minister of New Zealand, crafted the most diverse cabinet her nation had ever seen and made herself a worldwide role model for Covid management.[2] Sanna Marin, the thirty-seven-year-old prime minister of Finland, is part of a coalition government dominated by women in their thirties. Tsai Ing-wen, the first woman president of Taiwan, artfully mixes soft and hard power, pushing green energy one day, standing up to China the next. The number of women who are heads of state and government is on the rise, according to the most recent McKinsey & Company study, and researchers found that these women are stronger and better leaders than men.

Yet, as we dug into the subject, we also saw those same studies we just cited ring with ambivalence. McKinsey notes that "the state of women hangs in the balance." Sure, some metrics are better, but barely. The United Nations points out that the average number of women in government around the world is still only 25 percent. Ardern, a political star, stepped down citing professional burnout. As we write this, twenty-seven women are elected heads of government or state, which seems a respectable number, but at the current rate of change, gender equality for female heads of state won't be reached for 130 years. Um, what? That's way too long for our liking.

How about the everyday, infuriating, professional hurdles we all recognize? There's the woman who told us she was fed up with being asked to find the "perfect" woman for a job, because, of course, nobody ever qualified. What was wrong with a mediocre woman, she wondered, given that mediocre men had been succeeding around her for decades? There's the perfectly nice, "liberal" man who told us how excited he was that his daughter was going to a women's leadership conference, but who, in the very same conversation, complained that he couldn't get that board seat he knew he deserved because diversity programs have gone too far and, well, they only want women nowadays. Or the C-suite executive of a multinational company whose male board chair critiqued her outfit after a performance onstage at a board meeting. Or the almost partner lawyer who knows that part of the "checklist" for her ascension is a stint overseas, which she can't make happen given her family situation.

There were also all the women who admitted to us in hushed voices, that, yes, they were indeed the main breadwinner in their family, but please, would we just not use their real names. They didn't want to make their husbands feel even worse. There were the husbands who swore they would be willing to do half the household chores and half the child care duties, if only their wives weren't so darn good at it themselves.

We kept picking up fragments of a jumbled puzzle. It took us a long while to piece them together and realize these weren't trivial expressions of frustration that we should stoically ignore. No, each one of those stories points to the very reasons women don't have power. All of this came to us by way of reporting and conversations, but is backed up by the trends we found in the current academic and scientific research.[3] Men do exaggerate what they contribute at home. Neither women nor men want to own up to women earning more than their partners. Women are routinely passed over for promotion (especially Black and Latina women, because they lack an "intangible" quality or don't satisfy an opaque checklist).

We've felt this friction deeply ourselves. We've both been part of the power hierarchy in a multitude of ways over the years. Yet we've still struggled to fit ourselves into prescribed male molds in order to progress in our professional lives. We've experienced, as younger women, the sort of treatment that would certainly shock us now: we've been told to stop being so emotional, to calm down, to change our hair, our clothes, our wrinkles, our voices, our style—basically ourselves. We've brushed off inappropriate and unwelcome invitations from superiors; we've sat through questionable, cringe-worthy talks with other senior journalists, including one who refused to put a newsmaking interview we did on his program because, we were told by his producer, he was envious he hadn't done it. Well, it's the media business, we always thought. It's not like normal work. A ridiculous standard, of course, we now understand.

We're still seeing it happen. On an executive committee recently, one of us witnessed a male executive calling his Asian American female partner "crazy," *in front of the whole group*, for doing nothing more than behaving exactly as men always have—asking tough questions about the business. In a different industry, we saw the impact of one male leader exaggerating success and ignoring the welfare of employees to such an extent that the entire enterprise collapsed. We could go on.

For those who have always had it, power is intoxicating, but for many of the rest of us, today's power is toxic—not only for women and others who don't have it, but for men, too. The zero-sum nature of the predominant brand of power encourages narcissism, a lack of empathy, and emotional repression. We won't name names, but we know you can. No wonder many of us, of all ages, report that we don't want it. For most women, it demands that we bend, shape, shift, and amputate large chunks of our personal lives, our identity, and our instincts just to keep working, especially if we want to rise through the ranks.

This shouldn't be the only path for women, or for anyone.

We're far from alone in feeling uneasy about celebrating, or even simply accepting, this brand of power. There's a heightened level of discord in the drive for gender parity. Women have told us they are now nursing a steady diet of awareness, disbelief, and open animosity toward behavior they once tolerated, particularly women of color, who suffer a much higher rate of micro-aggressions than white women.

It's as though we've all tuned in to a different frequency. The last five years, with the rise of the #MeToo movement and Black Lives Matter, have awakened us to the fact that somebody's got to start calling BS more broadly.

Deepa Purushothaman, a former corporate executive and author of *The First, the Few, the Only*, has had hundreds of conversations with women of color over the last three years who believe that, despite recent changes, the system remains especially skewed against them.

"The women I work with are realizing that they get to the seat, but they still don't get the support they need. They don't feel powerful. Women are looking for a new definition of power."

Today's workplace, in short, is a sea of agitation, resentment, backlash, and burnout, with an alarming dose of ambivalence and anger thrown in, and the fallout extends to our home lives and bedrooms. Layer in Covid, #MeToo, Black Lives Matter, sexist, populist political movements, and nationwide social unrest—we are unmoored from the offices we once knew, with a more clear-eyed view about which structures of power do and don't support women, and all of us "others" who aren't cisgendered white men.

And what about those men? They too feel easily aggrieved and often don't hide it, annoyed because they don't really understand the new rules. For men, power has often meant making quick, unilateral decisions, employing equal parts charm and bullying to a respectful, unquestioning audience. Well, that doesn't really work today.

We are up against centuries of entrenched privilege, but it's not just that we're trying to take something men have always had, which would be a struggle in itself—nobody likes to lose. No, we are doing something far more disruptive. We are trying to change the very understanding of what it means to have power—who should have it, what the point of it is, and how to use it.

The good news, because there is some, requires a big step back. We're feeling heightened friction *because of* our progress. Indeed, we are in the late stages of a power transfer (however agonizingly slow it feels to us) and we're experiencing a collision of sensibilities as more women, more confidently, speak out and move into leadership positions. Mismatched expectations and misaligned views are having it out on power's cutting edge; it's a battle as much about values, stereotypes, and a bunch of other human proclivities as it is about power itself. It's about what kind of world we want.

Women just don't see power, or use it, the way men do. That fact, the central premise of our book, feels surprisingly intuitive—but it has profound consequences. More specifically, we tend to think "power to," while they think "power over." This is no tomayto/tomahto situation. The different mindset has affected our ability to rise, but what we're all witnessing now is an open clash between old and new, between two different concepts of power. A "reprogramming" of the power code is under way, and the new version has been mostly deployed surreptitiously, but deployed it has been, and it will continue to be, even more unabashedly, because no amount of molding us to the man-made version seems to dislodge our instincts to use power differently. Now it's time for it to see the light of day, to get its due, and, most importantly, to start collecting a paycheck.

It's a matter of time, in any event. "Do I think a different power style is imperative? Absolutely," one powerful Wall Street woman told us. "Our clients, and our juniors, are demanding it."

Our new code unearthed a range of abstruse questions, none of which match the tidy (though not necessarily unhelpful) power advice typically handed out to women—Learn golf! Talk first! Embrace bragging! Get a sponsor not a mentor!

Instead we grapple with what power really is, as a commodity, and what it does to our brains. We explore how to get more of it, and, ideally, not just more of the old concoction, but a fresh brew. We examine whether it has to be as corrosive and corrupting as so much of the research indicates it is. Are women immune to that effect in some way? And why are women still so ambivalent about power? Are we right to be? We dig into the hidden workplace hurdles for us to understand whether they are actually a product of men just not wanting to share, or of something deeper, of our different conceptions about power, and we ask whether the post-Covid chaos and political upheaval might allow for a massive reboot.

We look at our home lives, and explore why some women still hide their earning power, and whether we can ever really have power outside of the home if we don't get more help with pots and pans and planning inside of it. We look at what happens to marriages when expectations change and a wife suddenly becomes more successful than her spouse. And actually, how about all of that other stuff, *life* essentially, that falls outside work, and has always required "balancing" or solving, as if it's an annoying issue only women are really qualified to deal with? How is it that something so essential—the work of raising children, organizing families, and nurturing human relationships—caring for the world, essentially—hasn't been valued the same way "men's work" has? And we ask, as well, what of the men? If they can understand the benefits of sharing power, of a new conceptualization of power, surely it will make their lives richer, too.

We've taken a hard look at power, the way it has been, the way it is, and the way it can be. We now see the outline of new power emerging everywhere we look. Once you see things in a new way, you can't unsee it. That's what we're hoping you'll find in this book.

We also hope you will see that power is well within our control. There are things we can each do, individually and immediately, to get more power and even change the power we already have. It might be saying no to unpaid labor, speaking up on behalf of someone else, or asking your company, your colleagues, or your husband or partner to start to share and use power differently; there are things we can do to be part of this power shift.

We certainly want this book to change organizations, companies, political bodies—all areas of professional life where women of all backgrounds have traditionally been excluded. We believe your workplace, and our world, will be better, more inclusive, and more effective after a rethink on how power should be wielded. So yes, it is a manifesto for societal change. But it is also very much a guidebook for each of you. You are the foundation of that change, and ultimately, we want more women in positions of power so we hope this book gives you the means to get there. Throughout the book we turn the research into tools you can use every day to understand and muster the power you already have, and to see what you can do to get more of it. In short, we want this book to change society, but we also want it to change your life—to give you more impact, more satisfaction, and yes, more joy, at work and at home.

This is exactly the right moment for you to do that. This time of tremendous upheaval in the workplace can be an advantage; there is opportunity in chaos, chaos is a time to make change. What's at stake is much greater than the next job or a move up to the next rung. It's about being seen, our values being made clear, and a shift in the world's priorities. On a more individual scale, it's about agency, domestic harmony, and the desire for saner lives.

We are proposing something audacious. Women need to remake power, the domineering brand of it, on every front. We need to change our relationship to it, so that it flows from our goals and opens the door for the next generation. We need a new operating system that allows us to maximize our impact, for the sake of our own careers, but for the rest of society as well. We already know, in our bones, what to do with power. Women inherently understand that power doesn't have to intimidate or look intimidating. It can be about encouragement, and sharing credit, or getting the whole enterprise moving better. It can be less ego—and more joy.

The word "joy" isn't usually associated with power. And that's the point. Why shouldn't it feel joyful? We don't necessarily mean a Zen-garden, yoga-infused, sunset-view kind of joy. But we do mean something akin to that sudden burst of happiness, of great delight, when we're in our element, connecting with people, helping colleagues, serving a larger purpose, getting meaningful things done. When we're effective, and succeeding, and we know it. And we'd throw in laughter and fun along the way. Why not? That's joyful power. And we are convinced that anything we do with joy is bound to have more impact. We are all at our best and more effective when our actions bring us deep happiness.

So here, in these pages, we offer the new definition, the new power code, that we hope will feel, as you read it, like a moment of déjà vu—as if you've already been in this moment, and you're just repeating to yourself, and now to the world, what you already knew to be true. It's *our* narrative—an unapologetic and happily complicated version of the ape-to-superwoman legend. And, grounded in truth, like all proper legends are, once it's shaken out, and passed around, it can infuse, clarify, and direct our reality.

(Like so much else in our lives, by the way, the burden for getting this done, the way we want it done, the way it should be done, falls, you guessed it, to us. But this one is worth shouldering.)

THE POWER CODE

1

POWER SHIFT

Before we redefine, we should define.

Humans generally know power when we see it, or feel it—almost intuitively we think we know who has it or lacks it. We're aware of it on multiple levels every day, at work, with friends, even at home. Power can be political, corporate, domestic, or deeply personal. It can feel incredible to have it, yet also uncomfortable, even dangerous.

But what is the stuff we are talking about exactly? It's a notion, a potion—yes—and it's manifest in the organizational and political structures that we create. It's instinctual and evolutionary—yes, that, too—but ultimately, and most importantly for all of us, it's time to acknowledge that the strain of power we rely upon today is largely man-made. That surely means it can be remade and, as it were, female-made as well.

We found, as we did when investigating confidence, that in order to deeply understand why the current power imbalance remains so stubborn, and what to do about it, the underpinnings of power do matter. Moreover, we were already starting to suspect, based on early interviews, that men and women have different definitions of and expectations for power, and different uses for it, and so it was essential to journey back to the basics. We needed to dig around its roots, examine its lineage, and search for its origins. We set off to find the foremost academics, scientists, and experts who have made it their business to parse, poke, and deconstruct power.

POWER, WAY BACK WHEN

Over the centuries, no shortage of people have put forth big ideas about, made wise pronouncements concerning, and conducted deep autopsies on the subject of power. (The vast majority of them, you guessed it, have been men.[1]) Motivational maxims and warnings from history abound, and they reveal our centuries-long, complicated relationship with the stuff. One of the sages of ancient Greece, General Pittacus, who wrested his power from the Athenians and by most accounts governed the Mytilenaeans with great wisdom for ten years, actually offered an enlightened view of power, one you will come to see resonates with us today. In roughly 600 BCE he declared that the measure of a man is what he does with his power.[2]

Niccolò Machiavelli offered a different vision, solidifying the industry of political strategy with his now-famous (or maybe infamous) manifesto, *The Prince*, a guide to amassing political power (and keeping it). His take on power is that it demands strategy, hierarchy, and absolute control; broadly, it's one the world has essentially adopted.

More than three hundred years later, Lord Acton, an august nineteenth-century British thinker and moralist, offered this timeless warning, one still too often unheeded: "power tends to corrupt and absolute power corrupts absolutely."[3]

The kind of power these thinkers were examining, centuries ago, was largely political power. But political power is not the only force that governs our lives, and it's not, by and large, what we're writing about. There is also *scientific power*—the stuff that makes things move. The formal scientific definition of this kind of power is *energy transferred per unit of time*. This isn't the power we're inspecting either, but it is important to keep in mind because the power we're trying to dissect does seem to involve energy and action, cause and effect.

That brings us to the stuff we're really talking about, which is *social power*, a concept chaperoned by the founders of sociology in the 1800s.[4] Inspired by the scientific revolution a few centuries earlier, these prolific scholars were grappling with how to understand society through a scientific framework. French philosopher Auguste Comte coined the term *sociology* and argued that ideas, not just scientific theorems, require stages of assumption, critical thinking, and observation.[5] A few years after that, Charles Darwin placed humankind in the animal kingdom, hypothesizing that all human relationships can be viewed scientifically. A half century later in Vienna, Sigmund Freud changed the modern world when he posited that the human mind can be understood scientifically. We can't forget Karl Marx, who put his unique spin on the importance of viewing history, and society, as a long scientific march.

What emerged from these thinkers was a concept of power beyond the terrain that had been occupied largely by honorable or evil leaders, or a revolving set of important nations, beyond a grandiose political power that was only for the very few and the very great. As societies were moving toward more participatory political systems, there was a growing awareness of *social power* as an essential construct, as a critical part of everyday life, in relations at work and at home. Power as the grease, more or less, in the most basic interactions between people.

The study of power quickly became the centerpiece of all social science pursuits. Bertrand Russell, the celebrated British twentieth-century mathematician, philosopher, and Nobel laureate, proclaimed a love of power to be the central and essential motivator—a predictor of success in life. On the eve of World War II, he wrote a book on the subject, an attempt to understand this mysterious force that was dominating the century in new and terrifying ways. "The fundamental concept in social science is Power," he decreed, "in the same sense in which Energy is the fundamental concept in physics."[6]

So, social power is the essence of our society, but what exactly is it? John Locke, in the 1600s, had postulated that power is that which allows some entity to change or be changed by another. German sociologist Max Weber took a stab at answering that question a century ago in human terms, and his definition is certainly the way most of us still think of it. Weber decreed:

Power is the ability to exercise one's will over others.[7]

In the decades since, there have been a multitude of tweaks and clarifications. In 1957, Professor Robert Dahl, of Yale, gave it a mathematical formulation: *A has power over B to the extent that A can get B to do something that B would not otherwise do.*[8] Still others have called it: *the ability to influence behavior*, influence another party, or shape the behavior of another group.[9] More recently, scholars have broadened the definition to include control over people *and/or valuable resources*—a corporate budget, access to water, or critical information, for example.

But the basic notion, handed down through recent history, sees power as a kind of force exerted on or over others. It's lean, crisp, and hierarchical, with no window dressing or frilly values to muck it up. It comes with the built-in judgment that it would surely be better to be A (the one exerting the force) than B (the one enduring it).

THE POWER OF NOW

David Winter smiles, and the sun warms the light adobe wall and map of the United States behind him, while an abiding curiosity and a sense of adventure light his expression behind wire-rimmed glasses. In his early eighties and a professor emeritus at the University of Michigan, he's ensconced in his Albuquerque, New Mexico refuge, where he just arrived from the chilly Midwest. His expertise is political psychology, social motivation, and most things related to the psychology of power. When we tell him about our quest to chisel out the best few words to describe power (and why it may not be working so well for women), he explains that, in his view, the classic historical definitions are still apt. He reaches back to both Locke and Freud, and echoes Professor Dahl, for his own go-to definition: "to have power is to make something that is not part of me do what I want it to do."

"In a primitive sense," Winter says with a laugh, "it's literally, to get something to move. I have power over this coffee mug," he notes, wielding his blue ceramic cup, "because I can make it move, I can turn it around, etc. Now, it's trivial, because what the hell's a coffee mug, it's an object." He pauses. "I have power over a person, if I can make them do the same thing."

Power *OVER* a person.

MAKING people move.

Winter's framing was wonderfully simple and clear, but it also crystallized for us the domineering nature of that definition of power.

Then we met Professor Laura Kray. And got a more expansive take.

Kray teaches at the business school at the University of California, Berkeley, and is one of the nation's foremost experts on gender in the workplace. If you want to understand how the study of power is evolving, you speak to Kray. She's mined every concept of power that's been raised, analyzed, and argued about during the last half century or so. She has multiple studies in the works, and is especially focused on the kind of power that might better suit women. Offering up mountains of information in a warm conversational tone, she tells us something that feels central to our pursuit: "Power is a social force," she says, "and it likely has something to do with *the power to effect change.*"

Power *TO* versus power *OVER*.

We were intrigued. There is an element of this "making people do things" kind of power, described by David Winter, that's toddler-clear, an elemental push to establish control in life. We all practically slide out of the womb shrieking, "You can't make me do that." Kray's version puts more emphasis on the result—the "what for" or the "why."

Indeed, her take is what gave us our early feel for the outlines of a new definition, a new code, that unlocks the door to seeing and using power differently. Little surprise, perhaps, that such insights came from a woman.

Gray eyes sparkling, words flowing rapidly, almost urgently, Kray points us to research that shows men are both more hierarchical and higher in social dominance than women, which translates to "more for me means less for you."[10] Their notion of power infers control over and competition with other people, which is a "hierarchical conceptualization," she says, and they want "not just to be able to do things, but they want it to be better than you, which has implications for their value."

Women, she explains, are more likely to see power as the engine through which we get things done, as a more communal exercise, to believe that collaboration *with*, not control *over*, can lead to productive results. "We can both have power, and be collaborative," she elaborates, "because we see it as non–zero-sum, or win-win."

It's a critical distinction:

- Hierarchical versus communal,
- Zero-sum versus non–zero-sum,
- Win-lose versus win-win,
- *Power over* versus *power to.*

If fully embraced, this kind of power would necessarily create different organizations, cultures, operational styles, and even outcomes. But that's a big *if.* Moreover, even if women tend to view and use power differently to some extent already, it's still not the stuff that reaps the big rewards right now. So our attempt to sort this out isn't just a matter of finding the right definition. It's a matter of reimagining what kind of power gets noticed, emulated, and rewarded—and changing existing dynamics if they are not suited for our purposes. And we're pretty clear by now that, indeed, they are not.

POWER'S UNDERRATED COUSINS

It's hard to have any discussion of power that doesn't veer into the related topics of status and autonomy. Even as an academic subject, power has forced itself into a hierarchy, and these cousins are usually viewed as occupying lower rungs. Naturally, they have a lot to do with the way women think about power.

Autonomy, or personal power, is defined by independence and liberation. "It means," explains Kray, "you get to decide how you spend your time. You might be low in influence, but high in autonomy, and that contributes to a sense of power." She says women often prioritize autonomy over the traditional notion of power, in part perhaps because for centuries we've had to define ourselves through others and answer to everyone but ourselves.

Professor Joe Magee, a power expert who teaches "Power and Professional Influence" to MBA students at New York University's Stern School of Business, further clarifies the distinction between autonomy and power: "You're talking about an individual being able to do what they want. Power is more than that. It involves a relationship."

That made us wonder: Does the *relational* aspect of power feel riskier, harder, and more complicated to women? It suggests we have to deal with, or even overcome, other people to get it. Perhaps reaching for autonomy seems easier, less conflict-ridden? That's just about controlling one person—yourself. And sure, there might be a number of people who don't want you to have control of your own life, but it will certainly be fewer than those who have a thing or two to say about you dictating the terms of *their* lives. We might prize autonomy specifically because it offers a way to opt out of the traditional power hierarchy—it's an escape hatch, if the more direct execution of power, in its zero-sum form, doesn't feel appealing to us.

Status, on the other hand, isn't an opt-out. You don't get status by retreating into your own world; it's something you get from other people. By definition, status is communal; it's granted if you become a respected community member, someone with influence. In fact it's closely related to respect—you don't have it unless others choose to give it to you, and there's a positive reputational quality to it. According to Kray, status is something you get when you are fulfilling the needs of the group. That's a nuanced difference with power, but an important one. Of course, many people high in power acquire status as well, and vice versa. The two often go together. But power, as defined currently, doesn't require status. In other words, you can be a really bad boss, seek little respect, and stay in power. You can't keep your status, however, if you stop satisfying the community.

Kray told us something perhaps unsurprising. As with autonomy, women often gravitate toward status more than power (at least when the traditional definition applies). Perhaps because we typically seek to please, women also more instinctively prioritize respect. In real life, most people blend some amount of each, but there's a material difference—think senior advisor role versus chief operating officer, or Greta Thunberg versus Jeff Bezos. Kray has noticed something, for example, about those lists of the most influential and important people that come out every year in places like *Fortune* and *Forbes*. "Often women make those lists because they're high status," she observes. "Men make the list because they actually control things. And, you know, of course, status doesn't pay as much as power."

It may be less lucrative at the moment, but status interested us because it clearly seems to relate to *power over* versus *power to*—it lessens the emphasis on control. Conversations with one of Laura Kray's star graduate students helped convince us that for women, status is part of the new power code.

Sonya Mishra is a refugee from Wall Street, where she was confused, even shocked, by the lack of female role models in senior positions at her former firm. "I felt like I was in a version of *Mad Men*," she says, only half-joking.

Since she escaped corporate life, Mishra has been doggedly

looking for reasons to explain the dearth of women in power. She and Kray have discovered that women, as leaders, find that status is incredibly beneficial precisely because it's a quality that comes with respect. When women explicitly seek control, they often get backlash. But when women seek or gain status, explains Mishra, they don't, at least not as often.

Additionally, as we mentioned earlier, status seems to work for the greater good. "It's communal," explains Mishra, echoing Kray. "So it forces you to pay attention to people and makes you more 'other'-oriented."

Indeed, according to their research, when people have a lot of status they act fairly, because they believe consideration of others helps them maintain their status. Power alone doesn't require that effort. Power, Mishra notes, is "usually given to you from someone even further above you, and power requires less effort to maintain. However, status is conferred by a more diffuse community of people, and there's more downstream communication that is required to maintain status."

Mishra contends that women also gravitate to status-oriented endeavors because it's not a zero-sum activity. A single person can respect multiple people (in fact, we usually do), and many people can have status. Power, in a strictly hierarchical or control sense, is a more limited commodity.

Although academics have treated status and power as distinct, we believe that for women they are not—status is *part of* the way we see, interpret, and use power; it's what makes our power palatable, workable, and distinct. We earn the respect of others to gain power, and when we have power, we seek to maintain that respect. David Winter offered us an interesting formulation grounded in psychics: status as "potential power," money in the bank which can be drawn upon to produce "ready cash" of power. Whether the energy of status is latent or kinetic, we would posit that status, and therefore "respect seeking" are part of our new power equation. Just imagine if "respect seeking" were a prerequisite for power, and was as rewarded as power currently is? It's not hard to conclude that we'd have healthier power structures. Add to that idea our preference for *power to*, for asking *why*, and it's clear we might get different outcomes.

POWER AVERSION THEORY, OR *NO THANKS*

We hate to even put these words on paper, but a disturbing amount of research suggests that a lot of us just . . . shhh . . . don't like power that much.

We've dubbed this uncomfortable reality *power aversion theory*, because a) it's exhilarating to coin a phrase, b) it sounds more serious than the alternatives, and c) our ambivalence about seizing power is both unsettling and important.

Women seem to be fighting a war on two fronts. We're battling the current power structure to gain entry to the inner sanctum, and, at the same time, we're battling our own instincts, as we wonder whether we really want to be there at all.

Alison Wood Brooks, an associate professor at Harvard Business School, has been investigating women and power for years. Initially she was convinced by what's called "demand-side bias" theory. That's research demonstrating that women are viewed differently in the workplace than men. Women can say the same things, and do the same things, but people perceive our behavior differently, often negatively, and therefore our opportunities for advancement are limited. Essentially, she thought, the problem was with the men already in power, or, as she puts it, "the demand side." But then one day, after hearing a lecture on this type of stereotype bias, she had an epiphany.

"I walked out of the seminar, and I also found myself wondering about a supply-side bias, such that women have different goals in life, and different priorities, that might lead them to act differently," she says.

Is it possible, in other words, that women just don't want the same kind of power that men wield? That the "problem" isn't only men's attitudes toward women, but also women's attitudes toward power itself? Specifically, our distaste for what currently seems the necessary cost of gaining power—that is, becoming more like men?

Wood Brooks started asking these questions in a study with hundreds of men and women, and found that women do indeed want different things, in two critical ways: they have a larger number of life goals (keeping up with close friends, for example, being in a committed relationship, or exercising regularly)—and a smaller proportion of power-related goals (such as getting more "head count" to report to them or becoming chief executive).[11]

Among the key statements she had survey participants consider:

1. "as one of my core goals in life, I would like to have a powerful position in an organization"
2. "as one of my core goals in life, I would like to have power over others"

Women found both of those goals to be less desirable than men did.[12] When asked to imagine having significant power over others, and then to imagine possible outcomes, some negative and some positive, women expected stronger negative outcomes. Translated: women think power sucks.

"Our research suggests that the costs are too high," explains

Wood Brooks, "because the trade-offs are greater for women than for men. They would have to sacrifice on other things that matter to them that men don't care about as much. But it's also possible that they have different predictions about what the experience of having power will do to them."

Wood Brooks did at least nine versions of this study, trying to alleviate any obvious sample bias. In the end, she and her team surveyed more than four thousand participants. They included people who already have power, and people who would be deemed classically ambitious, such as Harvard undergraduates. They also tested their hypothesis on a variety of ages, expecting that the effect would disappear with younger respondents. But the gender difference always remained. Women were simply less sure that the pursuit of power would be worth it.

Claire: I'd always thought my sense of discomfort in the traditional power structure was a personal failing. To be sure, the professional world I inhabited for thirty years, of television and media, is not a classic corporate structure, but it's not so different in the end. I loved reporting, and found myself jockeying for position in traditionally male-dominated zones, like the White House. That was a prime power position. It was exciting, but also often uncomfortable, and frustrating. I was given multiple lessons on how to conform. How to look: "Lose the scarf" was barked into my earpiece. How to age: "Have you thought about Botox to stop that frowny look?" How to sound: "A slightly deeper register is more authoritative. We have a voice coach." How to play a part: "Think tough, crisp, gotcha for a big interview like this . . . your style is too soft."

For the record, I still have scarf PTSD; I tried Botox—but not being able to squint freaked me out. I actually liked my voice coach and learned a lot about recording narration, and after about ten years, I learned to trust my own reporting and storytelling instincts. I found, over and over, that my own style of so-called "soft" questioning yielded much more raw, unexpected, and newsworthy answers.

I also always had a sense that I had a slightly different lens on things. I fought to keep my take in the stories I would tell, which, as I think about it now, was usually a broader analysis of impact, maybe akin to that "why" Laura Kray talks about. But my inner voice was running on a constant loop, asking whether the battles were worth it. I was pulled into reporting by a love of storytelling and impact, but success in the industry depended on a healthy love of traditional power.

Once, when I was in contention for a top job, one which everyone was pushing me to grab, I realized it was just wrong for me. I'd given years to fitting in, but I'd reached my limit. My agent, who is still my good friend, told me at the time that I was his most unusual client. Not only was I *not* constantly demanding more airtime, but I was happy with less. I think he understood that I had some slightly different, and perhaps admirable, sense of the bigger picture, but I also felt, in that moment and many others, that I lacked ambition. How could I not want more power? Now I can see that it wasn't about me not fitting the power structure, but rather a power structure that didn't fit a lot of us.

Alison Wood Brooks's survey of attitudes about power, about women's ambivalence, is a breakthrough for those of us who've long looked at power and been turned off. (And you will see, we will come back to her research often in the book, because it also serves as an excellent concrete measure of what we simply know to be true—women do seem to place value on a much broader set of life's experiences than men do, and that matters. It infuses our choices and our ability to feel satisfied. Moreover, her work ultimately suggests a values disconnect that needs to be solved in our new power equation.) We should say that Wood Brooks also has an optimistic interpretation of her research. Women may overestimate the downsides of power, because it could be that the process of getting power may be harder than having it. And we do, in the next chapter, meet some incredible women who have figured out how to enjoy it, because there is joy to be found in the exercise of power, and what power makes possible for us.

But many women who have power also find it an anxiety-inducing experience. University of Texas at Austin sociologist Tetyana Pudrovska measured the impact of power on the health of those who have it. An expert on the link between health and work, she was startled by her recent findings: the more job authority women have, the more they experience symptoms of depression. And the men? Men with authority at work have fewer symptoms of depression than men without such power.

Women, on the whole, suffer more regularly from depression than men do anyway, but women in power see that rate significantly increase. [13, 14] "What's striking is that women with job authority in our study are advantaged in terms of most characteristics that are strong predictors of positive mental health," says Pudrovska. "These women have more education, higher incomes, more prestigious occupations, and higher levels of job satisfaction and autonomy than women without job authority. Yet, they have worse mental health than lower-status women."

Pudrovska believes the causes of increased stress and depression are clear: women in leadership roles deal with everything from negative social interactions, negative stereotypes, prejudice, isolation, and resistance from above and below. Not to mention the classic double bind: "Women in authority positions are viewed as lacking the assertiveness and confidence of strong leaders. But when these women display such characteristics, they are judged negatively for being unfeminine. This contributes to chronic stress." Women of color in leadership can find those stress levels magnified by experiences with racism, discrimination, and trauma.

The stress and mental health aspects of power are profound and troubling, and suggest that the women in Wood Brooks's study were to some extent accurately predicting what might happen to them should they take the reins of power. They understood the possible implications. Reconceptualizing power, we believe, would make everything about it, from conceptualization to acquisition to execution, less toxic and more appealing.

A NEW MODEL, LONG OVERDUE

We'd been examining power through an academic lens, and by doing some reporting on the front lines of work, had uncovered a distinct clash of definitions and beliefs. But, it must be said, it's hardly a new notion that the current hierarchy wasn't made for us. Feminists, thinkers, and historians, from different vantage points, have made similar observations. Actually, it wasn't made for very many people at all. Just think about the founding of the United States, which was built, essentially, to benefit wealthy white men. Some of that structure has shifted, but not significantly.

Mary Beard, the celebrated professor of classics at the University of Cambridge and a prolific feminist scholar, believes today's women are still battling for equity in much the same way our forebears did. It's a dubious honor, but in her eyes, we remain part of a centuries-old, always potent, story line. In Athenian drama, she reminds us, women were not role models as much as terrorists; most great Greek plays were tales about women needing to be put back in their places. Agamemnon's wife, Clytemnestra, is so powerful she becomes almost masculine, rules in his absence, and then helps to kill him upon his return. In the bathtub. She was a woman out of control, who could only be stopped, eventually, with matricide.[15]

Okay, scaling today's power hierarchy may not be quite that harrowing or melodramatic, but doesn't some of that stereotyping sound awfully familiar? The fear of women being too masculine, too powerful? Women out of control? We've all seen those themes play out.

What about the home front? Historically, one place women have wielded power is in our cottages or town houses or yurts, and studies show that we don't have the same ambivalence about domestic power. That may account for why women routinely control 70–80 percent of consumer purchasing.[16] The domestic world is one in which the traditional male power hierarchy model has been softened. It's not a *power over* zone. It's more of a *heavy influence* arena, with decision making often ceded, indirectly, to women. We may have felt more comfortable at home, but the bliss of domestic power has never been a completely satisfying or equivalent alternative to the *power over* construct, which is a subject we discuss more in chapter 7.

It almost goes without saying that our "control" on the home front was and is incredibly warped. For centuries women's power at home was limited by a lack of access to our own money. Poor women certainly had no way out of their dependence on husbands for financial support. Even privileged women didn't dare to rock the boat too much, for fear of annoying their husbands and incurring the risk of abandonment. Women couldn't afford either the social or financial burden of divorce. The modern version of domestic "power sharing" is still contorted, as women increasingly outearn their partners yet still act as COO on the home front. Domestic power today needs a massive definitional and functional overhaul, as we'll explore later, because what's going on in that arena is mind-blowingly antiquated.

The point is, indirect power, or the "power behind the throne" model that has been offered as a heartwarming alternative, has always been flawed, and is no substitute for the real thing, despite Aristotle's ancient shrug of support for the system. "What difference does it make whether women rule or the rulers are ruled by women?" he offered. "The result is the same."[17]

Oh, Aristotle! Really? Do we need to explain why it doesn't feel authentic or satisfying to live through someone else's power, the way women were forced to for centuries? Power like that is on loan; it can be and often was snatched away. Society wasn't good at accommodating women who tried to exercise more than a polite amount of power through their men. We were quickly divorced or ostracized, run out of town, or even burned at the stake as witches or martyrs—those "others" that Mary Beard discusses.

Beard's approach is historical and literary, but she reaches the same conclusions as the sociologists. The age-old conundrum, she notes in her book *Women & Power: A Manifesto*, is that "the conventional definitions of 'power' (or for that matter 'knowledge,' 'expertise' and 'authority') we carry round in our heads exclude women."[18] More importantly, she argues that women don't like the male version of power because it doesn't fit us; it has been, in her words, coded for men. In our words, if power *has* to mean power *over* rather than power *to*, many women may simply abstain from seeking it.

Feminist icon and thinker Gloria Steinem agrees, and echoes Alison Wood Brooks when she says it's not surprising that women would reject organizations designed by men for men. "Dispense with the word 'should,'" Steinem told a group of students, discussing feminism. "Don't think about making women fit the world—think about making the world fit women."[19]

So, what would something made for us, by us, resemble? Perhaps connection, communication, and listening would be essential values. Marion Woodman, the Jungian psychoanalyst and expert on feminine identity, believed they would. But she was the kind of rebel who went around openly declaring that caring is a virtue. Confession: Putting these words on the page feels dangerous to us. It's as though they betray some fundamental female weakness and clash with the ambitious professional culture we've been habituated to want to master. Can we really talk about caring and Jungian psychoanalysis and still be considered serious? Maybe. More than one male CEO has publicly embraced values like vulnerability and empathy. Which may have given us all a permission slip. (The irony isn't lost on us that when men embrace vulnerability it's suddenly okay.)

This is a risk, we realize, of authentically owning parts of who we are. But if power is formally expanded to include these "feminine" values, these broader qualities of human connection, it might be even more effective.

This historical foray led us again to what was becoming a foundational theme, audacious and yet obvious.

What would it truly look like if we could *redefine power* instead of *remaking women*? If the way women view power is different, then the structure holding power might need to actually change to accommodate us, rather than the other way around. Maybe it would resonate at every level of our society if we could learn to admire, respect, and follow leaders who talk a little differently than we expect, who don't sound like the masculine norm, who are out to write a new rulebook for power.

Consider this: Could it be that women are offering the world a better vision for the future of power, and not, actually, a lesser one? After all those years of living more or less without it, women might in fact know and understand something about power that men don't.

We can't afford to be naïve or blinkered in our analysis of the difficulty of the task before us. And the two of us are not. Years of maneuvering and skirmishing in the existing structures have taught us to be hardened realists. Yes, we still want to nurture that earlier image of women (and men, if they'd like to join us) stepping off the pescribed timeline, abandoning the current march to forge a new path. But we recognize we can't simply rip up several centuries of history and start over, building a full-on female utopia from scratch. We can't avoid the traditional architecture of power altogether if we want to change it. But we can, and have to, work to change power from within and without, and we can align ourselves with everyone for whom power has been even more unequally distributed. A redefinition helps us all.

THE POWER OF THE FEMALE GAZE

Change is already happening organically. The green shoots are on display in the academic world, where the study of the entire subject is morphing.

"The way people are writing about power is shifting," observes Stanford Graduate School of Business professor Deborah Gruenfeld, who's been monitoring the trend. "A lot of that is associated with women doing the research." It's the same process that's underway in coding, artificial intelligence (AI), or women's health. When women are building the algorithms, the results are different. When female researchers start to examine health questions, new areas of essential research (often focused on women) emerge. More women are involved not only in the execution and ownership of power, but also in the study of it, and that female gaze on the topic is creating shifts in the field.

Gruenfeld codirects the Executive Program in Women's Leadership at Stanford, and although there is little data on this yet, she has her eye on a burgeoning team of women academics who are digging into the study of power and approaching the topic so uniquely that their research might alter the definition itself.

Women like Professor Kray, who, instead of examining power through a traditional, hierarchical, hagiographic lens, are also considering the merits of power *to* rather than power *over*, and status. They are developing our nation's future CEOs at America's top business schools, and writing the books that politicians the world over will read. "They're more interested," Gruenfeld explains, "in the idea of power as making it more possible for people to do the maximum amount of good for the maximum amount of people. That kind of thing." The study of power used to be heavily strategic, she notes, focused on how to get more power, how power corrupts. Now there's an emphasis on what leads people to use it well, and women are driving that effort. Gruenfeld herself broadened her thinking and teaching in response to female students approaching her after class and saying they understood classic power intellectually, but could never use it that way.

RECODING

As if in a darkroom, we were experiencing the thrilling sense of watching a new power formula develop, clearer with each conversation.

"There are other ideas, other sides to the argument that dominance always wins," Gruenfeld told us. "That was believed for a long time, and recent research by a lot of women looking at this is showing that's not true. They are finding that there are status and respect–related strategies to power, which matter."

"I think that it would be absurd to say that this is the best of all possible worlds in terms of the way power works," David Winter told us. "It would be a good thing," he continued, "if power and our ideas about power changed, developed, were broadened."

We were coming to the same conclusion. Remembering that Professor Joe Magee had remarked to us enviously that, as reporters, we could theorize more *broadly* than academics, we're now using that particular power, in order to redefine.

We had identified three key definitional strands in a broader, women-forged brand of power:

1. *Power over* versus *power to*. *Power over* repels some women, feels zero-sum. *Power to* motivates us.
2. *Why?* Purpose is implied in *Power to*.
3. *Respect*. Status, or respect-seeking, is part of our power.

If the world's basic definition of power is, at the moment:

> The ability to exercise one's will over others, to make them do something they would not otherwise do.

Then our working definition would be:

> The ability to exercise one's will, to influence others, to effect change.

In this definition of power, the strict hierarchical nature and the idea of controlling other people has softened. The notion of status, or the necessity of seeking respect, is baked in. It reflects the way women see it: as more communal, with a focus on an end result, or the "why" of power.

For experts like Joe Magee, that "why?" is an essential question, and one he asks in all of his power classes, because he believes that motivations are the ultimate drivers of outcome. "I think we really want to understand people who acquire power for power's sake, when their end goal is to just have more power, versus people who actually want to get something done and improve the world with their power."

As we uncovered this alternative power definition, the outlines of our code started to come into view.

The ability to exercise our will—More Joy.

Influencing (not controlling) others—Less Ego.

Effecting change—Maximum Impact.

And as you will see in other chapters, more ingredients will funnel into and bolster those key tenets.

We were left, though, with many practical questions.

Can women really run the world operationally, if they don't fully embrace the traditional *power over*? Are men ready for a new version of power? Will they do what that might demand, at work and, just as importantly, at home? We still had plenty left to study. It was time, we felt, to take all of the academic theories for a road test. We were suddenly eager to discover what effect the female gaze, or the female grasp on power in the real world, is already having.

YOUR POWER CODE

As we reimagine power, and the way it could be more accessible to women and more appealing to everyone, we don't want to lose sight of your experience. In the end, this transformation will happen because every one of us understands and uses power in a new way. Power is not like optimism, or happiness, or even confidence. Those are qualities that by their very nature you can take ownership of independently and individually. You can boost your confidence by taking risks. You can increase your happiness by, for example, focusing on gratitude. You can reframe your experiences to become more optimistic.

Power is different. It's more of an external, relational force, situated in the worlds of domestic life, work, and society. But there are things you can do right now, on your own, and with others, to gain more power, to recognize the power you already have, and, ultimately, to change the way you and others understand and use power.

Our power revolution won't happen in a vacuum. It depends on you becoming more powerful. So in the chapters that follow, we will funnel theory into practice. We'll offer advice for women of all backgrounds, at all stages of career and life.

If you're at the top, we'll give you a template for what you can do to change what power looks and feels like in your organization. It's what you can do to help get more women into power and what you can do to enjoy your own power.

We'll have advice, too, for women who are still eyeing that daunting climb and wondering how on earth you can ever get to the top in a world where power seems both impossible and, frankly, unappealing. Sometimes you have to work within the existing power hierarchies; sometimes you can tweak them on your way up.

But, whatever your position, you can keep your eye on a new, more intuitive, authentic version of power—a power to do something meaningful, whatever that may look like. A power that is more joy, less ego.

Sifting through chapter 1, here are some suggestions:

Take Notice. Armed with all this new information, open your eyes to the different ways people use power. It isn't one size fits all. Once you start to notice, you'll see the distinctions everywhere—from everyday interactions to the highest levels of the power hierarchy. Pay particular attention to how power impacts people who've traditionally been excluded from it, and how they are changing the way power is wielded today. "Noticing" may have a trivial ring, but, in fact, neuroscientific research shows that our focus—turning our attention to things—is one of the most powerful things we can do to change our behavior.

Power goals. Think about using power yourself. Draw on Alison Wood Brooks's research and make a list of your life goals. Do you make a low priority of power-related goals (for example, getting a promotion, taking over a bigger team)? Do those goals feel stressful? Are you anxious about what it takes to win classic power and what it will be like to have it?

Flip the narrative. Imagine what you could *do* with power. Multiple studies show that women are more motivated to take risks, do hard things—on behalf of others, or causes. This may be why *power to* feels better to us. Test it out. If you were in a position to make change—to get three incredible things done—what would those be? Now notice—how do you feel? Does the "why" of power help?

2

THE POWER (AND JOY) OF HAVING POWER

It's hot in the office of Ndéye Lucie Cissé. Sweat-trickles-down-your-back-and-off-your-forehead kind of hot. Not that Cissé, perched on a shiny black leather sofa, seems to notice. She looks cool, oblivious to the humidity and heat. Perhaps a little perspiration is a small price to pay for a seat at the table.

The heavy brown curtains are drawn shut against the powerful African sun to give the aging air-conditioning unit its best shot. There's a planet to protect, Cissé reminds us. As if the second-term member of parliament in Dakar, Senegal, didn't have enough on her plate.

"Take this year's national budget, for example. The men in parliament want money for a mosque, or a town square," she says. "The women members, we want money to get electricity into maternity clinics so women aren't giving birth in the dark. We want funds for toilets with running water for girls in schools so they have somewhere private to go when they have their periods." For a brief moment Cissé's poise cracks, her voice rising in frustration. "Do you know, many girls here in Senegal are skipping school for almost a week every month just because they don't have suitable bathrooms at school? That alone makes it hard for our girls to keep up."

Ask Cissé what having power means to her, and it isn't some lofty, esoteric concept. It is a tool that, used well, can produce life-changing results: functioning sanitation for girls who are menstruating so they don't have to miss lessons, and electricity in a rural clinic so a midwife can deliver a baby with the help of a little light. It is an example of what power looks like when it's viewed and deployed as an instrument of progress, as a commodity that produces results. The power to do something—rather than power over somebody—builds stronger communities and lifts people up.

Shining a light on this distinction—what power in action looks like from a feminine perspective—is one of the intriguing questions that's taken us to Cissé's office in the capital of Senegal. After understanding, academically, that men and women may conceptualize power differently, we were searching for real-world role models, to see firsthand how women use it, whether it feels distinct.

The women in this chapter represent how the story of power can change when we rewrite the narrative. These women live on different continents, work in different fields, and come from quite different backgrounds. But they have a few critical things in common: they have significant power, respect for the responsibility of their power, and a way of deploying it that we believe illustrates the broader redefinition of power in real life. Furthermore, they relish having power and what they can do with it. These are women who are not trying to be more like men; they are women who are wielding their power decidedly as women.

THE POWER TOOL

In Dakar, Cissé agrees that power is a means to an end, indeed, to a better world. She certainly hasn't spent decades fighting for it in order to make herself rich or to give herself a lofty status in society; she wants power to improve people's quality of life.

She may just succeed because she has allies in the National Assembly. In 2010 this West African country passed one of the most radical gender quota laws in the world and took its National Assembly from 22.7 percent women to 42.7 percent in the space of just one election.[1] Political parties must be composed of equal numbers of men and women or they aren't allowed to run at all; the entire political party gets disqualified. Other countries have similar laws, but few of them have real teeth. Senegal's law does. So now, the hallways of Senegal's white colonnaded parliament building, with its soaring ceilings and slightly dated grandeur, have a decidedly more female feel. As a result, more feminine priorities are being passed into law. The power tool is at work, disrupting a long-established patriarchy to make things better for women and girls.

What's known in Senegal as the *loi de parité*—the law on parity—was years in the making and Cissé, a former teacher and union worker, was instrumental in helping to drive it through. It wasn't easy. Senegal is a predominantly Muslim, patriarchal society where women are still expected to prioritize the welfare of their husbands and their homes over their own jobs.[2] Even today, the parity law can provoke negative reactions in more conservative areas of the country, where it's seen as a dangerous bid by women to defy the control of their husbands. "Men won't ever give us power voluntarily," Cissé says. "We got parity in Senegal because women worked for it for years and years and in the end even the president couldn't say no."

After several failed attempts, Cissé and her fellow campaigners got a breakthrough when they teamed up with a group of lawyers who helped them formulate the constitutional merits of their case and shift their communications strategy to emphasize equality, or parity, instead of gender quotas. It was a subtle difference that played down the idea of women gaining power over men. (There it is again, less power over, more power to.) Senegalese female politicians were able to obtain that power to by conceiving of it differently than their male counterparts. Echoing the words of Professor Kray, who defined power for us in a less domineering way, they recast power as "collaborative" or "win-win."

When the law finally passed in 2012, the sixty-three women who joined Cissé in parliament as a result of the first election were still met with suspicion bordering on disdain from their male counterparts.[3] "They wondered whether we were just there for decoration, with our big colorful headscarves and long dresses," she told us. "They didn't think we would actually change anything."

Those men couldn't have been more wrong. The women had a plan. They didn't want to rest on their laurels, holding on to power just for the sake of having it. They wanted to use that power to change the country. Perhaps all those men who had sat in parliament unopposed for so many years, and had gotten comfortable with all the creature comforts that come to important people, simply assumed that women would want power for the same reasons they did—to benefit themselves. Perhaps they couldn't imagine power having a different purpose.

The new women members soon showed they were serious about the business of governing. "We stayed longer, we worked harder, we were more punctual, we asked more in-depth questions, and we were better prepared than they were," Cissé says with a wry smile. She describes looking around the assembly chamber when debates ran late into the night and noticing that those brightly colored scarves outnumbered the bare male heads.[4]

Senegal is a relatively poor country. People there earn an average of just $1,606 per year. Approximately half the population is illiterate. Yet, thanks to that change in the law, Senegal has achieved something the United States, the United Kingdom, Germany, France, and many other countries have failed to achieve.[5]

The women swept into parliament with an agenda that had a clear point: to improve life by making it more equal for women and families. They soon discovered that getting elected wasn't their final hurdle. The struggle for power continued even inside the parliament building. Cissé says the new women members weren't given positions of responsibility and had to battle to get seats on important committees, seats the men were reluctant to give up. But the first bill they passed changed the nationality laws so that mothers could pass citizenship to their children as easily as fathers could.[6] Then they toughened up an antismoking law to protect the health of nonsmokers. In 2020 rape was finally criminalized in Senegal, a law pushed for by female parliamentarians.[7] Was it all perfect? No. One conservative religious area of the country refused to abide by the law at all, and got away with it. "We can never take our foot off the accelerator when it comes to getting equality," Cissé realized.

Cissé and her female colleagues' initial goal was ambitious enough, but their efforts have also had a fascinating secondary effect. They have served as role models for young women throughout Senegal, but also, surprisingly, for their male colleagues, too. When she first took office, Cissé never anticipated that she and her fellow female rabble-rousers would change the way their male colleagues operated as well.

The men in Senegal's National Assembly, who initially complained about those brightly dressed women drawing attention to themselves, gradually came to admire them. Cissé remembers the first time a male colleague came to her not with a grumble, but with praise. He was clearly impressed with her dedication. Here was the force multiplier: Not wanting to be outshone, the men even started working harder themselves, in order to keep up. "They are men, they don't want to be left behind," she says, and chuckles.

Having women speak up for what women need has also opened men's eyes to problems they had little idea about. Take those school toilets for girls and the lightbulbs for maternity clinics. Cissé doesn't think they were excluded from previous budgets out of malice. It wasn't necessarily because the men didn't care about pregnant women and menstruating schoolgirls; it was because they had never lived those experiences themselves and so they simply didn't think about them. When the new female members of parliament wrote them into the budget, most male members were actually happy to vote for them.[8] It turned out that recasting power as "collaborative" and "win-win" wasn't just a clever marketing strategy to pass the *loi de parité*. Having more women in politics in Senegal has actually changed how power works in the country.

Cissé and the other women in Senegal's parliament aren't trying to be like men or look like men. They aren't bending their power to fit in with the men around them and they aren't apologizing for their power. It's hard work, and it hasn't all gone smoothly, but in Senegal, a different concept of power, a *power to*, is in the works, with the "*why*" on stark display through the women's concrete and audacious goals. This new power is transforming the men as well as the society.

THE POWER PROCESS

What most surprised Zanny Minton Beddoes when she was appointed the first female editor of the *Economist* magazine was the number of times interviewers asked her what it was like to be first.

Interviewers didn't focus on what she planned to do with the magazine, nor what her editorial leanings were—they wanted to know what it was like to be the first woman. She took over the job as editor in chief in 2015. She has since been followed by women editors at the *Guardian*, the *Financial Times*, Reuters, and the *Washington Post*, to name but a few of the global media organizations also to have appointed their own "firsts." Minton Beddoes can't wait for the day when that question doesn't come up anymore.

But what intrigues us about Minton Beddoes isn't that she shattered the glass ceiling, impressive though that is; it's how she demystifies power, and plainly articulates what it is like to exercise power day-to-day—literally, what the process is. It's something that could be very helpful to women who feel hesitant about taking power on. She doesn't aggrandize the stuff; for her it's practical, a lever to be pressed in order to get things done. In breaking it down, she makes it somehow more accessible. Less daunting.

We have known Zanny Minton Beddoes for years, but we never expected, when we interviewed her in her London home office, that her responses would remind us so much of Senegal's Ndéye Lucie Cissé. Yet throughout our Zoom conversation, Minton Beddoes reinforced many of Cissé's themes, chiefly a belief in fair process and a focus on doing the work that needs doing for the benefit of a bigger cause.

Minton Beddoes is one of the busiest women we know, but when we speak to her, she's not rushed. Her tidy study, accentuated with lilies in a vase visible over her shoulder and neatly stacked books we just know she has actually read, reflects the focus she brings to the conversation. When we ask her what it's like having power, she surprises us.

"Sometimes I think I'm paid just to make decisions," she tells us with a sudden laugh, as if the realization still both startles and delights her. "My day is really a list of decisions."

There are, she insists, plenty of people at the *Economist* who are more talented than she is at a range of different things—more talented writers and more talented editors—people who understand finance and politics better than she does. Her superpower is making decisions. Now, many leaders, of any gender, would probably say the same, but what interests us, as she guides us through her conception of power, is her approach to making those decisions.

As one of the top journalists in the world, Minton Beddoes chooses her words with care. It's not that she's guarded, but language matters to her. For a start, there's the word itself. "I never think about power. I never think about it as a term." She says she is happier with the word leadership. Exercised at its best, leadership, she tells us, gives her a profound sense of fulfillment and joy. Perhaps she prefers the word leadership because of power's negative connotations, but she clearly relishes her position and understands it.

As she sees it, all those day-to-day decisions are the scaffolding of her leadership; they are the things that keep the *Economist* standing strong and working well. So the way those decisions are taken, as much as the results themselves, is important. The way she makes decisions reflects her own understanding of how power should be used. In a way, those decisions are her power.

Today, she says, top-down decisions by fiat no longer work; they must be made following consultations. So her decisions are based on listening, which she describes as a critical stage of the process. Then, after she has listened and invited others' feedback, she recognizes that her position demands that she decide—on an editorial line, the title of a new imprint, a political endorsement, the image for a controversial cover page—whatever it is, she makes the final call. And she does so with confidence.

Minton Beddoes's power style is highly effective, and incorporates all of the elements of our new power definition: *power to*, *why*, and *respect-seeking*. Indeed her characterization of her attitude toward power reminded us a great deal of what Laura Kray's graduate student Sonya Mishra had to say about status, how it makes you "other-oriented," because you earn it from the group. Minton Beddoes has power, and she exercises it, but that power comes as much from the respect she has, and gets, from her employees as it does from her title. The way she talks about it, it's almost as if she is the custodian of this powerful role and it's up to her to fulfill its potential. "It might sound trite, but it really isn't about me. It's about the organization."

One concrete way Minton Beddoes leads differently than her predecessors, and attempts to reorder hierarchies, is how she runs the magazine's famous Monday meeting, a time when supposedly anyone on the editorial staff can pitch an idea. In the past, the meeting was in the editor in chief's office, with the EIC presiding from behind his desk.

As Minton Beddoes describes the meeting, it had "a clear hierarchy, in that the important people sat at the front, and the less important people at the back, and the interns would be trying to listen from the corridor, and it was always the same roster of men that spoke."

Minton Beddoes soon moved the meeting to a conference room and arranged the chairs in a semicircle. Already, she found this made a significant improvement, though she had to consciously ensure that the same voices weren't always taking up the most air. When the meeting moved to Zoom during the pandemic, she saw even broader participation because she was able to simply call on people based on when they put their hands up using the hand-raising feature (she does not require that cameras be on, to make sure all her employees are as comfortable as possible). "There's a kind of parity in Zoom," she says.

But Minton Beddoes didn't stop with those Monday editorial

meetings. Once every three months or so, she will also, in her words, "gate-crash" the daily meetings of other departments, such as the audio or video teams. She doesn't attend with any particular agenda, but rather to listen and to ask them if they have any questions for her. She finds that they always do.

Minton Beddoes says she sees the positive effects of her approach on a daily basis. "I think one of the most effective ways to be a leader is to make sure other people take the credit," she says. "Which, by the way, is also hugely motivating." She applies the same rule of not making it about her to the enjoyable decisions as to the hard ones, which helps when she has to do something difficult or unpleasant. "It's not about you, it's about what's best for the organization."

Her power as a leader depends on achieving the right balance between consultation and decisiveness. She still believes in the need for a hierarchy, even if remade, the need for making tough decisions, and the need, even occasionally, for being disliked. "If you don't consult, that doesn't work. If you second-guess your decisions, that doesn't work," she says. What is not an option is to punt on a decision. That's the difference, she says, between management and leadership. As we spoke, a clear picture of Minton Beddoes as a boss began to emerge. Leadership with listening and consultation, leadership in which she's also happy to take responsibility for the final call—this is her signature style.

As we wrap up our conversation, we ask her to describe the positive feelings associated with having power. She pauses for a moment. She is choosing her words carefully again, but having found them, she says them with total conviction. "If something the *Economist* has done is deemed to be really good, I take huge satisfaction in that. If we have collectively produced something insightful, it's an enormous reward. It's a sense of achievement but it doesn't have to be tied back to me at all. If we have two hundred and eighty-seven people at the magazine who feel their jobs are fulfilling, then I'm satisfied." Satisfaction, reward, achievement—the prizes of power well used.

POWER AS FREEDOM

The managing director of the International Monetary Fund, Kristalina Georgieva, has more experience than most of us with the consequences of exercising power—and of losing it. In high school she was put in a state-run institution in communist Bulgaria for appearing to make fun of military service. While participating in her country's mandatory army training, she had invented a sardonic military marching song and had the audacity to sing the subversive ditty during training. It landed her a three-week stint in a government facility.

She wasn't physically tortured, but she says she was scared the whole time. The communist authorities could be brutal and vindictive; they hated subversion, and Kristalina didn't know when she was going to get out, if ever. For decades she blocked out the memory of those three weeks.

Georgieva's experiences as a young woman in communist Bulgaria shaped how she views and wields power today. She sees it as a mechanism for self-expression in addition to being a means of achieving a common goal. For Georgieva, power must always be power to rather than power over, or power just because. She knows firsthand that power for power's sake can soon descend into violence and intimidation.

In the executive dining room of the IMF, she tells us another story from her youth we won't soon forget. When she was in high school, two of her fellow students were due to be transferred out of her prestigious state school to a lesser institution. "It was wrong, and unjust," she says. Kristalina already had a bad relationship with their teacher, who went by the wonderful title of Professor of Scientific Communism (only behind the Iron Curtain, she laughs!). She would regularly make fun of him, and one day he'd had enough of it. He hit her—she remembers that her glasses went flying across the room, and she couldn't see much.

Even in communist Bulgaria, that was considered out of bounds. The boys in her class were furious and ready to attack him, but, after retrieving her glasses, Kristalina persuaded them to hold off. She had a better strategy. Thinking quickly, she realized they could use the teacher's transgression to get justice for the two students who were about to be kicked out.

She calmed down the hotheaded boys and went to the school's director with a deal. Either they'd make their complaint public, which wouldn't reflect well on his school, or they'd keep quiet in exchange for the two classmates being allowed to stay. She got what she wanted. Her classmates' transfer was canceled.

She was just a teenager, but it was her first successful exercise in leadership and power. The boys in her class who bravely wanted to defend her didn't understand real power, at least not as Georgieva sees it. They understood retaliation, punishment, an eye for an eye, instant gratification. But Georgieva had seen power for what it truly was, a tool to reach a goal otherwise out of reach. She'd used her power, as gruesomely attained as it was, to right a wrong.

Now, after decades of experience, she sees positions of power as "an opportunity to do good." She recalled a time when she was the European Union's humanitarian commissioner and had an encounter with a Syrian refugee girl who longed to quit working in the fields and go back to school. Georgieva told the girl's story to a group of donors and within a month had convened a partnership that still today benefits hundreds of thousands of Syrian boys and girls. She used her power as a force multiplier for good.

Then, after a pause, Georgieva talks about what it means to her more personally. "It's a chance to finally say what I think from a position of authority so I get to be taken seriously. I came to this point of authority and what does it bring? I speak from a high hill. And what I say cannot be ignored." While this may be true of any boss and could be said of power of any stripe, Georgieva knows that it is even harder to ignore a leader who has earned her community's respect.

"I do want to call the shots," she says. "Not just for the sake of it. I want to do it for positive change."

Indeed, for Georgieva personally, power must be about *power to* rather than *power over*. Power over was what her cruel teacher and repressive government used against her. By contrast, Georgieva spends her professional life wielding the power to speak, to be heard, and to build a community in which others can do the same.

One way Georgieva has changed the nature of power at the IMF is by stamping out bullying behavior. When she arrived at the Fund, she found a tolerance for brilliant economists who behaved badly toward colleagues and subordinates. Not badly in sexual terms, but badly in the way they would shout at or intimidate people. "But they are such highflyers," she was told, as if that excused their tone. If they're really highflyers, she reasoned, they shouldn't feel the need to yell. She put a stop to yelling and quickly made it known that people who behaved badly, even brilliant people, wouldn't find favor under her leadership.

For the woman who spent time incarcerated in a communist institution, fear should never be how power is experienced; it's a tool for the weak. "It's key never to exercise power through fear but through excitement. Especially in a male-dominated world, it has to be your way, not their way." This is how Georgieva sees herself as molding power to a more female form.

But Georgieva admits that developing the confidence to lead this way took time. She wasn't always willing to be iconoclastic. In 1992 she gave a presentation at the World Bank. She was a young economist. The Iron Curtain had only recently fallen. In Washington, DC, it was still a white man's world.

She arrived at the World Bank headquarters on Pennsylvania Avenue in a colorful jacket. She still remembers it. It was brown with bright flowers on it. She walked into the imposing building and looked around at a sea of men in dark suits. The young Kristalina read the room. She walked out on her lunch break and bought herself a dark blue jacket.

Now Georgieva wants us to see, firsthand, how far she has come from that day in Washington. Toward the end of our lunch in the executive dining room, she tells us she really wants to show us her office before we leave. So after the lemon tarts and coffees have been cleared away, we head upstairs for a quick tour.

Her office is light, airy, and huge. The vast patterned rug is a riot of orange, red, blue, and yellow. The sofas are cream, with throw pillows that are coordinated, but not in a perfect, professional decorator kind of way. It's the kind of room you'd be happy to spend time in. Its warmth suggests that it belongs to a person as much as to an institution. We dwell on the décor because we've been inside hundreds of offices of male leaders and, we assure you, this one was noticeably, almost deliberately, different.

The executive suite of the head of the world's most important global financial institution is indeed beautiful. But what she wants us to see is a female leader enjoying, and owning, her place of power. And, just as important, consciously making it her own. Step into Georgieva's office and it doesn't shout its power. It doesn't need to.

As a metaphor for female power more broadly, it is unmistakable, and it's meant to be.

This is what Georgieva's power is all about: publicly role-modeling that there is another way. The distinctive design, the ban on shouting, the absence of fear—she's targeting the corrosive side of *power over* or power by fear from her elevated position. She also talks frequently about the benefits of being not the "first," but the "second" female leader of the IMF. It's a vote of confidence in female leadership, she notes, and, just as critically to women watching, it's a reminder that there's plenty of room for female talent, and it won't all look the same.

THE POWER OF OURSELVES

Cynthia Marshall's attitude toward power is perhaps the most liberating and refreshing we've encountered yet. We interview her over Zoom, and we can see that the shelves behind Marshall's large, leather desk chair are lined with impressive books, photos with important people, framed awards, the basketball logo of the team she runs, and a tiara—of the Disney princess variety. As she catches us looking quizzically at it, Marshall tells us with a grin that she loves her power, and that she'll put that tiara on sometimes, to remind herself, or others, that she's the boss.

"I was on a panel a couple of weeks ago," she told us when we asked her more about it. "And one woman just said she didn't really want to use the word *power* because it just didn't sound right. I'm like no, no, no, no, no, no, no!!! We have power. That power, that's queen-of-the-castle stuff."

Cynthia, who goes by Cynt (her nickname because it rhymes with *sprint*—she was a very fast runner in high school), talks rapid-fire. A lot of verbal exclamation marks. She exudes warmth and energy and optimism. She's one of the most powerful women in the very masculine world of men's professional sports.

Marshall was tapped by owner Mark Cuban to become the first Black female CEO of a major-league men's basketball team.[9] She runs the NBA's Dallas Mavericks, and she tells us she's had her eye on a powerful position like this ever since she was a child, witnessing her father beating up her mother. She doesn't indulge in self-pity, but the story still shocks us, and it turns out it's an important part of her own relationship with power. Marshall doesn't shy away from sharing the difficult realities of her early life. She doesn't shy away from encouraging others to do the same. Nor does she, after thirty-six years rising through the ranks of telecom giant AT&T and then taking over at the Mavericks, shy away from embracing the power she's earned. "I have the ability and the position and the status to do it."

Out of college Marshall had one priority: "I said I'm going to accept the job that pays me the most money because I want to help my mom get out of that apartment in the projects." But it wasn't just her own mother she wanted to help. "I wanted a job where I can be the boss so I can help take care of people and make sure they are treated right." It's the second part of that sentence that is really important to her, and that intrigues us. Power to make things right, power to protect and to take care.

Forty years later that is still what having power means to her.

Specifically, she says, power affords us two things: the ability to have people listen and the ability to effect change. Being heard, as Georgieva noted, is a big deal for women who have gone centuries being ignored or silenced—or have firsthand experience with the silencing effects of powerlessness. It's a theme we came across repeatedly. When we have power, people finally hear us.

Marshall has used her power to shake up the image of what it means to be a leader in the sports world, an environment that has historically been slow to change.

The woman with the big office, imposing desk, and sparkly tiara grew up in a housing project in Richmond, California. Marshall watched her mother being hit by her father and then going off to work with makeup applied to disguise her bruises. Her dad didn't stop with their mom; he beat his children, too. By the time she was in seventh grade, Cynt went to school with a police escort. It's what they did for victims of domestic abuse.

There's a powerlessness to being abused, as any person who has suffered from it knows. It is the extreme penalty of someone having power over you. It can crush people, but in Cynt's case it motivated her. Her mother, who finally divorced her father and juggled multiple jobs as a librarian and high school administrator, pushed Cynt to make the best of her chances with the mantra "It's not where you live, it's how you live."

She took up the challenge. She aced high school, applied to college, got five scholarship offers, and picked UC Berkeley. Originally, she wanted to become a math teacher, but she switched her major to business administration and human resources, all the while racking up firsts in her majority-white college: the first Black cheerleader, the first Black member of her sorority. All steps on her route to power.

And as a Black woman leader, in an almost entirely white corporate world, Cynt overcame particularly challenging hurdles to get there. There were the abundant stereotypes to knock down. "I've developed strategies so I don't come off as the angry Black woman," she says, with a broad smile. There was the casual racial abuse on the job that made her so mad she fired off a string of angry emails. It nearly derailed her path to the top. A mentor, an African American man, told her "You've got to get control of that anger because we need you to climb." Cynt did indeed learn and climb, but with a double dose of skewed expectations, and the burden of repeatedly being a "first." Today, her own power gives her the ability to speak her mind whenever she chooses, but she also knows that in corporate America that is still not a luxury available to younger people, especially people of color. So, drawing on her own path as a groundbreaking Black female executive, she urges them to own their power, but be judicious. "I'm very protective of some of the younger leaders. Because you want them to climb. You want them to move up. You don't want them to make this a strategic error that is going to cost them their jobs because they have to say something. It's like, you've just got to chill until the right moment."

Her climb, the patience it took, the lived experience she brought to it, created for Marshall another essential tenet in her power rulebook, one she can implement since she's now the boss: radical authenticity is not only okay in her workplace, it's required. She's used the "whole self" principle to transform the male-centered places she's run. She believes you cannot separate work from home, the personal from the professional, your corporate and true identities. It's all just life to her. Her approach can be transformational for women and people of color especially, and it hints at a more organic version of power that feels a lot more welcoming.

For years we've left our personal lives, our female selves, at the door because that was the way men had always done it; that was, we assumed, the only way to get ahead. Who would take us seriously if we talked about our families, or our emotional lives at work?

Marshall thinks that the whole concept is nonsensical. "I watched my mother go through all this stuff and I always brought that part of me to work, the part that says people's stories matter, what happens in their homes matters."

Marshall has an image she likes to paint for her team to get them on board with this whole-self idea; people don't get up in the morning, leave home, and then find a phone booth on their way to the office and slip inside to become a superhero. They don't put on an AT&T cloak or a Dallas Mavericks cloak and come to work disguised as someone else: "The people who get up out of bed are the same people who come into work." Here's where Marshall differs from generations of male leaders who found our home lives an irritating distraction—she wants us to be the same people we are at home; she wants our personal lives to inform our work lives. Bringing our whole selves to work—that's the real superpower, not some burdensome cloak meant as a disguise. It's not covering up or ignoring our home lives that makes all of us valuable; it's the opposite.

It occurs to us that women such as Ndéye Lucie Cissé, in Senegal's parliament, are changing politics by virtue of their unique experience. They feel no disconnect between what they know to be true from their lives outside of politics, and what they then deem important: lobbying for school bathrooms and maternity clinic lightbulbs. Cynt Marshall expands the notion—not only might our authentic lived experiences inform our work priorities, but showing our full selves, who we are at home and elsewhere, is not a problem; it's an asset.

"That's what authenticity is all about. We don't want the superhero cape. We want all the authenticity, creativity and diversity walking into our building," she says. She believes it's a leadership style that gives her an edge. If someone isn't performing well, she'll assess the specific work situation, but then her reaction is "what's going on at home. Is there something going on in their personal life that could be impacting their work?"

Her approach seemed not only novel and exciting, but the polar opposite of what we sometimes hear when we speak to the leaders of other large corporations. A few years ago, for example, a bank brought us into a partners meeting, and we laid out the business case for diversity. A group of people who think differently, have distinctly different backgrounds and mindsets and management styles, always collaborate better than a homogeneous group, we said. There is research that shows it to be true. We explained the confidence gap between men and women in the workplace and how it can hold some women back. We went through the structural barriers to entry for women in traditionally male institutions.

The few women at the meeting nodded enthusiastically. The many men nodded, a bit less enthusiastically. They gave us an hour, and they seemed to listen. They said all the right things about wanting more diversity. Then, as we discussed practical strategies, the head of investment banking said he had a question.

"How could we go to the best colleges and universities to recruit, and have a filter that would allow us to identify women who have the same qualities we've always valued in our associates?" he asked. "Women we know are going to fit into our culture?"

It took us a moment to understand the full significance of his questions. These white men, who had just spent a couple of hours earnestly talking about the merits of diversity, didn't actually want diversity at all, certainly not diversity in terms of leadership style. Yes, they wanted women, but only to solve a public relations problem, to boost their numbers and avoid bad press. They wanted women who "fit in," women who didn't disrupt the status quo, women whom they could rely on to act in a tough, hierarchical, testosterone-filled way, just like the men they'd always employed.[10] It was deflating, to say the least.

Marshall's strategy couldn't be more different. When Marshall took over at the Mavericks she made a point of spending time one-on-one with every single employee. She'd ask them, where do you want to be in five years? Inevitably they'd spell out their career goals, but she'd push back: "And where do you want to be in your life, with your family?"

She's noticed, over the years, that most of her male colleagues would not think to ask questions like that. Her male colleagues don't share her belief in bringing the whole self to work. Indeed, that is not something her male colleagues would think to ask. They've tended to practice a kind of separation of church and state, work and home, that felt more comfortable, perhaps even safer, to male bosses who didn't want to know about their employees' feelings, problems, or personal lives. Marshall thinks men tend to rush decision making, and perhaps that's also why they don't want to delve into an employee's personal life; it's a time-consuming process, trying to understand your associate's family life as well as their work life. But, in four decades, she's learned that it's time well spent. Showing empathy at work, as we've mentioned, is in vogue today, but it was anathema when Marshall started out.[11]

She can pinpoint moments when her "whole person" approach has benefited the company. In times of tension or crisis, really knowing your employees helps. For example, when George Floyd was killed by a white police officer in Minneapolis in May 2020, the Dallas Mavericks were better equipped, Marshall believes, to handle what it meant for their team, because people had already been honest about race and what it meant at work. They had laid the groundwork by instituting a culture where she really knew her employees.

As a young associate, Marshall learned that it made no sense to ignore people's personal problems, and she had the confidence to say it and—most impressively—to bring people with her. She'd discovered that a colleague had a drug problem. Her bosses wanted the woman fired. Marshall pleaded with the woman to get help, but she refused. So Marshall went to her superiors, all men, and explained what it meant to be an addict, what it meant to be going through a hard time in life, and what it meant to come from a different background. Initially they just wanted to fire Marshall's colleague. But Marshall was persuasive, to the point that those male bosses started rooting for the troubled colleague; they wanted to help her.

The story didn't have an entirely happy ending, though. The woman refused to come clean about her addiction, and it fell to Marshall to fire her. But when she did so, those same bosses were in tears. The young Marshall couldn't save that one woman's job, or her health, but she did something else very powerful: she changed the way her male bosses saw their colleague. She opened their eyes to something they wouldn't have seen before, something they'd been missing.

She challenged them to see their own roles as leaders differently, to show more of their own humanity. To their credit, they rose to the challenge. Just as Ndéye Lucie Cissé's male colleagues improved their performance in the Senegalese parliament when they saw how impressive the female lawmakers were, so Marshall's caring leadership made the men around her more attuned to this style of leadership, too. When we use our power well, we can create that multiplier effect and raise the game of the men around us.

Power over has no place in Cynt Marshall's repertoire. A focus on the why, on building and seeking respect, seems to come as naturally as breathing, and ties seamlessly into her focus on authenticity.

When we initially heard Cynt talk about authenticity, about the whole self actually, we have to admit that we saw it as an innovative management technique that would help bosses get the best out of their employees, and employees to thrive. A tool.

But as we continued to report, and listen to women, we had an epiphany. What if the "whole self" is an integral part of the new conceptualization of power that we'd been searching for? What if it is both the route and the endgame?

In being our whole selves at work, and in power, we could breathe more easily, we shed the classic power straitjackets, expend our energy for things that matter. We wouldn't have to exhaust ourselves fighting to fit into a prescribed mold. The route to power would become easier and more rewarding, there would be more of us in power, and power itself would become more effective and productive.

But more significantly, making authenticity a priority essentially declares the importance of connection, emotion, nurturing. It openly values that other, shadow power women have always wielded as we care for humanity. It offers, essentially, a gateway to our other selves, represented in all of Alison Wood Brooks's data, all of those "other" things we cherish beyond career advancement—family, friends, community, spirituality—all of those items we often refuse to jettison for more advancement at the office. Whole self at work seems to allow for the possibility of a sudden, magical integration of ourselves, a reality in which we wouldn't feel constantly torn between the conflicting demands of home and family and work and success, because at the very least we're not suppressing anything. We wouldn't have to ignore those myriad parts of ourselves that haven't been valued historically as professional assets. A boss pulling that stuff into the workplace, by the way, also helps men feel comfortable broadening their emotional operating system. And it certainly expands our sense of the qualities we want in a leader.

Authenticity, we came to see, is a critical part of the *joy* in our code. Being ourselves, everyplace, is inherently joyful, and it also attracts us to power in the first place.

POWER AS JOY

However you define power, the road to achieving it is not easy for any woman, no matter the advantages and disadvantages accorded to us at the outset of our journey. None of the women we interviewed sugarcoated the costs. If you want to be CEO, or senator, or editor in chief, or manager, or team leader, or department head, you will have to travel for meetings and work on weekends and catch up in the evenings. It's true of all leadership positions. You will have fewer moments for yourself. It will put pressure on your partner, and you will have less time with your children. We explored, in some depth in the last chapter, why women are so ambivalent about it.

Yet the women leaders we interviewed also show a different side of having power. They show us the satisfaction and pride and sense of fulfillment that come from leadership. It may be that, as Alison Wood Brooks said, having power could be easier than procuring it. These women, at least, made power look, well, . . . tempting. Like something that can bring joy.

Think of Cynthia Marshall and that tiara. "That power, that's queen-of-the-castle stuff." We want what she's having. Her brand of power is clearly fun. She makes a point of tying authenticity, bringing one's whole self to the office, into a creation of joy in her workplace. (The creation of joy, and the inability or ability to express it openly is something Black women in particular are grappling with at work, and is something we explore in chapter 4.)

Similarly, we were struck by the positive energy that infused Ndéye Lucie Cissé because she knows she's now got a seat at the table. Indeed, the more difficult the challenge she described, the more vitality we heard in her voice. Joy, for her, was tied to the meaning of her work, and motivating other legislators around her.

We noted the ease with which Zanny Minton Beddoes seems to carry the role. It doesn't stress her or weigh her down. She makes power seem accessible, almost, dare we say, simple. It's not that she doesn't work very hard; she does. As do all the women we interviewed for this chapter.

The satisfaction, and yes, moments of joy she experiences as a leader, especially when empowering others, is why, Minton Beddoes told us, she wants more women to join her in the top ranks. She often sees the result of the power aversion theory we outlined. She finds it harder to get her female colleagues to step up for promotions than the men. The reasons are varied. Sometimes they say they worry they won't have enough time for their families. Sometimes they just want more time to pursue other passions. Sometimes it's a partner who needs to live elsewhere. She knows they are all talented enough, and she knows that she has found having power doable, fun, and immensely rewarding, but those very competent women often look at power and choose to say no. Minton Beddoes relates to the impulse, but it's frustrating.

Kristalina Georgieva echoed these sentiments, telling us a story, much like Marshall's, about a panel she was on recently, where one woman seemed to shy away from the notion that power is worth striving for. "I want to get women who may be doubtful about taking power to be less doubtful," she said. Is power work? Yes. But she finds intense joy in building a healthy organization, and in presenting another face of power.

Georgieva recognizes, however, that the path to the top is hard, and that even when they get there, women often don't like what they see at the pinnacle of institutions—the jockeying, the egos, all the mansplaining that is an unattractive part of life in most C-suites.

She just doesn't buy the notion that the only way women can ever really achieve equality with men is by putting on those traditional power plays. She believes that even as women rise, if they are brave enough to exercise a different version of power, it can be uniquely effective, and in turn it can make power more attractive for everyone.

The women we have profiled in this chapter helped us to answer, quite clearly, the question we posed in Chapter 1—can women gain power, and use effectively, if we don't play by the old rules? In a word, yes. We also gained a critical component for our power code: Cynt Marshall's radical authenticity is an essential ingredient in the joy of power. And these women have the opposite of a scarcity mindset; they play the opposite of a zero-sum power game. They don't see other women in power as competition—quite the contrary. They actively want to look to their left and right and be surrounded by women. They know it will take a multitude of us to make permanent changes to the power structure, in any organization, to see our society and workplaces change for the better.

"*Patriarchy* is a slightly annoying buzzword," Minton Beddoes says. "But it is true. Men have been very comfortable in a world where they look up to leaders who look like them, are the same gender as them and the same color as them." Disrupting that system will be deeply threatening to white men in particular, she says, and it will take time. But she believes the system is overdue for disruption.

Cissé, Minton Beddoes, Georgieva, and Marshall all believe power needs a new operating system—one of less ego, more joy, and maximum impact. That's what they are attempting to create, in real time, and they want to recruit you to join them. The results, they argue, are enormously satisfying and do enormous good. You are heard more clearly when you climb up Georgieva's high hill. You cannot effect the same kind of change from the bottom of the pyramid as you can when you are "queen of the castle." If we use our power to raise up our communities, be they nations or newspapers, banks or basketball teams, our lives will be marked by successes, and feelings of satisfaction, that are simply not possible if we stay on the sidelines.

YOUR POWER CODE

We asked, in the introduction, whether women can run the world operationally if they don't fully embrace *power over.* The portraits of these women suggest yes, absolutely. They may have played the traditional power game to get to where they are, but they provide incredible templates for how to use it well, and differently, changing the hierarchy as they lead. A few more tips lie below, for joining the recoding process, if you already have some power. For women looking to power up their positions, the challenge might seem frustratingly out of your control. To be sure, there are structures and systems in place (as we've discussed) that feel antithetical to the cultures being created by the groundbreaking women above, but we hope that practicing these steps, or even being aware of them, might give you a view of what's possible, and allow you to role model a new path forward.

Get personal. One way you can encourage others in your organization to flip the switch and see employees' personal lives as an asset is to ask about them themselves. Keeping it simple and casual helps to normalize the conversation. "Peter, how's your son's new school going?" or "Mary, how's the marathon training?" are easy openers. Remember Cynt's success with this—when you bring the outside world into the work world, you are demonstrating that being a whole, rich, human being is not just okay with you; it's something to celebrate. Showing care and concern for colleagues and employees doesn't make you look weak; it conveys your values (relates to theirs) and deepens connections.

Power share. Power isn't finite—someone else's success doesn't diminish yours. So go ahead: celebrate the successes of other people.

That will help promote the collective nature of power—as Minton Beddoes says, it's not about you, it's about the team. Find opportunities to hand out credit—it will have a ripple effect across the group, affirming a culture of power sharing rather than power grabbing. And delegate, don't micromanage. There's science to show it works. When employees feel empowered, it boosts productivity, satisfaction, and feelings of being able to be authentic to themselves by up to 26 percent.[12] The more free range they are afforded, the more powerful they feel, and the more productive they are.

Stamp out fear. As Kristalina Georgieva says, fear has no place in leadership. It might create a short-term blip, but it won't increase retention or long-term performance. Amy Edmondson's book *The Fearless Organization* makes a distinction between having high standards (a good thing) and having employees who don't feel they can speak up or have their opinions heard (a bad thing). Creating a fearless organization starts with exorcizing bad behavior. Lead by example—if you don't yell, you're setting a clear standard. If you're in a position of influence, go further: ban yelling, bad language, and aggression when you see it in others. A simple "Andrew, nobody here is hard of hearing, you don't need to yell to make your point" could do. If you need to make a stronger impression, raise it one-on-one. "John, you're a brilliant accountant, but this organization does not tolerate bad behavior. You won't make management here if you don't treat people with respect."

The return on respect. When your employees don't feel they matter, it costs your organization. Research suggests that respect from leadership is the number one driver of commitment and engagement from employees.[13] The simple act of being treated with respect is more important to engagement (and therefore productivity) than having a clear vision, being given feedback, or getting development and learning opportunities. It's a pretty clear formula: people who feel respected work better, produce more, and quit less. Showing respect isn't hard, and maybe you do it automatically, but it is worth being conscious of.

Be authentic. Your associates will know if you're faking respect.

Be patient. Don't interrupt or speak over your colleagues.

Ask for opinions and really take time to listen to your coworkers and think about their input.

Don't confuse respect with lowering standards. You can and should expect quality performance while respecting your employees. Indeed, demanding high standards shows that you know they are capable of the best and that you respect their abilities.

Conversely, if your boss is, respectfully, demanding a high standard of you, don't take offense. It shows they know you have the ability to perform well.

Enjoy the ride. All the powerful women we spoke to had moments when being in leadership was tiring, stressful, and lonely (especially as a rare woman at the top). But they didn't regret taking the plunge and making the sacrifices to get there. Once they got power, they saw how they could wield it to change their organizations, and the lives of the people in them, for the better. (They also ended up with terrific support systems—teams, associates, even executive assistants who make having power a lot easier.) Focus on the benefits, the achievements, as much as possible. It helps your outlook, and, remember, you are role-modeling!

3

YOUR BRAIN ON POWER

Sometimes, in the course of scientific study, the most novel insights come from the most unassuming tools. Take a simple plate of cookies. It wouldn't seem to have much to tell us about how power affects human beings. But Dacher Keltner thought these tempting treats might be just what he needed to understand people's minds—amped up not on sugar, but on power.

Early in his career, Keltner, a UC Berkeley professor of psychology, was looking for the most basic way to study power and human behavior, to take it out of boardrooms, cabinet meetings, and wholly artificial lab settings, and apply it to regular people. The "cookie-monster" study, as he later dubbed it, has been replicated in many different guises over the years, with surprisingly similar results.[1]

Keltner brought people into his lab in groups of three, and randomly designated one person in each group to be the leader.

All three members of each group were given a fairly boring writing assignment. Then, about halfway through the process, he put a plate of four freshly baked cookies in front of each group.

You can probably guess what happened—at least initially. Each person took one cookie, leaving the last one, to be polite. Keltner wondered who would take that final remaining cookie. In just about every case, it was the person who had been randomly named the leader. One other weird tidbit: the leaders were more likely to eat with bad manners—lips smacking, crumbs dropping, mouths open.[2]

Keltner's study, and other leading behavioral research over the years, concluded that people with more power tend to be less empathetic and more self-obsessed. Power just seems to make people care less about other people and the shift from good behavior to bad behavior can happen surprisingly fast upon the assumption of power. That's a striking headline.

We were intent on understanding what power does to our brains, and where the impulse for it might reside. In our previous book on confidence we had become obsessed with the genetics and science of confidence. We even tested our own genetic predisposition to confidence (low, in case you're interested). For this book we didn't set out thinking there would be a particular scientific link between our brains and power. But we hoped to at least learn whether some people are predisposed to being powerful, as we had found with confidence. Could any part of our gray matter explain the mutual ambivalence women and the current power structure seem to have for each other? The neuroscience of power is more or less in its infancy, but plenty of behavioral science is already beginning to decode how power works, from the inside out.

THE UNHAPPY COUPLE: POWER AND EMPATHY

A team of social psychologists—Joe Magee, Adam Galinsky, Ena Inesi, and Deborah Gruenfeld—decided to test that cookie monster hypothesis in a different way—to focus more broadly on the relationship between power and empathy.[3] They started with a classic technique for behavioral scientists, called "priming." Priming means essentially helping a participant in a study "feel" a certain way, for a limited amount of time, even though that might not be the way he or she generally feels. It's a way of creating a situation, instead of observing people in real life. Priming is a limited stand-in for the real thing, and these studies are extrapolated to the actual world with caution. But they also allow for extremely controlled settings, which life does not.

In this particular experiment, priming was used to sort participants into two groups: one, the high-power group, was instructed to recall and write about a personal incident in which they had power over another individual. In the other group, participants assigned to a low-power condition were instructed to write about a personal incident in which someone else had power over them. For both groups, power was defined as controlling the ability of another person to get something he or she wants, or being in a position to judge, or evaluate someone else. (There is substantial evidence that priming someone to remember a time they were low or high status does temporarily make them act that way.[4])

The next step was a bit bizarre, but illuminating. All the participants were asked to write the letter *E* on their foreheads. Some wrote the letter as if they were looking at it, which would mean it was backward for others. Others wrote it backward for themselves, so that anyone approaching them would easily be able to read the letter *E* correctly. The researchers suspected that the power level of participants would dictate whether the subjects took the extra time to think about what the letter would look like from the point of view of others. They were right.

Participants who were primed for high power were almost three times more likely to write the letter prioritizing their own perspective rather than that of others.

The researchers also tested participants' ability to execute social judgment, think from other points of view, and read emotions—essentially, they were testing for empathy. In every experimental condition, they found that those primed for high power displayed a "reduced tendency to comprehend how others see the world, think about the world, or feel about the world."

So it seems there's an inverse relationship between power and perspective. More power equals less concern for what others are seeing, feeling, and thinking. Galinsky, Gruenfeld, and colleagues also teased out some other gems: power tends to make the powerful favor people who are useful to them, regardless of whether they're likable; it also inflates powerful people's sense that they can influence totally random events, such as rolling a dice (which, obviously, they can't). And here's a fun one: power tends to make people less inhibited, both socially and sexually. Cameron Anderson, a professor of organizational behavior at UC Berkeley, has found in his studies that power makes people overestimate how positively others view them.[5]

David Winter, the University of Michigan psychologist, offers a more historical, if extreme, take on this, reminding us that the German philosopher Friedrich Nietzsche uncovered this link more than a century ago, when he declared that power makes us stupid. "He said that power tends to lead you to a dehumanized view of people; if a person is like this mug I can move, then it's not really a person, not human, not deserving of moral considerations, unconsciously."

Power forces a view from above, Winter notes, causing the powerful to regard other humans in an abstract way, if they even see them at all. (No wonder "power over" might feel so natural, in some sense.) Also, as Winter suggests, "abstraction has a lot of costs. It's extreme to say that the Holocaust was a series of abstractions that people played out, but I'll say that there's a danger to abstract thinking."

But there are also benefits to abstract thinking, he and other experts remind us. A bird's-eye view is critical for managers who need to spot trends and act on them. Abstract thinking allows us to step back, and focus on the big picture. It can also allow for more creativity, because there is distance from more immediate matters. "I do think there's something to the idea that power makes people more abstract thinkers," psychologist Joe Magee offers. It's not that people with power are necessarily jerks, he says, or even uncaring. His take is less value-laden. To Magee, abstract can mean seeing what the ultimate goal is and not getting caught up in what some people would call the minor details (although he adds that details can also be important).

Other studies have pointed to similar conclusions: people with power tend to put themselves before others. For Dacher Keltner the cookies were not sufficient; he wanted to see whether he could extrapolate his findings elsewhere, so he looked at cars. One of his studies found that drivers of the least expensive types of vehicles—Dodge Colts, Plymouth Satellites—always ceded the right-of-way to pedestrians in a crosswalk, while people driving luxury cars such as BMWs and Mercedes yielded only 54 percent of the time; nearly half the time, they ignored the pedestrian and the law.[6] Other studies concerning power and behavior (we might call it common courtesy) come to similar conclusions. Keltner has also found that people in positions of power are three times more likely to interrupt coworkers, raise their voices, or get distracted with other tasks in meetings. The data helps to explain why many workers instinctively feel that empathy is in short supply in the corner office.

We asked Joe Magee the question that really worried us—whether people who are more abstract thinkers, and less empathetic, tend to simply become powerful more naturally. Or, could it be possible that people are less powerful *because* they are more empathetic? But he was adamant on this point: there's absolutely no evidence that abstract thinking drives people more quickly up the ladder. In fact, one study shows that as people are rising up the career ladder they actively benefit from displaying empathy and other so-called people skills. They just tend to forget those qualities once they get to the top.

The key for good leadership, according to all of the experts we consulted, is a balance between abstract thinking and empathetic engagement. The problem with power, as we know it today, is that it often tends to tip the scale toward the former and away from the latter.

So what does it mean, we wondered, that our world is mostly shaped, our fates so often decided, by people who seem to care so little for us, or at least rarely take our perspectives into account? If power were to fall more squarely into women's hands, would the results be the same? Would we take what we learned at the bottom, all those skills the powerful seem to lack or disregard, and apply them to create a different version of power? Or would we, in a female-dominated world, just re-create the same dynamic that men have created?

Based on the women we've profiled in chapter 2, and others we have interviewed over the years, we're convinced that power would look different. Our academic sources also give us reason to think so. Magee, for example, says it takes a certain type of leader to bridge the power/empathy gap. And it sounds a lot like—ta-dah!—a female type. "You've got to be someone who's either really focused on other people to begin with, whether it's because of some feature of the situation or because of some property you have as an attribute that you have as an individual," he explains. "That's when you see that happen." It's worth taking a moment here to talk about women and empathy, because this theme will keep coming up. The notion that women are more empathetic than men may sound like a stereotype. Substantial empirical research has found, in fact, that it is often the case, although there is an interesting a caveat.[7] The empathy aptitude doesn't seem to be based on "natural" ability, but rather, on motivation.[8] Or, put another way, societal gender roles. By way of example, in one particular study, participants were either subtly primed to be sympathetic toward a character in a video, or told nothing relating to empathy/sympathy. Of those not primed—men and women displayed the same level of empathy after watching the video. Of those primed, the women displayed substantially more empathy. The researchers posit that because societally, women are expected to display and use empathy; they tap into it more quickly. So, empathy may be a function of nurture rather than culture. Wherever it comes from, we'll take it, because it's an advantage, an essential tool leaders need these days.

We also found an interesting link between status, or respect-seeking, and empathy, in terms of the female mindset about power. Sonya Mishra, Laura Kray's PhD student, came across some remarkable data that shows a difference in the way power affects the male and female psyche.[9] She found that women, because they seek status, actually handle power differently when they have it. Mishra and her team were looking at a data set from a huge Fortune 500 company when they noticed that as men climbed higher in the hierarchy they suddenly adopted a less realistic view of their organizations, perceiving them to be more diverse, more inclusive, more equitable than they actually were. Moving up seemed to change their brains—it cut them off from reality. As women rose, however, there was no change in perception about any of the challenges their companies faced. "The women's perceptions were unaffected by their rank. But for men, we found this powerful effect where they would transform into 'company men,' as they ascended in rank." They would look down from their high vantage points and see their companies through rose-tinted glasses. Meanwhile, power didn't hinder women's abilities to acknowledge their companies' shortcomings. Women were able to see their companies for what they were, warts and all. (Early data also suggests that non-white women may perceive *more* organizational inequity as they rise in the ranks, but the possible causes of this effect, Mishra told us, need more investigation.)

Broadly, Mishra found that women maintained their ground-level, realistic view more often than the men. She and the other researchers then cross-referenced the data and found, specifically, that when *women had status* they were best able to maintain that connection to people, rather than adopt the fully abstract view that seemed to engulf the men. So, if we can master the power + empathy equation, maybe women really can wield power better than it's being wielded now. We just need the system to work with us instead of against us.

PRIMED FOR POWER

The neuroscience of power, although still emerging, is not only backing up the behavioral research but offering important new findings. Professor Sukhvinder Obhi is leading the charge to peer inside our heads to figure out how power works. He runs the Social Brain, Body and Action Lab at McMaster University in Hamilton, Ontario, and he's been taking the study of power right down to the level of neural activity. He's a Sikh, an immigrant to Canada from the United Kingdom, where he was also part of a South Asian immigrant community, and his other developing area of research involves issues of diversity, equity, and inclusion in leadership. He's in his midforties and, in a sky-blue turban and gray and black Adidas track jacket, has the demeanor of an approachable academic, captivated by and curious about the topic at hand. He offers immediately that questions of power and gender are "all incredibly important," noting he has two young daughters.

"I mean, I'm obviously a member of a minority group myself, a hypervisible minority. So I kind of have some sense of what it's like not to be in the dominant group," he explains. "And I think it's not enough to wait for systemic change—whether it's race or gender, or whatever it might be, because that's going to take, even if it happens, it's going to take who knows how long."

Obhi's research on the subject of power began when he became fascinated by what social psychologists were seeing in terms of a process called mimicking. Social psychologists have found that when you feel independent you mimic other people less, and when you feel socially connected you mimic other people more.[10] Moreover, Obhi noticed, this directly relates to power, and the behavioral studies on empathy we just discussed. "When I'm feeling powerful," he explained, "I don't mimic someone who is less powerful very much. But when I'm feeling powerless, I mimic a powerful person quite a bit. There's asymmetry in the degree of mimicry that people show when they are in a power-laden dynamic."

Obhi decided to examine this phenomenon on the *inside* of our brains, looking at a process called mirroring, and testing for differences inside the brains of the powerful and the powerless. To pause for a second and explain, mirror neurons are a buzzy phrase at the moment.[11] They swing into action in our brains when we take specific actions, but also when we see others doing those actions. For example, if you are a baseball player and you observe another person at bat, the motor areas related to swinging a bat in your brain will also light up, almost as though you, too, are at the plate.

As Obhi puts it, "If you watch somebody on TV who's in a fight scene and you're obviously not there, you're on your couch or whatever, you might flinch when someone gets hit or when they fall over. And what that's telling us is that, at some level, your brain is simulating the experience of the person that you're watching, and that's what we call mirroring, right?" Our brains actually show a similar sort of activation as if we experienced a blow ourselves. Mirroring is theorized to be important for empathy, although Obhi takes pains to note that it is not the same as empathy.

Scientists first discovered mirror neurons' function when studying the brains of macaque monkeys, and today they are viewed as having a critical role in social cognition, learning, and even power dynamics. To understand the relationship between mirrorring and power, Obhi and his team primed participants to feel temporarily more or less powerful.[12] Priming, as we mentioned earlier, is a technique that means, essentially, influencing people to temporarily adjust their mindset. In this case, they relied on a method pioneered by Adam Galinsky, of Columbia University, whom we mentioned earlier. It's called episodic recall, a process in which participants were asked to remember and write about a time they felt powerful.[13] "By reactivating memories, you are actually able to put yourself back in approximately that mindset," Obhi explains.

Obhi and his team then employed a transcranial magnetic stimulation (TMS) machine, which can be used to probe the excitability of the motor areas of the brain. In the participants who were primed to see themselves as more powerful, the process of mirroring all but vanished, suggesting that power truly affects how our brains respond to others, and who we need to pay attention to.

Obhi has since turned up even more interesting insights in the course of his research, and has come to believe that power is linked to a number of brain systems. One is called the behavioral activation system, which basically affects our propensity to get up and take action. For this study, his team again attempted to induce a feeling of power or powerlessness in the subjects. In these experiments, subjects were asked to recall events in which they felt they had power over others, or in which others had power over them. The neat thing about episodic priming is that everyone recalls something meaningful to them. They often included experiences like being in charge as a summer camp counselor or being entirely dependent on teammates in physical, Outward Bound–type challenges.

While we could see what that memory might do to our brains, and how priming for power might work in the lab, what about the lived experience of having power? "I think the work we do probably underestimates the effect of high power," he says. "My two cents is when you have high-level power, you're quite frequently made aware of how much power you have." All those cars, assistants, people agreeing with you—it could bolster your sense of power, and potentially the effects of power on the brain. "A lot of real-world priming goes on to remind people they have power. It's kind of chronic."

In the next step of the experiment, his participants' brain activity was assessed, this time using EEG, or electroencephalography. That technology, which involved electrodes glued to participants' heads, assesses patterns of electrical activity on the scalp thought to represent behavioral activation. Obhi's team found that the people who were asked to remember situations in which they felt powerless had less activity in areas related to the behavioral activation system, literally their left frontal lobes, meaning they are likely to be more tentative, less prone to getting up and taking action.[14] "Conversely," he said, "powerful people show more of this left frontal brain activity." In other words, powerful people are more likely to approach situations, to act. Another striking headline.

Some of the behavioral studies on power have also found a link between power and action. In a separate study by Galinsky, Gruenfeld, and Magee, participants who were given power in a group setting were more likely to take a card in a simulated game of blackjack, more likely to react against an annoying stimulus, in this case, a fan, and more likely to take action in a social dilemma.[15]

All of these findings have major implications for the self-reinforcing nature of power: in real life, people who have less power may be more cautious, and therefore create fewer opportunities for themselves, whereas people who are already powerful would generate more action and therefore more opportunity. (This also makes clear that systemic issues can create a profound disadvantage; people boxed out of the current power structure start well behind in the power-generating cycle.) It's intuitive that having power might give you more "energy," or propensity to action. The implication of this, that power begets power, is also intuitive. But seeing it play out in studies is transformational for the study of power.

When we heard this we started having flashbacks. This heavily echoes the work we wrote about in *The Confidence Code.* Confidence, we had found, is not only about action; it's created when we take risks and act, and even when we fail. We'd found in our research on confidence that women tend to be more risk-averse. Now we were starting to see that lack of confidence could be cross-linked with lack of power. We wondered whether women in general have less activity in their behavioral activation systems (the action centers of our brains) and how Obhi's results broke down along gender lines. When we followed up, Obhi told us that women have the same results as men when primed for power, but that, independent of power, women had lower left-frontal activity than men.

We asked him what that might mean. Are men somehow more "primed" naturally for action? For power? Or, perhaps, is action more relevant to their version of power? Obhi says it's impossible to answer any of that with the current state of research. "But it's worth exploring," he notes.

Claire: I experienced what I think was the "power produces action" phenomenon recently, although I didn't fully recognize it for what it was until we had this research in hand. I've recently become involved in the business of women's sports. I had assumed it would be largely a feel-good time investment. Instead the team was soon engulfed by a coaching and management scandal, and the male owner had refused for months to listen to all outside advice, including mine, on how to be more inclusive; he'd also rejected suggestions that he stop hiring male executives without consulting anyone. (Kind of Management 101, yes?) I had grown increasingly shocked at his head-in-the-sand leadership style. Then, although he was being forced to sell by the league, he still refused to sell to his female co-owner, who he felt had been too "pushy." At one point he suggested to me that if the female owner would just "stay in her lane," focus on "taking the players to dinner" and the like, all would be well. I tried hard to imagine the kind of mind that would think that a wildly successful businesswoman and entrepreneur, who had been brought into the organization for those very reasons by this very owner, should stay in the lane he had in mind, and take no interest in the struggling business. I told him, fairly gently, that his notion was unrealistic. He never reached out to me again.

I wasn't sure at that point what change I could make, and

honestly it was deflating, as angry as I was. I was one of twenty outside investors, without a lot of obvious power. There was a billionaire waiting in the wings with an offer to buy the team, and most in the league saw him as the easy fix. But I started to help pull our investor group together, the women especially, but some men as well. Slowly we were able to get the league to pay attention, and then other owners, and then the public. As we gained power, inch by inch, I felt much more able to DO, to ACT and just keep pushing what, for a long time, had seemed a quixotic cause. I ended up spending about nine months helping the female co-owner battle for, and finally win control of, the team. I distinctly remember, about midway through, understanding that I possessed a kind of power—because improbable things were actually happening! I didn't think of it as power in the traditional sense—call it influence, or outrage—but looking back now, I realize that it was the recognition of my own power that activated me to exercise even more power. Power begot more power. Maybe we just don't always recognize our power—our power to—in the first place.

It's important to know that the kind of power Obhi was using for priming was of the classic variety: participants were told to remember a time when they had *control over people's outcomes.* Would substituting influence change the results? He thought it might. "For women," he notes, "women may use a completely different means. You've spawned the thought in my head that we should pay attention to this. I do think the term *power over* is understood a certain way and could be quite gendered actually."

This also suggests that if women were told to remember a time when they had *influenced* a group toward an outcome, our behavioral activation systems might also light up, perhaps even more if our hypothesis is correct about *power over.* Under that condition, we might feel more motivated to act, just as Claire did when she decided to try to influence a change in her team's trajectory. If discussions of power were oriented in this way—and if the stories we shared demonstrated this sort of power—we might find many more situations in which women were acting with power to get things done. With this reframing, we might begin to see ourselves as powerful and thus use more power and thus generate more action toward the outcomes we want to achieve, creating a perpetual-motion machine of *power to.* It would become a virtuous circle.

Just because scientific research finds that something *is* the case doesn't mean it has to remain that way. As we discovered with confidence, simply because we start out with less tolerance for risk doesn't mean we can't find ways to shift that reality when it's useful (while also recognizing the virtue of caution). All of this research, actually, could be especially important in helping us to find a way to alter a system that isn't working as well as it could—to use our knowledge of our brains to change the power dynamic.

What if acting powerful, for example, could become a healthy habit that might produce results? And acting powerless could be a habit we could learn to avoid? What if, using techniques like cognitive behavioral theory (CBT) or other priming methods, we could learn to rewire our brains for action-packed power? No doubt neuroscientists like Obhi and others will continue to track these questions through their research, not just for the benefit of women but for everyone else, too.

POWER IS A VERB

Clearly, power, as we know it today, *does* things, bad and good. It encourages action and seems to motivate us. We were starting to understand that power can do a lot for us, both at home and at work, if we think about it as a tool. Like confidence, it seems to help grease wheels to make things happen. Adam Galinsky notes another power effect: power offers a patina, or rather seems to encourage us to give ourselves a halo effect. "Power changes the way that we perceive ourselves in social situations: people who are high power inflate their importance compared to those who are low power; those who are high power see themselves as able to get away with more," he says. That's not all good, obviously, but women could stand to recognize our halos, occasionally.

There are other positive power side effects, such as optimism and higher self esteem.[16, 17] Feeling valuable, good, and capable would encourage action, and, in the right hands, with a healthy dose of empathy, that's no bad thing. Likewise, research suggests that a lack of power correlates with depression and pessimism.[18, 19]

Joe Magee agrees that seeing power as a tool is essential: "One of the key points we make is that power doesn't necessarily corrupt. What power does is allow people to accomplish their goals."

Knowing powerful people's goals is essential, he continues. "Because what you can be sure of," he warns, "is that they're going to be more likely to achieve whatever their goals are. And those goals could come from lots of different places." In other words, for selfish people, or people who value power for egoistic reasons, Magee says power corrupts because it lets them meet "self-interested ends even more quickly."

All of this research gives us a scientific basis for the argument that we clearly need people with good intentions to have more power. "For people who really want to do good in the world, power is great. Those types of people can be multipliers," he says, "creating positive results for many other people around them, and society."

It can even be liberating. Jennifer Jordan, an organizational psychologist teaching at the International Institute for Management

Development (IMD) in Switzerland, says research suggests that power not only fuels action, but also might encourage authenticity.

"There tends to be this notion that power corrupts," Jordan says. "But actually, we know just as much that power can lead to positive behavioral effects on people as much as it can lead to negative. We also know power brings out the person inside. So you feel more free to be yourself when you're in a powerful role and you feel less constrained by social norms." This echoes Galinsky's research (the two often collaborate) with an affirming twist. Obviously, depending on the hierarchy in which you exist, there will be limits to the lack of limitations you feel, or the authenticity you can display, but the point is—power, in its pure form, can induce some good feelings. And it could be that helping women understand that would provide an incentive for seizing it.

Katty: Jennifer Jordan's work rings so true to me. As I've risen in my career, and gained more respect, and, yes, more power, I've felt freer to act on my own instincts. That feeling impacts small everyday things, like which meetings I schedule and which I say no to. Even the language I use in emails has changed. I've learned to avoid using "just"—a needlessly apologetic word. For example, I no longer write "I just want to check . . ." but "I want to check . . ." The note of apology, of somehow not wanting to bother someone, or take up space, has gone—it's a subtle but significant difference. But the feeling of authenticity impacts bigger decisions too—which assignments I take on, how I conduct reporting interviews, and how I delegate to team members. Whether the actions are small or big, I find myself carrying them out now from a bedrock instinct of what feels right to me. I somehow know that if something doesn't sit right, then it's the wrong thing to do—not just for me, but for the organization and wider world in which I operate. I'm no longer trying to fit into someone else's agenda. And because I have as much power as I want, I'm freed from acting in negative or inauthentic ways in the hope that of winning more of it. I don't need more of it. Which all meant that when I recently found myself in a professional situation that went against my values and instincts it was easy to say I didn't want to be part of it without agonizing. This kind of power is incredibly liberating.

Even being able to operate a bit more as our authentic selves, without seeking approval, is appealing. It's exactly the environment Cynt Marshall is encouraging, by championing "whole selves." And it's also a state of being, we realized, we observed in our powerful women. Remember Cynt Marshall's crown, Kristalina Georgieva's pleasure at being heard, Zanny Minton Beddoes's satisfaction in the success of others, and Ndéye Lucie Cissé's surety about what her nation's priorities should be. Utterly themselves. Joyful. This—we thought—might be the scientific root of the joy of power. Multiple studies demonstrate that the ability to be authentic, to act freely, to encourage others, creates opportunity for joy.

For women, who spend so much time pleasing people and deferring to men, this is a really useful outcome—like a breath of fresh air. Jordan believes women, in fearing power, may overestimate the costs and underestimate the emotional upsides—it's almost exactly what Alison Wood Brooks told us. Indeed, Jordan's basic description of those benefits reads like a blurb on a bottle of happiness elixir from some magical apothecary.

This formulation "allows you to be able to act without needing approval from others, to do more of what you want and be more of yourself."

Wow. Who doesn't want that?

That's the kind of advertising old-school power should have been doing all along to attract women. It's clear we need to think about power activating as well as corrupting. Power can spur a range of behavior, and reactions, obviously, but it can also have lots of benefits for women.

How's this for a rebrand of that famous Lord Acton warning that we mentioned in chapter 1?

> *Not: Power tends to corrupt, and absolute power corrupts absolutely. Great men are almost always bad men.*
>
> *But: Power liberates and shared power succeeds absolutely. Great women are almost always good women.*

We'd buy that model.

What power does to our heads, to our behavior, the understanding that it starts as a neutral force, leads us back to that essential definitional and hierarchical discussion from chapter 1. Power has a bad rap because of the way it lives in the world now. Not many people see power and joy tied together, for example. But if we can unshackle power from the current structure, from its relationship with ego, from the pursuit of it for its own sake, it can be harnessed to create meaningful impact, joy, and broader appeal. We've seen in this chapter how much mindset matters, and therefore, how we define power at the outset, how we see it, is important in terms of whether we choose to seek it, and also how we choose to use it, and set the norms that will govern it. *Power over,* as Laura Kray told us, is an extremely zero-sum game. Hoarded, scarce commodities produce fear and anxiety rather than joy. *Power to,* however, suggests that power can focus on purpose, can grow exponentially, can be shared.

The most intriguing part of the science dive to us is more granular. Researchers are close to uncovering some basic strategies to override the brain's power propensities, much in the same way that mindfulness and other techniques can be used to change our reactionary or fearful thinking patterns. That might allow for people low in power to jump-start the process of acquiring it with simple mental exercises. And those mirror neurons—just imagine their potential! If we tend to mirror those with more power, then more women in power, behaving and leading well, might lead to more people everywhere generally behaving and leading well, and so on and so forth, which means . . . change.

The science of power surprised us. We didn't expect to find so much data to underscore its inverse relationship with empathy and its direct links to action and to authenticity. All of that helped us to reinforce our code. Jordan's research, and her positive take on power, and Obhi's studies showing power as a behavioral activator, also helped us see scientific grounding for the joy of power. Marshall had helped us find a connection between authenticity and a better power, a more joyful power, but here was another essential link. Power activates, allows us to exercise our will, which also allows us to be more authentic, more of ourselves, more liberated. And that, multiple studies demonstrate, creates opportunity for joy.[20, 21]

Likewise, the behavioral research on the fraught relationship between power and empathy offered more support for our conviction that *Less Ego* is a critical component of any new code. Maintaining empathy, in addition to respect seeking, helps women guard against the negative influences of power. *Less Ego* had seemed, initially, like a fringe benefit to the way women use power; now it seems like a basic safety requirement.

We came across a take from bestselling author, academic, and vulnerability expert Brené Brown that helped us to see the elements of our code as mutually reinforcing. In her book *Dare to Lead*, Brown outlines a similar divide between *power over* and *power to/with/within*, noting that the latter conceptualization encourages connection and humanity, and helps empathy-driven agendas to thrive; when the focus turns to empathy, community, relationships, meaningful work, that is when authenticity and joy ensues.[22]

So *More Joy* makes power more appealing, more authentic, which attracts women, who create *Maximum Impact*, who focus on purpose, which in turn nurtures joy and authenticity. And *Less Ego* supports all of it—*More Joy* and *Maximum Impact.*

Our code, our definition, our supporting pieces, at this juncture, stacked up like this in our minds:

- Exercising our will, being liberated to act with authenticity, to access our broader values, offers *More Joy.*
- Using influence, respect and empathy, eliminating the hierarchical power over, all result in a safer power with *Less Ego.*
- Focusing on the why, inherent in power to, in purpose, creates *Maximum Impact.*

That is our code, the outline of a better power product, for us, and, indeed, everyone.

There are, of course, just a few limiting factors in its wildly successful rollout; a roiling workplace full of old-school anti-women obstacles, a work-life tug of war that refuses to find balance, a dark ages domestic life for most of us, and a lot of male angst. We choose, in the following chapters, to see those as opportunities.

YOUR POWER CODE

Science is still evolving, but there is already plenty of research to draw on to help you build a more powerful mindset. Remember, your brain is plastic, is malleable, and with behavioral exercises there are ways you can mold it to think and feel differently.

Speak it. Words matter, and just a few choice phrases can actually prime you and others for power. It can be as simple as using words that sound positive, are motivating, and give your associates a sense of mission and control. The aim is to prime your employees for leadership, no matter their current level. Try it for a week and note the impact.

Words to embrace: helpful, goal, team, leader, integrity, efficient, excellence, vision, performance, character

Words to avoid: stressful, task, pressure. Phrases like "just follow the instructions" take control and power away from people.

Practice priming: Before a big job interview, or any other important work event, set aside fifteen minutes. (Schedule it in your calendar.) Then recall a time in your life when you have felt powerful.[23] Think, specifically, of a time when you've felt powerful *in relation* to other people—a time when you were influencing others to make a change.

Next, write it down. Don't just write about the actual event; write about how it made you feel.[24, 25] (That will get your behavioral neurons firing.[26])

Spend at least five minutes writing about it. Neuroscientists say writing on paper is more effective than typing on smartphones or tablets because it takes you more deeply back to that memory, and connects your brain with it.[27] But you need a few minutes of writing to retrieve the memory.

This exercise will prime you to feel more powerful, and act more powerfully. It's not necessarily a long-term fix, but it will last through that interview or presentation. And bit by bit it will become habit forming. Other people will notice your more powerful self. Adam Galinsky found, in studies of interviews conducted with primed subjects, that not only did the interviewees feel more powerful, and write better cover letters, but the interviewers picked up on their power.[28] Those who had primed themselves for power had better outcomes.

Prime yourself for goals, joy, and confidence. You can also prime yourself for the psychological qualities that help to support power—things like goal seeking, happiness, and confidence.

To prime for goal seeking, take five minutes and list your goals. The time frame doesn't matter. You choose whether it's your goals for the next week or the next year. Make a written note of how those goals make you feel.

To prime for happiness, remember moments of intense joy—sit in those feelings.

For confidence, make a list of your recent accomplishments. Study it—go back a year or two even. Again—focus on the feelings as well as the events.

Goals, joy, confidence are all things that "activate" us and help get us into power mode. Researchers, by the way, have also found that people primed for power impress colleagues, and it's not a fleeting boost.[29] Weeks later they still make a powerful impression.

Make power priming a habit. Because power can have reinforcing benefits, putting yourself in a position to have some of it on a regular basis can make a difference to your life as a whole. Social psychologist Pamela Smith, who teaches at the University of California, San Diego, says the roles we have can change our basic cognitive processes.[30] She's found that when people are assigned to managerial roles, whether in a real organization or a simulated one, they are more likely to act decisively, take risks, and think optimistically.

If you have opportunities to wield power at work, take them.

Even if you haven't been eager, maybe these power benefits will convince you it's worth a try.

If you are in a powerful role already, pay attention to any behavioral benefits you are feeling—that might help counter any stress that comes with having more authority.

If you don't feel you have much power at work, look for a role outside of work in which you can take the lead. It might be a volunteer opportunity in your local school or church. Once you start feeling power in that role, you'll be in a better position to take on power at work.

Micro-primers. Actions and tasks aren't the only way to let yourself experience power. Listen to what you tell yourself and make changes in your own language.

More: I can, I have, I will.

Less: I can't, I've never, it's impossible.

Primed for opportunity. Armed with all of these power-priming habits, and the research on power's benefits, you may start to shift your mindset. You're offered a promotion and you see possibility rather than peril. Yes, that new job will mean a bit more strain at home, but you already juggle the multiple demands of family and work anyway. And actually you do it pretty well. Will one rung up the ladder really be so different? Take it one step, one promotion, and one new job at a time.

It might not be as bad as you think at work: you may not be able to hire new staff immediately to help you achieve the goals of your new position, but you can draw on the social capital, status, and respect you've built with peers and other department leaders to help you stretch your resources. Power priming—and this kind of positive (even just non-catastrophic) thinking—can have lasting impact.

4

WHAT HAPPENS WHEN EVERYONE'S FED UP AT WORK

Luckily, Clara Green tells us with a firm smile, she doesn't scare easily. She hadn't been naive enough to believe that every person would be on board with the changes she and her team have been driving. Still, she hadn't expected to receive something as threatening as hate mail.

Green is the chief diversity, equity, and inclusion officer for Regions Bank, a retail bank with offices throughout the southeastern United States. She was brought into the company to diversify the bank's twenty-thousand-strong workforce. She is a disruptor, a woman on a mission to change a largely white, predominantly male financial institution in a region steeped in the worst atrocities of discrimination and segregation.

Regions Bank, under Green's steerage, and with the backing of a very determined CEO, has done a commendable job diversifying its workforce. From 2019 to 2022, they've deliberately changed the makeup of their senior leadership group. Whereas Regions had only 20 percent women in senior leadership roles, three years later they had 32 percent. The number of people of color in the group has gone from 8 percent to 19 percent in the same three years. It was a commitment we noticed when we spoke at their women's symposium. When it comes to things companies can do right, Regions has a lot to share (see chapter 7). But the story of that hate mail underscores how fraught the disruptive journey is.

Green's story reveals a constellation of current workplace tensions: sexism, racism, ever-shifting gender boundaries, and the new rules of post-Covid work. On top of all that, she's in charge of not just distributing but *re*distributing power more equitably. That means she's juggling every single constituency that feels shortchanged at work, which these days seems to be pretty much all of them.

NOBODY'S HAPPY

Over the last few years we have interviewed hundreds of people in dozens of professions. Male and female, Black, white, Brown, old, young, senior executive, junior associate—nobody is holding back about the way the working world is failing them. What we've heard is a catalog of complaints, the discontent often veering into sexism or racism.

"I would apply for that London job, but they only want a woman, or someone of color."

"If one more man tells me they can't find a qualified woman for the job, I'll hit them."

"He just competes with me *all* the time. It almost makes me want to quit."

"They'd never tell a man to be less dramatic."

"White women aren't much better than white men. They don't share power with us, either."

"I can't afford to make a single mistake. I'm the first woman to have this job."

"I should get a seat on a board, but I'm a white man so that's never going to happen."

"I'm all in favor of diversity, but not when they choose people who aren't ready."

"I'm done with massaging their egos. We do all the work and then we have to make them feel good, too. It's exhausting."

"What does #MeToo mean for flirting at work? Is that forbidden now, too?"

There's the frustrated white guy who feels he's being denied opportunities because he's, well, white and a guy. The woman of color who can't find allies among her white colleagues, including white women. The woman who found herself, during Covid lockdowns, juggling work, kids, and everything that comes with running a home while her husband blithely ignored the domestic side of things. And *all* the women who tell us they are done boosting egos, being perfect, and ignoring patronizing putdowns. They just want to do their jobs and get an equal shot. They are increasingly certain, in fact, that they do their jobs quite well, even better than the competition.

This sudden discord, the open expression of dissatisfaction, is the result of the multiple upheavals that have rocked the working world in the last few years.. The Covid pandemic brought unparalleled disruption, forcing all of us to rethink structures and systems that had been taken for granted for decades. The #MeToo movement pulled back the curtain on women's reality in ways that could no longer be ignored. Add to that the anger and the urgent call for racial justice that was sparked by the Black Lives Matter movement after the murder of George Floyd.

Also throw into the roiling mix women's long-running frustration that our progress has stalled, and that women still face unique burdens at work, especially women who are in an "other" category. Just a few examples: Women of color are interrupted or have their judgment questioned at a higher rate than white women do.[1] Black women are far more likely to be coping with the impact of racism and racial trauma. Latinas are less likely to earn flexibility in their jobs, and they have even less flexibility at home. Asian women feel unfairly overlooked at work, especially in terms of leadership; they have fewer interactions with senior leaders, and are not noticed as individuals. Lesbian women often have their judgment questioned, get negative feedback on how they present at work, and are often told they are too outspoken and confrontational.

No wonder we're all disgruntled as we face a reckoning about what it means to hold, and withhold, power.

BACKLASH

A by-product of today's raw, tumultuous workplace: women and minorities are less afraid to speak up—about everything. And when you challenge the status quo, backlash is never far behind.

In 2016, before "MeToo" was even a hashtag, Stefanie Johnson, an associate professor of management at the University of Colorado Boulder's Leeds School of Business, was studying sexual harassment in workplaces. She surveyed 250 women in the US to understand how harassment impacted their work. Then #MeToo rocked the world and she decided to do a second survey. In 2018, Johnson, along with three colleagues, talked to 263 women, some of them from the original research, to find out what had changed.[2]

Because not all incidents of sexual harassment are the same (ask any woman), she measured it in three broad categories, in ascending severity: gender harassment, unwanted sexual attention, and sexual coercion.

In those two years—before and after #MeToo—she found that incidents of *overt* sexual coercion (pushing a woman to have sexual contact with a colleague) and unwanted sexual attention (ogling, leering, touching) did indeed decline. But reports of gender-based harassment (sexist remarks, inappropriate jokes, showing sexual material)—stupid, annoying crap, in other words—all of that actually *increased*, from 76 percent of women saying they'd experienced it in 2016 to 92 percent in 2018.[3] That's quite a jump.

Johnson thinks that increase is partly the result of women speaking up more about everything, but even more likely it's men behaving badly because they were threatened by the movement. "It's a backlash towards women post-#MeToo and a sense of men having reverse discrimination," she explains. "Men say they feel their boss is being inclusive and so they feel they are experiencing discrimination and have fewer opportunities."

Many men told her they also felt wrongly accused by a movement that didn't discriminate between bad guys and good guys. It didn't even seem to matter whether an accusation was actually made. "It's obviously not true," Johnson says. "Women don't think all men are sexual abusers. But I think there's a feeling among men that 'just by the nature of my gender, I'm guilty.'"

Backlash against #MeToo may limit our upward trajectory in more concrete ways. Research by the journal *Organizational Dynamics* has found that men have become significantly more reluctant to interact with their female colleagues:[4]

- 27 percent of men avoid one-on-one meetings with female coworkers. Yep, that's right, almost a third of men don't want to be alone in a room with a woman.
- 21 percent of men said they would be reluctant to hire women for a job that would require close interaction (such as business travel). That number was up from 15 percent in 2018.
- 19 percent of men would be reluctant to hire an attractive woman (and more than 10 percent of men *and* women said they expected to be less willing than before to hire attractive women).

Meanwhile, the threats that Clara Green at Regions Bank experienced are just one demonstration of how the fight for racial justice has also created serious tensions even as it has catalyzed change. The head of human resources at a different major financial institution, whom we'll call Gwen, put it this way: "George Floyd changed the world. . . . [His death] made us all look at our promotion rates and say, 'Let's go!' Our promotion rates are higher than they ever have been." But she points out that many diverse candidates are still getting stuck on the way up, and that the push for change is sowing noticeable discontent among some white employees.

It's also true that change is, in fact, still slow. After George Floyd was murdered, American companies pledged $67 billion to racial equity programs.[5] But a study by Creative Investment Research shows that as of August 2021 they had actually delivered only a small fraction of that money.[6] If you're a Black woman, the post-#MeToo and post-BLM world is particularly burdened with disappointments. Gwen described a conversation with a CEO who questioned why the bank was even bothering with diversity. His question to her was, "What's in it for me?" In one quick swipe he managed to devalue diversity efforts as a whole and also her entire job. Black women leaders may face added frustration because they happen to be more ambitious than other women. Fifty-nine percent of Black women leaders say they want to be top executives, compared to 49 percent of women leaders overall. But they are much more likely to get signals that it will be harder for them to advance, and to say they've been passed over for opportunities because of personal characteristics, including race or gender.

"There's definitely backlash about everything, it's happening," says one head of a major law firm who wants to remain anonymous, and whom we'll call Susan. The worst human behavior, she notes, "happens when people are insecure." She still hears gripes about women who seem too "full of themselves," or complaints that "males don't need to apply" and general grumbles about no ability to advance in the company.

On the other side, Susan also hears anger from women who don't want to be boxed into corporate roles that traditionally have gone to females, so-called staff jobs like general counsel or head of human resources. Nobody, Susan observes, feels "relaxed" about their options these days. Perhaps that's wishful thinking in the world we're living in.

EVERYDAY POWER DISSONANCE

The turmoil of this moment has made many of us less tolerant than we used to be. We notice commonplace inequities with a fresh eye and a deeper sense of grievance. Those moments aren't typically full of dramatic clashes—they are more subtle, as several women helped us understand.

Louise (not her real name), a successful film director, was recently filming a high-profile TV show in Europe when she bumped into another director who was also there filming. She'd known this man for ten years; their kids were in the same class at school. When she told him what she was doing there, he looked shocked. "How come I didn't know you were a director, too?" he asked, with distinct irritation. She knew exactly what he did for a living. He didn't know what she did. But somehow he implied that it was *her* fault that he wasn't informed. In the past, Louise says, she might have responded with an almost knee-jerk apology; perhaps she'd failed to inform him. But his casual rebuke made Louise realize he had never really taken her seriously as a peer, or even as a potential competitor, in a way that he would have taken a man seriously. Now, in that European capital, he finally acknowledged her as his equal. It was a small thing, but it made Louise surprisingly angry, and it's changed her behavior at work.

She had been bothered by this kind of subtle slight for years, but had accepted it as the kind of background noise women learn to shrug off. The male-dominated TV industry is full of blatant misogyny. (Did you know there is one camera shot, a medium close-up, known as a Two Ts—"two tits"?) But thanks to today's climate, and to her success, and after that run-in with a fellow director, Louise decided to do something different. When she feels she is treated by studios, or producers, or crew in a way that wouldn't happen to a man, she immediately texts the people who hired her. She no longer cares whether it makes her seem "difficult." She has noticed lately that when she complains, things do change on set. At least for a while.

Claire: I was sitting in a meeting a few years ago, pre-pandemic and post-#MeToo, discussing the best way forward in a serious challenge our organization was facing. I noticed something I'm not sure I would have focused on in years past. One of the women started to offer her opinion, and she was, within about a minute, interrupted by one man, and then another. Both enthusiastically broadened her point, but it felt to me like she was just there for the benefit of offering them a launchpad, so we could listen to their really profound analysis. I felt a surge of indignation. I'm diplomatic by nature, and in the past, even if I had noticed questionable behavior, I might have wanted to address it later, privately, and gather consensus. Instead I interrupted. "Kate didn't actually finish her thought, and I'd love to hear the rest of it," I said. "And then perhaps we can take turns speaking." I felt my armpits sting in the hushed pause that followed. But then Kate dove in, and, for the rest of the meeting, everyone turned to me, looking for a kind of unofficial nod to speak. In this case, my anger was channeled into speaking up and demanding that another woman be heard. As awkward as I felt, it was for the better.

The difference between having power and not having power, as Kristalina Georgieva said in chapter 2, is being able to speak up and be listened to. Louise is at the top of her career, and Claire has amassed plenty of power and status. But younger, less senior women rarely feel they can challenge the ways and means of the workplace.

Consider Elizabeth's story (she asked us to change her name). She's twenty-four and works in the offices of a Democratic Party committee, prepping an executive for press interviews. She replaced a twenty-eight-year-old man who got promoted, and within weeks he was deliberately making her life hard. "It started out that he'd cut me off, or steal my chair when we're sitting in the chairman's office." It got progressively worse. "He'd kind of put his body all over the meeting table so the chairman wouldn't be able to see me. Small, petty things like that."

Even her bosses, who were both women, would roll their eyes when they saw what he was doing. "They're like, 'We understand. We get this all the time.'" And they were his superiors. "Do we just have to accept that men are going to behave in ridiculous ways?" Elizabeth wonders.

She is just trying to get her job done, but this guy is still operating by the same old playbook. Like so many men, he's resisting change, and in doing so he is contributing to a heightened feeling of discord, because Elizabeth is aware of how wrong his behavior is.

She's aware, awakened, but squeezed on both sides. There's the guy in her office who's constantly, in her view, playing power games, and then there are her female bosses, too busy or too cautious to make her problem their problem. She just hopes that by working hard and being the best she can be, she'll get to bigger and better things. "It's the battles versus the wars, and I'm not going to battle over everything."

Where have we heard this before? Elizabeth's good intentions—to just do her job excellently, and not cause trouble—are exactly the same sentiments we've been hearing for the last few decades. In some ways, not much has changed.

A partner at a top strategic advisory firm, in her late fifties, whom we'll call Amaya, says that pattern is remarkably familiar. "I'm Hispanic, and I mentor a lot of young women at the firm, and there's an overwhelming sense of we don't want to rock the boat, from all women, but in particular women of color." says Amaya. "They want to get promoted. They want a raise."

Cole (not her real name), a twenty-five-year-old television journalist, notes it can be a double burden to "perform" at work as a mixed-race woman. "Are all of your interests the same? You have to think about the way you might talk with the boss, or connect, talk about the weekend—how you make small talk. Also, any flaw or chip in your performance is just likely to be taken more seriously. There is pressure to be kind of squeaky clean in a way."

We would like to think that after all the upheaval of the last few years, and the enormous focus on the #MeToo movement and racial justice, younger women wouldn't think twice about rocking any boat they chose. And many say they want to. But the reality is more nuanced. Sometimes, yes, women in their twenties feel empowered to speak up when they encounter bad behavior, but often they don't; it is just remarkably hard to do. So there's still a lot of "going along" with crap in order to "get along and get ahead." And maybe it's too much to put all this on the shoulders of younger women, especially women of color, to expect them to conduct a power revolution by themselves. If even Louise or Claire, with decades of experience, finds it draining to publicly call out misogyny in real time, little wonder that Elizabeth or Cole do.

Perhaps a better way to see the situation is as a continuum of positive change. Back in the 1990s, when we were in our twenties, we simply ignored bad behavior. It upset us, but it wouldn't have occurred to us to complain—it was the price of having a job at all. Over time, and with more women taking leadership positions, we started noticing when men belittled us. We found allies, commiserated with our female friends, and sometimes we spoke out. Today young women tend to find allies sooner and seem to have fewer qualms about calling out bullies, rejecting stereotypes, and demanding changes, big and small. There is progress. But let's not kid ourselves that it's easy.

During our careers, we, too, have employed keep-your-head-down self-preservation tactics just like Cole's and Elizabeth's. The difference is that we used to feel somehow that we were the ones not playing the power game right. Elizabeth, in her twenties, is more clear-eyed: she sees the guy's tactics for what they are. But the fact is, we're still largely in an increasingly maddening holding pattern when it comes to measurable progress.

Just a few numbers to be aware of, lest you believe your situation at work is unique:

- Far from rising, women's participation in the labor force has actually plateaued.[7]
- Attitudes to gender equality are no more advanced today than they were in the mid-1990s.[8, 9]
- The gap in pay between men and women, which declined rapidly in the 1970s and 1980s, narrowed a bit in the 1990s and has largely stalled in this century.[10]
- In 2020, for every $1 earned by a white man, white women earned $0.79, Black women earned $0.64, and Hispanic women earned $0.57.

Even though:

- We now do better in school than men.[11]
- We get more bachelor's degrees, we get more graduate degrees, and we even get more PhDs than men.[12]
- We have fewer babies (so as not to interfere with career advancement) and we are having them later.
- The changing nature of the modern economy favors us, too, as

brain-powered service jobs have replaced physical labor as the main driver of employment and higher wages.[13]

On the face of it, women should be miles *ahead* of men at work. On the basis of our résumés, more of us should be CEOs, more of us presidents, and we should be getting paid at least as much as, if not more than, men. Remember, we are better educated, in an economy that values analysis over muscle power. Indeed, in today's world of intense automation and AI, we could argue that the most important thing humans add is their empathy, emotional intelligence, and analytical reasoning. In theory, this is the perfect moment for our skill set.

Yet even women navigating the very pinnacle of power still see the obstacles, and perhaps in more stark relief these days. "I just thought we'd be further along as a group by now," sighs a top woman in finance, whom we'll call Jeannine. She scaled the ladder, expertly, landing in a coveted senior position few women reach, and can't believe, given her substantial power, that she's still dealing with the same treatment. "I mean, I wouldn't call my colleague a misogynist, exactly, but he instinctively thinks women are less qualified." She says he recently went behind her back with clients, and gaslit her in a way that she found stunning. Her real-world conclusion about different approaches to power is the same as ours: "It is something I would never do. Women just don't play the game the same way." She echoes Laura Kray's analysis, explaining, "We don't think of it as a total zero-sum game. You don't have to lose for me to win."

A psychology professor at a top northeastern university, whom we'll call Camille, is heavily focused on stereotypes, bias, and people with threatened identities in her research. She hasn't found the magic bullet for rupturing the status quo, despite her expertise. She notes that in her world, the existing hierarchy (largely male) still resists change and maintains a tight grip on what constitutes academic excellence. She's got multiple degrees from similarly elite universities, and a stellar pedigree, but she's still had to combat a steady refrain of comments and questions, especially early on, about how valuable or scholarly her work was. "Honestly, the thing that's helped me most, as a woman of color, in the sciences, is having been an athlete. You drive to the hoop, and there are so many people out for you. I realized I'd seen and felt all of this before. I actually knew how to deal with it." Her strategy now is straightforward: avoid the obvious pitfalls, or places she can't feel "psychologically strong," like large faculty meetings with very few women or people of color, and keep her focus on the realms in which her perspective is valued and needed.

Susan, the head of that law firm, said she had a revelation about different operating styles at a high-profile breakfast meeting she recently attended with many prominent, mostly male, titans of industry. Before the event started, she noted something she had overlooked before—most of the men were strutting around like distracted peacocks, holding small audiences with each other as they jockeyed for prominence, one eye always scanning the room for somebody more important, while the women largely found their seats and stayed there, not at all performing the same ritual. "Why are these powerful women not using that networking event in the same way?" she wondered. "Why did they go right to the tables and sit down instead of joining the men?"

She understood then that even women who have risen to the top, but are still outnumbered, continue to feel out of place in situations that have been orchestrated by men, for men. At the moment, she would argue, we still need to play by those rules, and she offered a tip from her personal handbook when she's navigating events that take place in the evening hours, and struggling to hold her own in the male arena. "Purely based on my size, I just can't drink heavily for two or three hours," as is the usual practice. "I was advised and have deployed the 'finding a plant' method." We imagined the plant method as something complicated, subversive, having to do with "planting" an idea and perhaps slipping out early. Planting a friend to help. No. It was purely old-school—"Sip, but mainly pour my drink into the plant."

We couldn't stop thinking about her anecdote. Susan is in *the* room (ideally one full of well-placed plants), the room where it all happens, but it still feels inhospitable. She has power but still feels, in some ways, not part of the club. Her stories, among many, led us to wonder again about the need for a different structure. Our first instinct was that maybe women should just get up from their seats at that breakfast, fight the uncomfortable feeling, and strut around the way men do. Or, for other occasions, learn to drink. But we realized that what Susan was reporting may not be a situation in which women just need to "catch up," or "learn technique." She may be witnessing a clash of power styles.

Perhaps we should establish a parallel operating style, the finance bigwig mentioned, one that, to Jeanine's point, feels organic and, as Jeanine mentioned, non–zero-sum; we might stay in our seats, invite a few others to join the conversation, and then our different, more welcoming way of interacting might become a signal for other people to drop the exhausting preening and sit and talk with *us*.

We imagined what it would be like to design something entirely new. It would have a completely different—and we think more open—feeling to it. If we want a world where everyone shares power at the top and then uses it to change the organizations they lead, we need to work toward creating a space where everyone can express their strengths rather than operating within opposing systems. The world isn't binary at all; it's moving beyond labels. The halls and rooms of power should be, too, and not only in numbers but also in attitude.

We believe this is the right moment to get there, because so much is up for grabs. Is it too pop-culture to offer some wisdom here from Littlefinger, beloved *Game of Thrones* villain, and remind everyone (picture a sinister smirk), "Chaos is a ladder"? Expectations of work and the workplace itself have been upended. But we need to be both idealistic and realistic. We know we can't design a utopian parallel power structure, and ignore the one that is currently in place. The challenge is to rework the existing system by identifying the most formidable obstacles in our path (gory, frustrating details to come in chapter 5) and, brick by infuriating brick, remove them, and build what *we* need all the while adding what we want as we go.

YOUR POWER CODE

If you've already got power, use it to make life at work better for those who don't. You can afford to take risks and speak up. The more you do it, the easier it becomes. If you've survived the anxiety of calling out bad behavior once, it will only be easier the next time. (Psst—using your power for others adds to your store.) If you are still starting out, how do you battle a system that feels rigged against you? There are things that you can do right now to tip the playing field in your favor.

"Let her finish." Start complaining in real time. You can make the world better for those below, and for yourself, when you call out biased behavior as it happens. It creates a small ripple, and it's remarkably effective. Trust your instinct; it's a useful, well-tuned radar. If something feels wrong, it probably is. Jeannine, that high-powered finance executive we spoke with, is one of the only women at the very senior levels at her institution. She gave us blunt, fearless advice about the way to call things out. When you're in a meeting and Joe talks over Jamilia, again, use your power to jump in and say, "*Let her finish.*" If you like, you can add a "please," or, "Let's hear what she was about to say." Or try, "*Let me finish,*" when you're being cut off. We wondered, when we heard her formulation, whether it's too "aggressive." Our instinct, as always, would be to soften the edges. No, Jeannine explained. It's quick, to the point, almost like it's not a big deal. She has found that's the kind of language men respond to. When you add a lot of explanations it can sound "whiny," which is, in her view, not as effective. Practice it at home. We've employed it lately, and it's intoxicating.

Cancel code words. Listen for language that disparages women and call it out in real time. Some phrases are obvious: "emotional" or "overreacting" or "difficult" or "bitch." Others are less obvious and offered under the guise of "good fun," but are equally damning: "prima donna," "Negative Nelly," "Debbie Downer." Plan your real-time comeback in advance—sometimes humor helps: "Bob, you're dating yourself. We haven't used language like that to describe women since the 1960s." Or remember Claire's new go-to: "I don't think we call women colleagues crazy anymore." You'll be surprised how much thanks you'll get from female colleagues, and how many men will start turning to you for gender etiquette advice.

Flip the code. Research shows that in performance reviews men are more often described as "competent" and women as "compassionate."[14] Humans are both. When you're overseeing performance reviews, use it as an opportunity to introduce the new code: "Suzie is an effective leader who cares for her team." While you're at it, praise Dave for his compassion, too. That's a remarkably effective way to encourage men to step up their own empathy game.

Share space. Look around and notice who might have an even harder time climbing the ladder. Black women, for example, are almost twice as likely as women overall to say that they can't bring their whole selves to work and more than 1.5 times as likely to say they don't have strong allies. One young Black woman described to us the frustration of feeling as though she's putting on a mask every day at the office. Be aware, even in everyday interactions.

Meanwhile LGBTQ+ women are underrepresented in management positions, and they also face more sexual harassment and obstacles to promotion.[15] Make a conscious effort to power share and distribute it widely. What does that mean? Actively checking in on colleagues after difficult headlines. Publicly advocating for racial and gender equality. Calling out discrimination. Offering to mentor and sponsor women of color. Or do some of the inclusion work. When a slot comes up on the DEI committee and your superior turns to your queer or trans colleague, your Hispanic colleague or Black colleague, step in and offer yourself, or better still, offer Steve, the white guy in the department, the spot.

5

POINTLESS PERFECTION AND OTHER BURDENSOME BIASES

Our bold new world of work would start with an office thermostat that works. For us. At the moment said thermostat forces us to huddle in our cubicle in a thick sweater in the middle of August because some neanderthal engineer didn't think to include women's lower body temperatures in the calculations for where to set the standard temperature of most offices. Offices just weren't built with women in mind, in ways big and small. We could perhaps overlook the dumb physical stuff—the height of podiums for presentations, the lack of private places to pump milk, the absence of convenient parking spots for pregnant women (more of these "fun facts" in our Flawed by Design section ahead)—what we can't ignore are the more pernicious systemic hurdles that keep women from the top. Our gaze, in this chapter, is on some very specific barriers and biases. We've identified them in our many years focused on women and leadership, and we believe they are keeping women out of command and control positions.

Flawed by Design

- Most modern offices set their temperatures based on an average worker who just happens to be a forty-year-old man weighing 155 pounds.[1] This was fine in the 1960s, which is when the temperature formula was arrived at, when the average worker was indeed a forty-year-old man weighing 155 pounds. Today about half of all office workers are women. But no one has thought to change the thermostat. That is why we sit and freeze. Offices aren't designed for us. Literally.
- Companies typically don't reserve parking spots for pregnant women near the office entrance.[2] It took a heavily pregnant Sheryl Sandberg arriving at Google to get the company to change.
- Speaking podiums are designed for men, not women.[3] Anyone who has ever done any public speaking knows what it's like to arrive onstage and realize that the monolith of a podium comes up to their chin. It's hard projecting authority when the audience can't even see you. Good public speaking is an important qualification for almost anyone who wants a leadership position. The podium matters.
- Work gear, from body armor in the police force, to personal protective equipment (PPE) in hospitals, to safety harnesses on building sites, to the weight and size of tools, even the bulky dimensions of an architect's portfolio (no women have arms that long!)—all those work tools are designed with a man's weight and build in mind. When it is adapted, it's just sized down, but that still doesn't take a woman's build and bone features into account.
- Women are 17 percent more likely than men to die in car crashes because most cars are safety tested with male dummies.[4] We are actually safer drivers than men.[5] We're a lot less likely to be involved in a crash, but because car companies are stuck in some ancient world where women don't drive, they haven't bothered to make them safe for us. Indeed, women are known in the industry as "out of position" drivers

because we sit farther forward than men—translation: it's really our own fault if we die. We were doing it all wrong.

- Don't get us started on how tech doesn't work for us. We know men think big is better but do smartphones really have to be the size of a minor planet? Women's hands are about one inch smaller than men's, which makes the ever-increasing size of our devices hard for women to grasp.[6] Fitness monitors don't include the steps we use up doing housework. Fitbit doesn't even recognize the activity of pushing a stroller.

The impediments are formidable largely because they are nebulous—hazy customs and cultural artifacts that work against us. They are double standards and bedrock assumptions about leadership that apply to women alone, and they reflect our need for a broader conceptualization of power. We have to focus our efforts on calling out and dismantling those obstacles because change at the top creates outsize change everywhere else. The good news? We now see them for what they are. Even just a decade ago, the two of us might have assumed some of these roadblocks were legitimate—that the fault was ours, somehow, as women. There is power in seeing how warped they are, and crying foul.

Remove these stumbling blocks and our ranks will swell: our brand of power will flourish as a matter of course. Here are barriers that apply to women only:

- The cost of free labor
- The perfect woman peril
- The promise-versus-performance paradox
- Checklist Charlie

Free Labor: It's Essential, but You Don't Always Have to Do It

Think back to Clara Green. She is the DEI executive charged with making Regions Bank more inclusive who got threatening letters in the process. The security team investigated and the CEO gave her his full support, but the culprit or culprits were never found. But none of that was as tough as what unfolded in 2020. "That was definitely the hardest year for me. It was a year of me trying to process what I was thinking about the senseless deaths of George Floyd and Breonna Taylor and Ahmaud Arbery. I was trying to process that in my own personal space of having a Black husband and a Black brother and Black nephews and trying to think about how they were coping," Green says. And as if processing it all personally wasn't enough, she found herself with another load to carry: not only her Black colleagues' emotions, but also her white colleagues' emotions. "To come to work and have to coach other people through that," she recalls, "that was probably the most trying time for me ever at work."

The burden of having to educate her white colleagues through that time of upheaval compounded the anger and the concern she was already feeling. They didn't know what to say, or whether to say anything, or what language to use when they did say something. Somehow it was her job to guide them through it on top of dealing with her own sorrow and anger—and because she is kind and diplomatic, she did it with grace. She looked after them. As women, Black and white, so often do. What Green was doing, in some of the toughest circumstances, was emotional labor.

It's become a buzz phrase but what exactly is emotional labor? In her book, *Fed Up: Emotional Labor, Women, and the Way Forward*, Gemma Hartley defines emotional labor as the combination of the management of emotions and the management of life. "It is the unpaid, invisible work we do to keep those around us comfortable and happy," she writes. Emotional labor has to be done in marriages (obviously), in friendships, in families, and, yes, at work. In professional organizations it often takes the form of sending out birthday messages, organizing celebrations, or simply smiling a lot. In service and retail sectors, and any client-facing industries, emotional labor is an essential part of a company's performance. (A hotel with scowling staff won't get many customers.) It drives profits. But honestly, it's good for business everywhere.

For a start, high doses of emotional labor in a company make for a solid retention strategy. When managers actively support employee well-being, those employees are 19 percent less likely to feel burned out, and 38 percent less likely to consider leaving the company. They're also 33 percent more likely to recommend it as a great place to work, according to McKinsey's Women in the Workplace research.[7] And, little surprise, senior women leaders were 60 percent more likely to provide emotional support to their teams, particularly during Covid.[8]

The constant nurturing is necessary, especially in times of stress, but tiring. One female manager summed up her role during the Covid pandemic this way: "I feel so much responsibility for my team's well-being. There is no line between the workday and the after-workday. I'm taking care of everybody. I will regularly have conversations with my team, 'How are you feeling? What do you need? Can I remove barriers?'" As one female vice president told researchers from McKinsey's Women in the Workplace study, "I definitely think emotional labor is being taken for granted. We're so focused on revenue as opposed to the skills required to manage teams remotely in a Covid world." That makes no sense to us, because in a world where managing talent impacts profits, emotional labor is a bottom-line issue.

Here's a curious twist to women's emotional labor story. There's evidence that once we have power we stop doing it—at least one element of it. Alison Wood Brooks of Harvard Business School has found that women in low-power situations laugh more than men—not because they are happy, but as a way of being deferential and amenable. Once women get into positions of power, their inauthentic laughter completely disappears.[9] They stop trying to please people; it's as if they are liberated, at least in this one specific way. As we've mentioned, for women, *getting* power can be more exhausting than actually *having* it.

When women aren't laughing at men's jokes, or otherwise tending to their emotions, they're spending a lot of time on other unpaid, unrecognized tasks—what have become known as nonpromotable tasks, or NPTs. These are the jobs, not unlike emotional labor, we do at work to keep the organization running smoothly, but they also aren't things that will get you noticed or rewarded.

Nonpromotable tasks are things like sitting on a governance committee, acting as an informal mentor to junior staff, taking notes at a meeting, or onboarding a new hire. Take a second to think how often *you* do those thankless tasks. According to research by a foursome of female academics—Linda Babcock, Brenda Peyser, Lise Vesterlund, and Laurie Weingart—who wrote a book together, titled *The No Club: Putting a Stop to Women's Dead-End Work*, women are asked 44 percent more often than men to do work that doesn't lead to promotions, and they are 50 percent more likely to say yes.[10] The authors found that women don't particularly like doing these extra tasks, and, interestingly, they aren't necessarily better at them than men; we just say yes more.

Amaya, the senior strategic consultant, told us that Zoom and remote work in some ways made the practice disturbingly clear. "What I found astonishing," she says, "was you'd be on a screen full of boxes after a meeting, and you know, we'd have to do follow up on scheduling, or organizational work like that, and the male partner would look at the screen and then nine times out of ten pick the woman, even another partner, and say 'can you make sure we all get together next week.'"

By definition, time spent on these kinds of necessary but undervalued, low-profile activities means less time spent doing the high-profile things that lead to promotions, like building contacts with a new client or spearheading the marketing strategy for a new product line.

Here's the really irritating thing: When women do say no to these thankless tasks, it hurts our careers. We are seen as unhelpful, or not a team player.[11] And, you guessed it, the same negative consequences don't apply to men, simply, say the *No Club* authors, because men don't get asked to do these tasks in the first place.[12]

For now, even when this work is officially part of a company's mandate, it doesn't seem to change how it's valued. Many companies have programs to help promote diversity, equity, and inclusion—and guess who's participating in them? Senior-level women leaders are twice as likely as senior-level male leaders to take on this important work, which is often undertaken in addition to their actual jobs and carries no formal recognition or increase in salary. Eighty-seven percent of companies think the work of supporting employee well-being is critically important, but somehow that doesn't translate into actually treating it that way. Only 25 percent of them say initiatives in this area are substantively recognized. When it comes to DEI-focused work, those numbers are 70 percent and 24 percent.[13]

How do men and women handle this unrecognized labor in practice?

We spoke to Gwen, the executive at a multinational finance corporation, about the way she sees it play out in her company. She told us about two people who both run major divisions in the organization; one is a woman we'll call Carrie and the other is a man we'll call James. Both of them have team meetings as a part of their purview, but the way they approach them couldn't be more different.

James holds one meeting a week for his entire group, and it's structured as a kind of "call out" meeting in which people update the team on what they're doing and where they're hitting roadblocks; it's a meeting where staff "report out" on their work, rather than a meeting in which team members collaborate to get things done.

Carrie, on the other hand, holds five team meetings a week. Not only that, but each one has a structured agenda that guides people to come together to identify and address specific challenges in specific areas like HR, operations, consumer issues, and more. In other words, she's doing work before each meeting—of which there are many more—to ensure that her team is as well informed, prepared, productive, and supported. James, as Gwen put it, operates on a far more casual "just tell me your problems" level.

This contrast plays out in other ways, too. "We just hired someone and he had a birthday. Carrie made sure he had candles and cookies. She's automated sending birthday notes to twenty-five thousand people and people respond to that. I've worked with James for twenty years and he's never even recognized my birthday." Not only is Carrie performing far more unseen labor to make sure her team gets good work results, but she's showing that she cares about them as individuals. It builds loyalty and shows them that, to her, they aren't just cogs in the corporate superstructure.

Research shows, however, the emotional labor Carrie engages in, along with the nonpromotable tasks she fulfills, will not count when it comes to promotions and career growth.[14] She may lead a happier, more diverse team, receive higher employee retention rates, and earn higher marks when it comes to leadership traits such as "emotional intelligence"—all metrics that most progressive companies say they value these days. But when it comes to getting a power seat at the table, little of her effort seems to matter.

For better and for worse, women tend to see their role in the workplace differently than men do. We feel it's part of our jobs to support and empathize, to say yes to extra jobs, and even if, as *The No Club* suggests, some of us don't particularly enjoy it, we still take it on. The office, to us, is a place filled with real, complex people to be invested in; it's not simply a battleground filled with toy soldiers whom we can advance or leave on the field. If they aren't formally recognized as valuable, as part of a promotable portfolio, we certainly need men to share those tasks so we have enough time to focus on the things that do get us promoted.

We can't help but think that if companies made sure men did more of this work, the way it's viewed would change as well. Instead of being quiet, crucial, but low-value work, it would indeed factor into performance reviews and promotions, rewarding everyone for taking a broader, more holistic approach while creating a healthy, sustainable work culture. Of course, if men did take on more of it, women could do less, shifting the imbalance just that much more. That in turn might make it easier for women to start saying yes to high-visibility, career-building activities and experiences.

The Perfect Woman Paradox

This gets us to the "perfect woman" problem. This is a dilemma that was amusingly illustrated for us by Canadian CEO Josipa Petrunic. We met Petrunic at a women's conference where someone asked us how we respond when male executives say they would love to promote a woman but they just can't seem to find the "perfect" candidate. At that point, Petrunic piped up, "I'm fed up of being asked to find the perfect woman for a job. Now I just say, 'Find me a mediocre woman.'"

We all laughed. Petrunic had hit on something important. Plenty of men get promoted who are pretty average, but women, well, they have to be perfect, and then some. So we were intrigued by this notion of a mediocre woman. We followed up with Petrunic, speaking to her a couple of months later from her home in Toronto, where she is director of CUTRIC, a Canadian transport systems company. She fleshed out the perfection paradox with a story of her own. She was contemplating a career in politics, a move that was prompted by a cabinet minister she'd recently met.

"I think he's a great minister but he's great because he's reasonably above mediocre and has competence. And guess what. There's a thousand women who are just like that," Petrunic told us, a clear note of defiance in her voice.

She's right, of course. It would be absurd to think that every man who has risen to the top is a genius—and the great majority are certainly no more of a genius than the average woman. It's simple math. Some people are amazing, some people are useless, and most of us are somewhere in the middle. But somehow the corporate world still insists that women have to be exceptional to be trusted with the same positions of power that average men have held for generations. And it's even more extreme for women of color.

It's not just the achievements we have to rack up; it's the very way we have to behave. That has to be perfect, too. Perfectly male.

When gender expert Michelle King was researching for her PhD what holds women back at work, she interviewed dozens of men and women in two large multinationals and asked them to describe their perfect employee.[15] Consistently, both genders described someone who works long hours, dedicates themselves to the organization, competes for promotions, is on the whole an extrovert, and, oh, isn't encumbered by caregiving responsibilities.

Adam Galinsky, whose research on women and power we cited earlier, pointed us to a related finding: when we do seek power, women are often more careful and thoughtful about it. Slower to seek it. He saw this looking at statistics on women running for office, which don't always show an obvious gender gap. But, he adds, "there's a huge gender gap over time. Women are much less likely to run early in their careers, but then they're actually more likely to run later than men are." Galinsky says when women who run for office have more experience, they don't get the same degree of backlash or stereotyping. And experience is always, of course, useful. More of it may make us better leaders. But there's no question that all that time we spend planning and preparing puts us behind men who, as the research in chapter 1 suggests, seem to have fewer qualms about stepping up to the starting line even if they've had less experience and less preparation. Does the pressure to be perfect come from external forces? Or is it self-imposed? A little of both, we'd argue. But we're convinced the working world is driving this, with unrealistic expectations, and that has to change.

The need to appear perfect, to never try too much too soon, makes every stretch assignment feel risky and potentially damaging to our carefully acquired reputation. "If you dare to do something, the consequences will be severe, or people won't believe you, or your reputation will be ruined, or no one will follow you, or no one will support you," Petrunic says. It's no longer that women are told they can't do things; it's that they are reminded of all the things that could go wrong if they do. Understandably, that puts them off even trying to run for office, or go for a top job, or stick their head above the parapet in any way. We then fall into the perfection paradox ourselves, fearing we are never quite good enough.

In the end, Petrunic gave up on a career in politics because too many party bosses told her she'd have to spend months knocking on doors and running coffee mornings to earn her stripes. That was something, she knew for a fact, several senior men in the party had not done. Prime Minister Justin Trudeau's cabinet, she told us, is full of men who parachuted into cabinet positions from careers in the private sector. A path open to a man, it seems, but not a woman.

"I don't think men accept that a woman doing less is okay. We've created a standard where women doing one hundred and fifty percent is the norm," Petrunic concludes with an exasperated sigh. "I think we need to get to the point where we don't expect to have to hyperachieve to be considered good enough. And by the way, what is mediocre for a lot of women is actually already above and beyond the vast majority of male candidates."

She Needs Performance, He Just Needs Promise

David Leonard had a revelation when McCarthy Tétrault, the Canadian law firm he runs, tried to promote more women to equity partners, and came up with just one. One out of seventeen. One woman and sixteen white men made partner. That was *after* the firm had declared its intention to do better.

David was not happy. Rather than just accept that the women in his firm weren't good enough to be promoted, which is what some of the other male partners were suggesting, he launched an investigation and he found a systemic pattern. Time after time the male candidates were being promoted on the basis of what they could *potentially* achieve, while the women were being asked to demonstrate what they had *already* achieved. It was the difference, he says, between promise and performance. No wonder the men were making partners more often; it was so much easier for them. The women had to have jumped through all these hoops already—the men, well, they just had to show they had the potential to jump through them one day.

Insights like the one Leonard had aren't isolated events. Research shows women often fall into this pitfall of performance over promise. Professor Kelly Shue at the Yale School of Management examined data from a major American retail chain and found that every year women are 14 percent less likely to be promoted than men at the company—in large part because the women aren't seen as having leadership potential.[16] This is despite the fact that they get better scores on actual performance. So, women do their jobs better, but don't have leadership promise? Yes, crazy.

What Shue found is a bias in what constitutes "potential." To have potential, employees had to have characteristics like assertiveness, ambition, charisma. Those are traits more often associated with men. They are also very subjective and lead to a pretty strong bias against promoting women. That is why the retail company had fewer and fewer women at every rung up the ladder. Female leaders, by the way, were just as likely to downgrade the potential scores of their female subordinates as male leaders were. Biases are tough to dislodge, for all of us.

At McCarthy Tétrault, Leonard used the company's promotion results to force changes. "We had a bit of a crisis there and I think a good crisis always allows you to move things forward," he told us. He put in place systems to ensure that different standards were not being used for women. "Where we would take lots of bets on men, now we take more bets on women."

We don't want to single out law firms—these kinds of biases exist in every industry—but Leonard's experience did remind us of another story we heard from a major global legal practice. That firm, which spoke to us off the record, realized it had the same problem: hardly any female partners. So the CEO, whom we'll call Mr. Marcus, tasked the head of the commercial litigation division, whom we'll call Peter Smith, with improving the numbers.

Smith was assiduous. He found some great female candidates, he encouraged them to apply, he sponsored them through the process, and, when it came to the time for new partner selection, he was confident that he'd found a whole group of great new women partners. Not so fast. Not a single one of those super-impressive women made partner. He was stunned (welcome to our world, we hear you say). When he asked the management committee what happened, he discovered that every one of those women were seen as having "issues." One hadn't worked outside Europe; one didn't seem committed to the firm; one had no experience in mergers and acquisitions, one had young children and, you know, might struggle with the hours; and one was too new and hadn't proved herself yet. The reasons went on and on, until one by one each woman was turned down.

"They had just confirmed the problem. Men get promoted, women have drawbacks. It was staggering," he said. "Not a single one of those 'issues' would have been enough to disqualify a man." It left him wondering whether the CEO really wanted more women after all.

Amaya, that senior partner at the advisory firm, told us "forget promise, performance isn't even recognized."

A woman she's been mentoring is brilliant, strategic, loved by clients, and has been at the firm thirteen years. "She manages up and down seamlessly, clients love her, partners love her, often saying when she's on their team, they don't have to work." The mentee was up for a promotion, and there was no question in my mind she should be promoted," Amaya told us. "But I was told, 'Well . . . we don't know. Can she really bring in business?' 'Yes,' I said, 'she already does.' 'Can she really talk to CEOs?' 'Yes, she's already advising CEOs as we speak.'" Finally they offered this breathtaking flaw: "'Well, she has a resting bitchface on Zoom.' I was like, 'Really, you're kidding me, right? What does that mean?' I said. 'Well, like, she looks unhappy.'"

So. No promotion, another year, and a coach for said employee. A male at the firm, also talented and far less experienced, got promoted. He had threatened to leave. The woman? Disappointed and mad. But she will stick it out, because she feels she invested too much time to walk away.

These "issues" are disturbingly vague, hard to counter, and remarkably tenacious—all hidden barriers women face and men don't. However much promise we have, we are never perfect when we have "issues."

Checklist Charlie

Let's come back to the lawyer who didn't make partner because she didn't have experience with mergers and acquisitions (M&A). At first glance that might sound reasonable. The firm had always required that candidates for partner have experience in different areas of the company's business, and she lacked a qualification that was seen as essential.

But was that particular experience really so critical? Maybe she had skills in other areas that made up for that gap. Most of the hoops we have to get through to secure a promotion, the official or unofficial "checklist" that exists in almost every place of business, have been constructed over the decades by and for men, with little question as to whether said checklist is the only method for evaluating performance and securing promotions.

This list of requirements, whether made public or not, presents special hurdles for women—not due to our poor skills, obviously, but due to the assumptions underlying the checklists themselves. They tend to include requirements such as a posting overseas, experience in a specific department, the ability to travel frequently at the drop of a hat, or the ability to work fourteen-hour days. Their very structure is biased toward a traditional model of work, which is done by men, with men, for men—with women as "helpmates" keeping the home fires going.

Consider a senior executive whom we'll call Sally. Sally works for a firm we'll call BBB, a big multinational corporation with hundreds of thousands of employees. You'll know it, you've probably been a customer there, but she's asked us to change the name to protect her position. BBB has a rule that highflyers can't even be considered for the CEO job unless they've run one of the company's foreign operations for a few years. This usually involves a three- or four-year posting anywhere from South Africa to China. Ambitious candidates are expected to live wherever the company wants them to, whenever it decides. It's an exciting prospect, but it's also a career block for most women.

On a recent call to discuss candidates who might be in the running for the top job, another senior female executive pointed out the inequity—and the fact that the company had never had a female CEO. Perhaps the two issues were related, she said. How many women with a working spouse and school-age children can suddenly uproot the family for a few years in Brazil? The ruling simply excluded women from the race. And anyway, was it really so critical? she asked.

The CEO listened but was adamant. Mothers could do foreign stints just as well as fathers, he insisted. It was essential for a thorough understanding of how BBB worked around the world. Several women joined the dissent, but he wouldn't budge. One by one they went through the list of potential candidates for the top job. One by one female candidates were struck off the list because they'd either made it clear themselves—or worse, it was assumed—that they couldn't do one of those overseas postings. Having started with a list that was fairly evenly split between men and women, in the end only male candidates remained.

What's happening in BBB and so many other companies is maddening.

First, the premise is flawed. The idea that one foreign posting really lets you understand the whole world is silly. You can learn about the Latin American market just as well from the US as you can from a posting in Japan. Second, the CEO clearly didn't know, or didn't care about, the data. Men who make it to the top tend to have wives who don't have careers. Women who make it to the top tend to do so in spite of having husbands with jobs of their own. It would be wonderful to live in a world where men were as willing to change their expectations and roles in the household in order for their wives to succeed (and we'll have a lot more to say about why they don't in chapter 7), but it's not the reality. Only two in ten women in the top 1 percent of earners have husbands who stay at home, compared to seven out of every ten men.[17]

This experience caused Sally to question her future at BBB, and, after realizing she'd never have a fair shot at the top job, she left. It is their loss. Although this example of an unenlightened "checklist" has to do with foreign experience, it might apply to any number of items that have traditionally been the stations of the cross for executives moving up the ladder.

And who wrote that damned checklist anyway? We need to create a new checklist, in the open, that feels like fair play.

The checklist wasn't designed with us in mind, and why, really, is it the only way? After all, that God-given, immutable item on the checklist—"Everybody must be in the office five days a week"—is gone, and, no, the corporate world hasn't fallen apart. Indeed, it now seems almost absurd to think it was ever a rule. So who's to say that lots of other items on that checklist can't be revisited, too? We clearly need a more flexible, transparent, and organic understanding of what "requirements" are really necessary to get us into positions of power. But more than that, in fact, those requirements need to change. They've never integrated, supported, or valued the unique strengths that women bring to the workplace—the power to act on many values simultaneously, to focus on the end result rather than focusing primarily on gaining power over, to give just one example.

The discord, the seismic change of the last few years, is uncomfortable, but within all this disruption, this workplace cauldron, lies opportunity. And we have to seize it. We can take advantage of this rupture from the status quo to tell the honest story of how we feel about our working lives. Maybe the truth is that no one wants the old kind of corporate culture anymore—men included. Covid is like a blacklight we've turned on to our workplace, exposing all of its unappealing distortions. Women have come away with a greater conviction of what is not working for them, and we're more willing to express it. But, actually, everyone is now questioning what it really means to be fulfilled.

We shouldn't, though, rely on an act of God to change the workplace. That's horribly inefficient. Values that have been typically associated with women are spreading (think back to Alison Wood Brooks, to Cynt Marshall and authenticity), and we can fan the flames. If we could remove stubborn obstacles, figure out how to accommodate the ways women tend to work, the way we more naturally want to use power with less ego and more impact, and get real with each other about the way we *all* would like to operate and lead, no one group would control the room. More and different paths to success would open up for all of us.

We know that diversity within companies produces success, so it's only logical that having multiple paths to the top will result in better outcomes for companies and the people who work at them. This is the world that would come from having a broader definition of power, different concepts of leadership, not as competing in a zero-sum game, but as essential elements of a better whole.

YOUR POWER CODE

These systemic challenges are deep rooted; no simple tip list for individual women is enough. We highlight some innovative organizational solutions in chapter 9—but there are things you can do to start to chip away at the status quo.

When they want you to be perfect. In a way, your internal battle with perfectionism is the easy bit. You still need to overcome the system's unfair expectations that all women must be exceptional. But there are ways you can help yourself do that, too.

Cut yourself some slack and recognize that there is indeed a double standard. Even this knowledge can reduce some of the pressure you put on yourself. And remember that the playbook for perfection was written by white men, for white men, over centuries, but that doesn't mean it's the gospel truth.

Enjoy the fruits of your hard work. (Remember, there's joy in power!) When you have success, tell your boss about it. That's how you'll get the full benefit of all those hours toiling away. Women are more prone to underselling their achievements than overselling them—so don't worry about bragging. Promoting yourself will change perceptions of you. One reason Robert is already seen as perfect is that he doesn't hold back on touting his achievements.

When you see a perfection paradox, call it out. If doing that publicly is hard, use the performance review, or ask for a one-on-one conversation with a superior. If you know a male colleague has been given an opportunity denied to you, but hasn't got any more qualifications than you, ask why. Even raising the question can alert your superiors to an inequity.

Good enough. We cannot say this often enough. Do not allow your employer's "perfect woman syndrome" to become your own. You will never be perfect. There. Now give up trying. There are lots of useful tips out there for overcoming perfectionism—embracing the idea of failing fast, testing the waters with small, less-than-perfect steps. Once you embrace good enough, it is fantastically liberating. Those extra two hours noodling on that report? Spend them sleeping, exercising, or just watching TV instead.

Own your assets. Know the data. You've got the message by now that the corporate image of "perfect" has been pretty one-dimensional and basically male. We're changing that, and as you remember with Cynt Marshall in chapter 2, authenticity can be powerful. Take authenticity one step further by not only owning who you are, but also recognizing and then promoting your particular strengths.

Choose your style. Jeannine, the top New York financial exec, puts it this way: "You can't just imitate others. Try styles out if you like, until you find what feels genuine. Then go with it. I still often start my conversations with 'I could be wrong about this but . . .' and it's not ideal, but it's part of my thing now. Remember, other people can smell a fake."

Get educated. There are lots of tools online for assessing your own particular strengths. To sell them as an asset, you need the research to back up your pitch. If you're more of an introvert, for example, have the information on why your particular quality is useful to the organization. For example, a *Harvard Business Review* study shows that people who feel they have been heard are less anxious and perform better, and that listening is better than feedback as a leadership tool. Use nuggets like that to make your case, to sell that less tangible quality of "promise."[18]

Limit free labor. Emotional labor, nonpromotable tasks—it's all essential to the running of any good company and your bosses need to value it—but you don't have to do all of it. You have to do some of it, but probably only about half of what you're actually doing.

The first step is to recognize it for what it is. Literally make a list of all the tasks you do that fall under the category of free labor. It will look something like this.

Organize Sam's going-away drinks.

Research new data software.

Write up notes from DEI committee

Shepherd summer interns.

Order coffee/pastries/lunch/dinner/birthday cake—any type of food delivery is a classic NPT!

The second step is to say no to any more NPTs. Yes, it's hard. Yes, it has to be done. So, try this:

Start with a good positive response (Sam is such a great colleague, we are really going to miss him) followed by a no, ideally one that subtly shows how valuable you are in other areas (I am busy with the marketing project and there's a tight deadline) followed by a helpful alternative (I know Chris has time, he'd be great at this).

If you really can't manage an immediate no, buy yourself time. ("I'm really busy right this minute, let me get back to you on that.") Then talk yourself into the No Code. Remember, getting rid of things you've already said yes to is much harder than saying no in the first place. Amaya, the senior consultant who told us what she observes on Zoom about tasks being handed to women, suggests handing the task back to the person who handed it to you. "Can you handle the follow-up, Jim, because I'm back-to-back all day today? I just won't get to it." She did just that recently, and her recounting of it made us laugh out loud. She knows that not every woman will be ready to do this, but she's been gratified to have younger women call her afterward and tell her how great it made them feel even to witness this audacious exchange.

No laughing matter. Women go the extra mile to make those around them comfortable. It makes a nicer atmosphere but it can be tiring work. Some of this work is essential. But not all of it. We mentioned earlier, for example, that women often feel compelled to laugh at work. Try this: stop forcing yourself to laugh and smile when you aren't feeling like it. As the research shows, male peers aren't doing that. Your female bosses aren't doing it, either. It doesn't mean you have to scowl or be rude; you just don't need to spend so much energy being jolly (or ending every sentence of an email with an exclamation point to show how cheerful and energetic you are!). See how that feels.

The nudge. You're growing more confident in your own power and valuing your assets for what they are. Now it's time to nudge your peers in the same direction. Women are great at complimenting and listening to each other. Take action. When you see a peer shying away from a position with more power, taking on yet one more unpromotable task, or procrastinating because only perfect will do, nudge them in a new direction. Studies show that one respected person suggesting to a woman she should take on a new role often makes the difference in her deciding to take the risk. You'll be their ticket to power.

Men matter. Jeannine also suggests the power of kindness when bias is spotted. "Just because they've said or done something wrong doesn't mean they are bad people." When you take the time, after a meeting, to perhaps offer more advice, or raise issues, she has found most men really are grateful and want to learn. "They are often relieved to talk, and the floodgates open. Humor helps a lot." Yes, the burden is on us, again, but it's in our interests to guide. If a man asks how he can help, here's what she tells him: "Stop interrupting. Ask what a woman thinks. Give women good assignments. If a woman is doing a lot of the work, but you are called on, say something like 'Ellie is the real expert here.' Men validating women is really powerful."

6

THE BLEND

Mariana Atencio is immaculately put together. Makeup, clothes, shoes—we have never seen a hair out of place.

We don't usually mention the way women look or dress, but Mariana makes a point of telling us that being well turned out, every minute of every day, takes focus, effort, and, critically, time. In other words, it's work. The thirty-eight-year-old businesswoman is disarmingly honest, and an intrepid risk taker.

From her hip, sun-filled office in Miami she bubbles over with energy and enthusiasm. Mariana left a promising career as a correspondent in network television to set up her own media company. She and a cofounder are taking on the corporate world, having grown their company, GoLike, into an exciting force in the media content business. She is in demand to give speeches and host conference discussions; she makes documentaries and podcasts and is ferociously committed to promoting other women. Especially women of color. Being her own boss, nurturing her company's growth, becoming a successful female CEO in a largely male world—this is how Mariana uses her power. She doesn't mind that it requires a 24/7 commitment. She has big plans to "build an empire."

What Mariana does not have plans for is children. When we press her on that stance, she doesn't waver.

"My work, my company, it's my priority. It would be a tremendous hurdle for me to have kids—and have power," she tells us. Indeed, when she founded her company, she split up with her boyfriend of eight years because he wanted to start a family. In their Latin community, her decision was particularly unusual and difficult. "If you don't have kids you are failing. It's a very conservative culture." Of her thirteen good female friends, who are all Latin/Venezuelan, only four are still working and only two of them have kids. The other nine are stay-at-home moms, with three kids each. (Yes, all nine have three kids each—what are the chances?!)

Mariana stands out as a fusion of the old power code and the new one. On the one hand, she still feels that she has to make a choice between a career and kids. It's something most men haven't had to do because their wives do the heavy lifting at home. But she embodies the new code in that she's unusually confident about her choice, openly ambitious, and quite clear-eyed about the limiting factor of time for most women. And she also, by the way, walked away from a testosterone-fueled hierarchy when she saw it would limit her progress, and wasn't in line with her *power to* goals.

For Mariana, giving up her professional dream is inconceivable. "We put one hundred and fifty percent of our time into this job," she explains. Running the social media side of a content company means round-the-clock posting. "People want to see what you eat, what you read, what your bedtime routine is. And as a woman, particularly in a Latin culture, you have to look amazing in every post." (Hence the time-consuming hair and makeup routine.) Women are pulled in so many different directions, she adds, and as female founders of a start-up they are expected to be even better than men.[1] So even when women reject the established hierarchies and start their own companies, they still can't escape the perfection paradox we unearthed in the previous chapter.

As Mariana sees it, the only way she could realistically have a child would be with a dad who stays home more. "Yes, please," she says jokingly. "Help me find a supportive stay-at-home dad who also makes me laugh and stretches my mind." She fears, before she even finishes the plea, that the chances of finding such a person are slim. Mariana describes herself as a hopeless romantic who would love a relationship, but she won't even entertain the thought of dating someone who doesn't support her ambition. Are men put off by that? we ask. "Woof! Latino men especially," she chortles. "They've even told me they find it a turnoff."

It's not just in the Latin community. In more communities than we like to admit, ambition is not generally seen as an attractive quality in a woman.[2] It took Mariana a long time to even say out loud the words: "I am ambitious." Full disclosure: we can't understand why anyone would miss out on an opportunity to be with her. She's remarkable.

But it's not Mariana's romantic life that interests us, or at least not her romantic life in isolation. We're intrigued by her choice to pursue a career over motherhood, and, more importantly, by the fact that she has to choose at all. Are we really still talking about this—the choices women have to make between love, work, and family? Yes, clearly we are. And, yes, it still seems ludicrous. Mariana's decision is her own, and we would never second-guess it, but we do ask, why, in the twenty-first century, is the way we work still forcing such tough trade-offs on women and families?

One way to think about this tension is that women, as we saw with Alison Wood Brooks's research, place value on a broader array of life goals. We are pulled in many directions because the range of things we find important is so big. The standard answer is we have to choose: get a babysitter, or, as Mariana believes, a husband who is a stay-at-home dad.

What if there was a system that actively valued and even compensated a focus on nurturing our families and communities, as well as valuing and rewarding fierce work ethics and bold business minds? In that power hierarchy, we, men and women, would be able to thrive without having to make such a radical choice. Our pull toward achievement in multiple venues, our abilities to nurture, care, keep a focused eye on the next generation or the welfare of a group, is part of our *power to*—it's the uncompensated power we already wield, and is critical to society and our lives. But it needs integrating, needs to be part of our Blend. (And, as we discuss in chapters 7 and 8, men would be happier embracing it as well.) We need to work toward a culture where our brand of power, one that includes women's many strengths and interests, is universally appreciated—rather than seen as something that needs to be tamped down.

GOOD RIDDANCE, WLB

We're as tired of talking about work-life balance as anyone. We really didn't even want to deal with it in this book. First, it feels so retro, so 1990s. Shouldn't it have been consigned to a dusty, clichéd exhibit at the Smithsonian's American history museum—something featuring a frazzled plastic replica of Modern Woman: nylons, briefcase, heels, baby, pan full of bacon?

More than a decade ago, we wrote a book called *Womenomics*, which took a deep dive into issues of workplace flexibility. It was full of thought-provoking new data on the value that women bring to corporations' bottom lines, and the productivity returns of allowing women, and men, to work flexibly. It made a compelling case for more control, more time away from the desk, and more family-friendly work practices. That book was written when we both had toddlers around the house and were trying to figure out for ourselves how to have fulfilling jobs, careers, and enough time for our families. We described a new way for women to look at their careers by seeing them not as a ladder that needs relentlessly climbing but as a wave where sometimes you dial it up and sometimes you dial it down. At the time, it seemed that corporations, employers, HR, governments—everyone was on the WLB case.[3] Change was afoot.

Now our kids are essentially grown, and the puzzle, sadly, is still far from being solved. In fact, a recent study by Deloitte confirms that 38 percent of women across ten countries rate their work-life balance as "poor or very poor" (we rather wonder who the other 62 percent are). Recent data looking specifically at burnout in women is concerning. According to a survey by LinkedIn of almost five thousand Americans, 74 percent of women said they were very or somewhat stressed for work-related reasons, compared with just 61 percent of employed male respondents.[4] The pandemic laid bare that number, making plain what women already knew. We have intensely competing priorities that Zoom calls from our cluttered kitchen tables have exposed for all our colleagues to see. Balance, suffice it to say, has not been achieved.

The second reason we didn't want to tackle work-life balance, we realized, is the discordant sound of the term. Post-Covid, it rings empty. With a new employee mindset and a younger generation more interested in putting life before work, the notion of a tenuous balance between the two seems out of whack. At the moment, yes, many of us do still feel sliced and diced, but we don't really want a precarious old-school balance, or to choose between things we value. We want something more organic.

Here's what that looks like: time for intellectually satisfying careers *and* time (that is not rushed) for looking after our children and elders, volunteering, building satisfying relationships, and having strong bonds of friendship. We want the ability to be ourselves, with all those elements of ourselves, every place we go. What stresses us out is less the work itself and more the tension between all the different things we do, whether it's raising children, taking an ailing parent to the doctor, or creating a fantastic presentation for the board of directors. We want the radical authenticity Cynt Marshall is modeling, and we want to use it to more fully embrace and integrate our broader value set—all of those things that Alison Wood Brooks discovered are making us wary of the traditional power climb. Getting this Blend right, in other words, is essential to the success of the new power code.

We're constantly being pressed to make binary choices—childless career or stay-at-home partner. Our employers want us to put work first, or, if we can't, to quit work and focus on family. Our families, and even society, may assume we'll be there 100 percent of the time for them, and if we're not, then we're somehow lacking as mothers, wives, and daughters. That's one reason women are more likely to say that they are stressed for work-related reasons than men.[5]

Just take a look at Japan if you want to see what happens to a country that has made even less headway than the US in finding a satisfying solution to the demands of work and home. Japan has many jobs that demand serious hours, long commutes, regular after-work drinking sessions, and an antiquated view of family dynamics. Japanese women don't typically get help at home. It's not culturally acceptable for dads to do the cleaning, drop the kids at kindergarten, or make the evening meal. That's why Japanese women are increasingly concluding that it's impossible to combine work with family life. Here's what's new. In the past, they almost always chose children instead of a job. Today, like Mariana, increasing numbers of Japanese women are choosing a childless career instead.[6]

The result is a country with lots of old people and very few young people. Economists describe the situation in Japan as a gathering demographic storm. Soon there won't be enough young Japanese to do the jobs needed or to pay the taxes the government relies on to look after their elders.

In 2013 the Japanese leadership stepped in to try to solve the problem, stealing our book title and calling their program, guess what, "Womenomics," in an effort to not only increase the number of women at work, but make their working lives easier, with incentives such as more available childcare.[7] The number of women in the workforce did inch up, but a majority still leave, never to return after having children, and many who do stay in work say they have to battle a sexist, macho culture that makes life miserable. It's a disaster for two simple but intractable reasons: Japanese jobs aren't flexible, and Japanese relationships aren't flexible. Japan is an extreme example, but it's not impossible to imagine something similar in Western democracies, where birth rates are also dropping, if we don't fix this.

Just as Covid has provided an opportunity to reshape norms in the office, it's also providing a chance to redefine the concept of work-life balance—perhaps even to get rid of the construct entirely. Indeed, we're so eager to redefine it, rework it, stop talking about the need for it, that we're coining a new phrase (thanks for your faithful service, work-life balance): the Blend. What women, what *people*, need is not the precarious balancing of work and life, where the different components constantly threaten to crash to the floor, like so many plates in a frantic spinning test. What we crave is a *blend* of work and life. Forget those fragile plates; we're thinking smoothies—something fresh, where the combination always tastes so much better than the individual ingredients.

It's more apt, we think, for capturing what people are after at the moment: an authentic, holistic and realistic approach. It's not based on moving back and forth between the realms of work and family, but on integration and flow.

Covid has revolutionized the world of work and as with any revolution, the results are messy, but also full of promise. Everything we understood about the way offices function is now up for review—the hours we work, where we work, how we communicate, how we create, think, and thrive. What is increasingly clear from the reluctance, even refusal, to return to the old normal is that our former work lives weren't working.

At last the flexibility women hankered after for years has arrived. We no longer have to hide that we have multiple priorities (nor could we even if we tried, thanks to Zoom). But we still don't have the flexibility equation exactly right yet. As one foodie British CEO put it to us, "We don't just want a smaller slice of the same old pizza; it didn't taste very good anyway. We need to come up with a whole new recipe and that means thinking carefully about all the different ingredients so that they taste good together." Multiple executives told us, in fact, that the workplace revolution will be one of the most important lasting effects of the pandemic. We just have to be vigilant that what we build now allows *everyone* to thrive.

THE FLEXIBILITY BONUS

A key ingredient for our new pizza, or for the Blend, must be workplace flexibility—flexibility of location and time. We reread *Womenomics* again recently and found that it's stood the test of time remarkably well. Depressingly well even. Mothers are still just as overwhelmed and demoralized. Companies, which promised to do better and spend big dollars on diversity programs, have made little headway and say they, too, are frustrated by the slow progress. One of the biggest hurdles to women's professional advancement is still the "broken rung"—the step on the ladder that takes us into management. It's no coincidence that it's the step professional workers often take in their early thirties, exactly when many women are having children. According to McKinsey, in 2019, for every 100 men promoted to manager, only 85 women get the same shift up. The gap is far wider for women of color. Only 58 Black women and only 71 Latinas were promoted to manager for every 100 of their male colleagues.[8]

Flexibility is one of the best ways to keep women who are caregivers in the workforce. For many working mothers, the only real alternative to working flexibly is reducing their work to a part-time schedule, but that diminishes a woman's income and her long-term career prospects.

The Netherlands is a good example of the false hope of a part-time job. The country has the highest rate of women working part-time of any industrialized nation. It's the result of conscious government policies dating back to the 1980s, which were designed to get more women into work in a nation that had a very low rate of female participation in the labor force. And it was successful. Today, according to the Organisation for Economic Co-operation and Development (OECD), more than half of Dutch women work part-time.[9] It's considered normal, and it certainly makes managing a family much less stressful.

But the experiment proved more complicated and less satisfactory than the government intended. A 2020 survey showed that Dutch women are underrepresented in managerial positions. Indeed, the Dutch government has done a 180° on part-time work and now actually sees it as a weakness in their labor force because it stops women from getting into senior jobs. "If you want to reach the top, then you have to work full-time and more," concluded the researcher Ans Merens.[10]

The Dutch lesson suggests that there really isn't a viable route to senior power positions when women only work two or three days a week. At least, not while we still live in a world where men are able to work five days and more, and in which there is no creative, equitable path to the top that values part-time work, and encourages it as a possibility for all. Since part-time work comes at such a price, remote work and/or flexible hours seem to make more sense for women who want to keep their careers moving. Covid lockdowns in 2020 showed us it's possible by launching the biggest-ever global workplace experiment in history.

Almost overnight, workers left their offices and retreated (with their laptops) to the safety of their bedrooms and kitchens. Suddenly a whole new industry was born around allowing everyone—men, women, parents, people without children—to work from home. At least while we were in the thick of lockdowns, the mommy-track stigma that comes with working from home simply evaporated. When we researched *Womenomics* we discovered that when flexible work schedules are targeted just at moms, they stigmatize mothers and young women in general; they're seen as a problem, not an asset. But this time, everyone was doing it.

This is not to say everyone in the C-suite loved it. Some bosses hated not having their workers in eyesight. Ten months into the pandemic, the CEO of Goldman Sachs, David Solomon, called working from home "an aberration that we're going to correct as quickly as possible."[11] Wall Street titan Jamie Dimon (another white man in his late sixties), CEO of JPMorgan Chase, said working from home didn't work for people who are ambitious: "It doesn't work for those who want to hustle."[12] His argument was that old one about watercoolers, culture, and the spontaneous generation of ideas and creative thinking that comes from all being in the same physical space.

We have some skepticism about this notion. We aren't alone in suspecting these sorts of responses are as much about a fear of losing control of the old ways as about what actually works best for companies and all their employees, which is what this tumultuous moment in time calls for.

"Who are those people who are able to have those long watercooler chats?" asks Professor Heejung Chung, a labor markets specialist at the University of Kent. We interviewed Chung from her home in the south of England. It was late in the evening for her, and she had just put her young daughter to bed. In a corner of her living room reserved for work calls, she sat with a glass of wine, winding down after a full day of teaching. We'd scheduled our Zoom call for thirty minutes, but more than an hour later we were still talking. We apologized for keeping her up late but Chung brushed our concern away; she is on a mission to solve this puzzle.

Chung says that the idea that creativity comes from moments when people are spending extra time at work, casually chatting round the cooler, is both inefficient and alienating. Lots of people feel excluded by the competitiveness of being in the office for long hours and schmoozing the boss—not just mothers, but people of color and even many white men who feel they can't voice their dissatisfaction with that whole macho culture. Also, not many people really have time to linger around watercoolers, or anywhere else for that matter. Most people in offices today either have their heads buried in their computer screens, are stuck in endless meetings, or are hurrying to get to the train station for the long commute home.

We would also dispute the notion that nothing creative happened in companies during Covid. One financial services executive told us that his large corporation had never been more creative. He put it down to the satisfaction people got from being able to work from a place they really wanted to be. If an employee can live at the beach, in the countryside, or in the mountains, he said, and really feel good there, they are actually more likely to be creative. Indeed, we talked to a lot of business executives throughout the pandemic, and they were all desperate to figure out ways to hang on to the innovative thinking that Covid unleashed. Yes, having all their workers suddenly stuck at home on Zoom had its challenges, but it also sparked new ways of thinking and working that executives appreciated.

Communication and collaboration are obviously important, as is some sense of company culture, but most companies now seem to understand that the cost of being in the office five days a week is high. Some are moving permanently to hybrid work, with regularly scheduled days in the office for focused collaboration and brainstorming.[13] Some of their decisions are by choice, because they recognize the benefits, but some of these moves are happening because employees are demanding it, it's a simple talent retention policy. If and when unemployment rises, companies may be able to demand that their employees return to the office, indeed some are already doing so, but survey after survey shows younger workers in particular value a more hybrid approach.

One boss did insist to us, eighteen months into the pandemic, that his workers weren't giving him the hours he was due when they were working remotely. He felt they were just making excuse after excuse for not coming back to the office because they could get away with doing a part-time job for full-time wages.

But the data doesn't support that.

In the summer of 2021—a full year and half into the pandemic—researchers from the University of Chicago, Stanford University, and the Mexico Autonomous Institute of Technology released a survey that suggested productivity had risen in the US during Covid, not declined.[14] They tracked thirty thousand workers, ages 20–64, for more than a year of the work-from-home experiment and found that 40 percent of workers said they were *more* productive working from home than they had been in the office. Only 15 percent said the opposite was true. The study concluded that the overall productivity of the American workforce rose 5 percent during the pandemic, compared with pre-pandemic office life.[15]

That's especially astonishing when you take into account that millions of parents were working from home without child care at that time. Stanford's Nicholas Bloom, one of the researchers, even suggested that working from home was *far more* productive than he or anyone else had anticipated. (Cutting back on commutes alone was a massive time saver. Every day, Americans saved 62 million hours of time by not traveling to and from an office.[16] Then they spent about 35 percent of those saved hours on work—no wonder they were more productive.)[17]

We didn't really need the pandemic to teach us this. Studies conducted prior to the shutdown showed that remote work led to productivity gains (indeed, we wrote about some of the earliest surveys in *Womenomics*).

Flexibility is increasingly seen as the cornerstone of a new healthy office, of a "life first" mentality, for women and men. A post-pandemic survey by FlexJobs found that 80 percent of women said working from home ranked as one of their top job benefits. The men surveyed weren't far behind; 69 percent said it was important.[18] But—remote work is not without its challenges.

THE FLEXIBILITY TRAP

In the midst of the pandemic, we spoke with a number of women about how things were going for them—whether the forced flexibility of the lockdown was making their lives easier or harder.

While many of the women we spoke to appreciated the chance to be at home more with their families, they'd also found that their days had gotten, somehow, even busier than before.

The accounting firm Deloitte confirmed our reporting. Sixty-five percent of women said they had more household chores because of Covid. Seventy percent said the burden had negatively impacted their careers.[19] None of this should come as a surprise. Before the pandemic even began there were warning signs that working from home might have unintended consequences.

A 2019 German study by the Hans-Böckler-Stiftung foundation found that mothers who work remotely end up doing more child care than mothers who do not.[20] They are around the house more, so everyone assumes they *can* and *will* pick the kids up from school and oversee their homework. But the same rule doesn't apply to men. Fathers who work remotely don't seem to feel the same responsibility toward household duties and child care. Indeed, they actually do *less* child care than men who work in offices. Instead, they use the time at home to increase their paid work hours—as do professional women without children. It is only women with children who do not follow that rule. Working mothers are too busy picking up laundry, cooking meals, and overseeing bath time to do more office work.

It got so bad during Covid that some professional women chose to leave the workforce entirely. In 2020, mid-pandemic, McKinsey produced a Women in the Workplace study revealing that one in three women were either planning to downshift or leave their jobs entirely.[21] Forget leaning in—they were jumping off the ladder entirely. It was the first time in the history of the six-year-old report that so many women had expressed such a strong desire to work less.

For some women, the change was welcome. They listed child care problems as their number one reason for downshifting and said they were relieved to have more time to look after their children without being frazzled. Yes, they were aware that it sounded a bit old-fashioned, and some were even hesitant to admit that was the decision they'd made.

But for many women it wasn't a positive choice, and women leaving the professional ranks when they would prefer not to, because they feel there is no other option, isn't good for anyone. The IMF has calculated the hit to gross domestic product (GDP) that comes from women not being fully engaged in the workforce.[22] Their research shows that if women participated in the labor force to the same degree as men, national incomes would rise—by as much as 5 percent in the US, 9 percent in Japan, and some 15 percent in poorer countries where women are currently not engaged in paid work much at all.

Amaya, the strategic consultant, was stunned by what was unfolding at her firm during Covid. "I was on the promotions and remuneration committees and it really woke me up. The numbers kept coming back that seventy percent of the people not performing well were women. I took it upon myself to do a deeper dive, and many were single moms in the middle of a pandemic, who were attempting to do everything, or married women still attempting to handle everything at home. I had to really speak bluntly and say we can't ease these women out, this isn't where we want to be."

As the immediate crisis of the pandemic receded and many CEOs mandated and cajoled their employees back to the office for at least a few days a week, flexibility and remote work remained a double-edged sword for women. A global survey by Future Forum, a research group run by Slack, found that after the pandemic white men were the group most keen to return full-time to the office.[23] As Angelica Leigh, a professor of management at Duke University, pointed out, those results are not surprising given that office culture was originally created to accommodate the needs and sensitivities of white men. Sian Beilock, who was the president of Barnard College at Columbia University in New York at the time, pointed out the irony. At the women's college she was running, the majority of workers are women.[24] But who showed up to the office first after Covid? Her male employees. And that costs women.

Writing in *Harvard Business Review*, Professors Mark Mortensen and Martine Haas described the in-office bonus like this: "Working in the same space as the boss increases the likelihood that employees' efforts and actions will be recognized and top of mind."[25] When men go into the office and women stay home, the former get more face time with bosses, more in-person encounters that lead to interesting assignments, and more chances to impress and be seen. It's as simple as being in the line of sight and it pays off. Even pre-pandemic, a lack of face time and interaction with leadership was an issue for workers who took advantage of "flex-time."

In Amaya's firm, it's still women paying the price.

"The child care situation, whether it was school or actual child care, was very iffy, and if somebody got Covid it was the mom who handled it and couldn't show up just when people were going back to work," she told us. "Women weren't in the office as much as the men because of those sorts of responsibilities. So even today, if they aren't in the office, they aren't getting thought about or sought after or promoted, or getting to do the cool work."

Furthermore, of course, the more women work from home in a world where men have returned to offices, the more male-dominated those offices will become, meaning they'll continue to be inhospitable for women and other people who don't fit the old male-dominated mold.

Getting the Blend right will depend on a mix of ingredients: flexibility about how and where the work gets done, new metrics for evaluating work performance that's done remotely, and creative solutions that pull employees together, whether remotely or in person. That Blend may well encourage everyone to take advantage of flexibility and so erase the stigma for mothers. It should definitely include a heavy dose of Cynt Marshall–style authenticity, so that life doesn't have to stay at home. The recipe is still evolving. But there's no question in our minds that for the new Blend to succeed, we have to take on something essential, that, for all its good intentions, work-life balance never even touched: how *much* we work.

GREEDY WORK IS IMPOSSIBLE WORK

Women will never have balance, sanity, our new Blend—any of it—unless we can solve the problem of overwork. It's a mountain that stands between us and power.

"Women did everything right. Then work got 'greedy.'"[26] That was a 2019 *New York Times* headline that we can't stop thinking about. The article described a phenomenon where it becomes virtually impossible for mothers to stay in top professional careers because those jobs have become insanely time-consuming. However much flexibility we carve out, however much we insist on working from home, however hard we struggle to balance competing priorities, very few working mothers will be content in a world that increasingly demands fifty- or even sixty-hour weeks. Neither will a lot of women without children. Neither, indeed, will a lot of men.

Claire: In large part, our writing career was forged in the fiery pits of the kid/career conflagration so many pass through. It was made clear to me, however, at the TV network where I was a full-time correspondent, that my job, essentially the ability to cover the stories I wanted to cover, was an all-or-nothing proposition. For years I had proposed endless counteroffers to this model, but I kept being told, in no uncertain terms, by a top executive that "when we like you, we need you all the time, every day, and we need you able to go wherever we need you to go, whenever we ask. We'd have you on the air nonstop if we could." He continued: "Part-time won't work. And Claire, you should feel flattered. We don't like everybody."

It was such an odd, dark, Lucifer-like compliment, and it was of course also meant as a shut-up-and-just-be-grateful-and-more-ambitious pep talk. I felt trapped. I also didn't buy his argument. Simple math suggested that some of the "valuable commodity of Claire" would be better than none. I started working part-time anyway, because I felt I would never see my children otherwise. I was partially buoyed by my writing work. But over time, my boss's prediction proved accurate; my television career quickly became less lucrative and compelling. There was no easy middle ground.

Overwork and overwhelm may well be the last weapons of an increasingly outdated zero-sum power hierarchy, wielded despite the mountain of evidence to suggest these crazy hours don't do anything to increase our productivity. According to a Stanford University study, after working for fifty hours, our brains need a rest; loss of focus and reduced productivity set in. After sixty hours a week, you may as well just stay on the sofa and watch TV since you really aren't producing anything worthwhile at all. Indeed, you'll achieve exactly the same amount in seventy hours as you would in sixty hours.[27]

Greedy work is a revealing case of the "power over" code. (Even worldwide, thoughts considered worth recording still came from mostly men.) It implies an endless loop of competition—beating out colleagues and climbing over any obstacles, including ridiculously inhumane and unsustainable, unproductive work hours—in order to get ahead. The "power to" mindset is more specific and concrete. It's not about the show; it's about the results.

The world of greedy work makes it almost impossible for women to make satisfying choices. When we try for balance, the already significant gender pay gap widens. By our midforties, a male college graduate earns 55 percent more than his similarly educated female counterparts.[28] As we noted earlier the pay gap is biggest for women of color. If a married mother quits altogether because the sixty-hour weeks just aren't compatible with raising children, she loses all her earning power. If the couple separates, the ramifications of that decision are acute.

Every stressed-out woman and overstretched couple is left to cobble together their own solution. They find individual fixes when what's needed isn't the single, lonely Band-Aid—it's a radical redesign. We shouldn't be making tweaks around the edges to enable some people to work sixty-hour weeks. Or making women choose between kids and a good career. (Lots of men don't like bearing the burden of greedy work, either, something we address in chapter 7.)

It bears reminding that the US is extreme among Western nations in its worship at the altar of work. What was, until the 1970s, just a job has morphed into a religion. Derek Thompson of the *Atlantic* was the first to coin the term *workism*.[29] It's the notion that work stops being an economic necessity (I work to live) and becomes a centerpiece of one's identity (I live to work). Workism dictates that policies to improve human welfare must focus around encouraging and enabling more and more work. In recent years it's gotten out of control.

Katty: As a European I've never understood the American attitude toward work. When I first came to the US I used to hide the fact that I took proper holidays, like three or even four weeks off in the summer. I was surrounded by people who bragged about not having taken off more than four days in a row in years. Twelve-hour days are routine, weekends barely happen. I stopped feeling like a guilty slacker a long time ago, though, when I realized my more "European" attitude to work was actually really effective. Looking at the evidence, I've had a high-profile anchoring job, become a well-known political commentator in a highly competitive field, and written six books, four of which have been *New York Times* bestsellers. And I've done it while taking at least six weeks vacation a year and working no more than forty- or occasionally fifty-hour weeks. I've even taken a couple of long sabbaticals to do interesting things like go to Senegal with my family for a few months. This is what life should be like. My real accomplishment hasn't been the books, and the anchor jobs; it's been blending work with four kids in a way that gave me an interesting job while allowing me enough time to enjoy the thing I love most, my family. I'm willing to bet that this model would work for a lot more jobs than people think. The culture of killing yourself for work has to change because it is, quite literally, killing us.

According to a 2021 study by the World Health Organization, long working hours cause hundreds of thousands of deaths every year around the world. The WHO defines unhealthy work hours as regularly doing more than fifty-five hours a week, and they've studied the impact on mortality rates. Working more than that (so 8 a.m. to 7 p.m. every day) resulted in 745,000 deaths globally in 2016.[30]

Few countries understand the dangers of overworking better

than South Korea. Workers in the East Asian nation clock up more hours than anyone else in the industrialized world. In 2019, South Koreans worked an average of 1,967 hours, 241 hours more than the average OECD employee. They work longer than people in Canada, Japan, the United Kingdom, or even the United States.[31]

In 2017, concerned for the health of his nation, the president of South Korea launched a campaign to get people to work less. He introduced a working-week guideline of fifty-two hours a week—down from sixty-eight hours a week. Think of that—sixty-eight hours as a workweek guideline.[32] No wonder South Korea has a word for the malady of working yourself to death—*gwarosa*. Every year, the government believes, hundreds of people die there from working too hard.

Comparisons with other countries suggest this work ethic is not required for a successful economy. Here's a global picture, courtesy of 2022's World Population Review, of countries where employed people spend less than forty hours a week at work.[33]

Netherlands	30
Norway	33
Germany	34
Denmark	34

Netherlands, Norway, Germany, and Denmark. Not exactly slacker nations.

Germany also has a word attached to its workweek—a much healthier word, *Arbeitszeitgesetz*. It's the Working Hours Act, which sets out fair conditions for employees and puts them into law.[34] It mandates that no working week can exceed forty-eight hours a week or eight hours a day, over a six-month period. In other words, you can do a short stint of crazy hours, but then you'd have to slack off for a bit in order not to clock up more hours than the legal limit. One of the largest trade unions in Germany, the powerful metalworkers union, has won a legal fight for the right to a twenty-eight-hour week.[35] Yes, twenty-eight hours a week.

How does this all stack up against the USA? In 2021, the average German worker put in 1,349 hours, while the average American worker clocked up 1,791—that's about 30 percent more time at work than their German counterparts.[36] The attitude in Germany is that if you're working more than forty hours a week, it's a problem. It's a different approach to efficiency. If you can't get your tasks done in a reasonable amount of time, it suggests there's a problem with the worker or with the job specs. It's such a different approach from the US, where if you aren't at your desk (or remote computer or, in both our cases, on TV) for long hours, you're seen as lacking ambition.

You might wonder, then, whether all those extra hours end up making the US economy more productive than the German economy, where workers spend less time every week at their desks and take about six weeks paid holiday every year. The data is a little complicated to analyze, in terms of apples-to-apples comparisons, but the best answer is that the two are comparable.[37] Both Germany and America are fully developed, highly productive countries, but German workers do it with a lot more time off simply to live their whole lives. *Arbeitszeitgesetz.*

WORK THAT WORKS

Professor Chung completed her master's degree in South Korea and learned the meaning of *gwarosa*—the South Korean phrase for death by overwork. She didn't die, luckily, but sometimes she almost felt like she might. She now describes the way she worked there as doing "stupid hours." Literally, hours that made her more stupid, not less.

Fortunately, she then moved to the Netherlands, where the attitude toward work was very different. After a few weeks, her Dutch professor came to her with a complaint about her long days. He told her she wasn't being productive, because she was working too many hours! It wasn't a badge of honor, he explained, it was a waste of time. The experience made Chung reexamine her life, and the whole issue of work and life more broadly. She came up with a new theory of work. One that actually works.

"I've noticed that if I work late at night, I'm useless the next day. If I work on weekends, I'm a no-go on Monday. You can't be creative and work these insane hours. We all need restorative time," she says. Chung knew all that in theory, but it was her professor's reprimand and then having her own first child that forced her to become more aware of her time management. "I'd read about it but it's another thing to feel it."

Her new approach to time management hasn't deterred her own rise. She is now a full-time professor at the University of Kent, in England. "I'm successful for my age and I do have balance. I coach soccer. I have a dog and I play in a punk band!" All this as well as a career, a partner, and a daughter.

Along the way, she's identified where time is wasted in offices. The biggest culprit is what Chung calls performative work. That's time spent doing tasks with the aim of showing we are working. We may look busy for our bosses, but we aren't necessarily producing much that's worthwhile.

In the performative bucket Chung places many of the meetings we all found ourselves sitting in, quite a lot of the emails we send, and definitely the extra time sitting at our desks trying to look important. Meetings, she says without a shadow of hesitation, are the biggest time waster. She reckons most companies could cancel a good chunk of meetings with *zero* negative impact on output.

So what's the ideal productive week, we ask? Is it forty hours, thirty-five hours? Her answer surprises even us. Six hours a day, or just thirty hours a week. Chung is confident that 90 percent of top professional jobs, not part-time low-level jobs, but top management positions, can be done in that amount of time. Cut out the performative stuff and you get to just six hours a day of actual valuable productive work.

Chung's research is just one snapshot of what might be possible. And, prompted by the Covid pandemic, lots of companies are testing new ways of working.

In June 2022 the United Kingdom launched the biggest study of a four-day week, with 3,300 workers at seventy different companies committing to work no more than thirty-two to thirty-five hours a week for the same pay as a forty-hour week.[38] The results were a boost for 4 Day Week Global. Ninety-one percent of the firms taking part have decided to continue with a four-day work week, citing lower attrition, higher levels of employee well-being, and stable revenue and productivity. Oxford University, Cambridge University, and Boston College, which helped to run the study, intend to sift for hard numbers on productivity, but previous research in Japan, the United States, and New Zealand has shown that productivity increases when you give workers an extra day off.[39]

All companies should attempt to understand this concept soon, because younger workers are starting to vote with their feet. Indeed, when, in 2022, Elon Musk famously gave Twitter employees an ultimatum to go "extremely hardcore, to work long hours at high intensity" or leave, many chose to leave. Musk's approach was widely ridiculed as retrograde. Young workers are also voting, more subtly, with their effort. Quiet quitting, a trend outlined by the *Wall Street Journal*, is on the rise.[40] It involves workers dialing it down on their own accord, opting out of hustle culture, picking assignments or jobs that demand no extra emotional energy—essentially, choosing to do the bare minimum at work so they can have more life.

Less work, more life. Perhaps most critically, more joy in both realms. It would certainly make the path for women to the top much more feasible, and place less strain on competing values. And it's essential for the Blend to succeed. But it still seems to separate our lives into competitive corners. So let's think even bigger, about a real blend of the heretofore siloed work/life. What if, in this moment, we looked at all of the skills and values women typically put into action outside of work, in our lives, and see they aren't competing efforts but rather complementary. Our time as parents, caregivers, community builders actually reinforces our value at work.

Even bolder, since we're whiteboarding it, what if we pressed reset, and created a world in which work and life carried equal importance and supported each other, a world in which our lives enhanced our careers, and vice versa? Not just for women, but for everyone? This is, in fact, the very essence of the Blend we envision. Imagine a limitless swirl of components from various parts of our lives, all coming together to create something new that reflects who we are, what we value, and what we're hoping to achieve with our *power to*. We're proposing an added layer to what Cynt Marshall is attempting to unleash. By bringing the "whole self" to work, she is placing overt value on the other roles people play. We want to tap into that notion we mentioned in chapter 2 of authenticity as a gateway. Let's recognize the work we value as a society in terms of family and communal care—just plain recognize our societal values, and stop demanding we silo our lives by location, grueling time demands, or gendered expectations. Imagine the power of this end result—men worrying openly about a daughter's stressful playdate, or choosing doctor visit over meeting. That's new power. Instead of an arrangement in which so many women feel they're doing too many things and none of them well, we could create a joyful world in which women (and men) can play multiple roles without apologizing for it. About joy, for a minute. Gwen, that global HR executive, told us something she's observed in recent years, and which she knows from experience. "Black women have a particular hunger for joy, even at work. Despite the fact we so often find the opposite, it remains a priority, and something we are determined to bring as leaders. Maybe it comes from a place of faith, I'm not sure. But it's a thing. And it's especially important these days." So, let's all follow that wisdom, and Cynt Marshall's example, and finally create something better than balance—a life Blend that actually works, and opens the path to power, with joy.

YOUR POWER CODE

It's what you do, not what you say. You can tell your employees a thousand times that you run a family-friendly culture, but if you fire off emails on Saturday, Slack at 11 p.m., or schedule meetings for early evening, you're sending a very different message. Your employees will feel compelled to respond right then and there, and soon they'll feel compelled to model your behavior.

So ask yourself: Is that Sunday morning email really essential or can it wait until Monday? If you can't resist the urge to get the question off your chest, write the email but select the delay option so it doesn't reach your employees until Monday morning. If you really, really can't resist—at least give your message the subject heading "not urgent" or "only address on Monday."

Create creativity. The serendipitous watercooler encounter that sparks the next brilliant innovation strikes us as a remarkably inefficient (not to mention exclusive) way to generate creativity. That's a lot of time hanging around the company corridors on the off chance of having the one conversation that produces a breakthrough. In a world where not everyone is in the office at the same time, let alone in the kitchen waiting for lightning to strike, you will need to create occasions for creative, in-person encounters. We've heard of various different approaches. When everyone is together, make time for informal gatherings; have lunch brought in and keep the conversation informal. It doesn't mean you can't get input on a challenge your organization is dealing with, but it's also a good time to chat about families, hobbies, and vacations. For more focused time together, bring your core team together for an in-person mini-retreat. The agenda can be a mix of work challenges but with some time reserved for informal conversation.

Stop the meeting madness. Here's an exercise. Make a list for one week of every single meeting you attend. Then go through each one and determine how productive it was on a scale of 1 to 5. Anything 2 or below is not worth the time and should be cut. A meeting that scores 3 needs, at the very least, reimagining to make it more productive. Here are a few of the tips we've heard for cutting back.

Take a hard look at recurring meetings. They can be the easiest to cut.

Ask whether the issue could be better addressed with an email, Slack, or a quick call instead.

Cut the length of meetings. Most of the time, thirty minutes is sufficient—the same goes for conference calls. Don't default to thirty-minute increments when twenty minutes might be just as effective.

Block out chunks of time that are meeting-free and reserved for deep work. It might be possible only one or two days a week, but don't let other people's priorities drive your day.

Meeting manners. It's not just the number of meetings we hate; it's the nature of them. It's the way the same group of people dominate the debate, making it hard, or at least exhausting, for people who are in the minority in the room to be heard. Meeting culture has to change. Here's what you can do.

Limit the size. Research suggests that twelve people maximum (jury size actually) is the sweet spot where everyone can still add value. Send an agenda in advance, so there's a clear goal that everyone is aware of.

Nudge those who haven't spoken with an encouraging invitation: "Alice, you've done a lot of work in this area, we need your input." (Need, not want.)

Be a listener. Amy Edmondson, author of *The Fearless Organization*, urges leaders to be "humble listeners." Ask attendees what they see and probe for their opinions, and then really listen. Edmondson advises being a "don't knower," literally saying, "I don't know. What do you think?" as a way to encourage reticent people to give their thoughts.

Express appreciation for contributions, particularly from those who make them less often.

If Joe steals Jane's idea, talks over her, or interrupts her before she's done—call it out, firmly and clearly. "Joe, from what I understand, that is exactly what Jane just suggested." "Joe, Jane was talking. I'd like her to finish."

Declare the value of meetings starting and ending on time. Set talking-time rules in advance: a minute or two per person, for example. Stop a long talker: "Sorry to interrupt, we've only got a minute for each comment." Or "Joe, great thought. Can you write that up and send it around? We're out of time." If you have to, set a timer.

Do show up. Working from home five days a week may seem appealing, but if your colleagues are in the office and you aren't, you will miss out. It's called proximity bias, and it has real implications for your career. You do need face time with bosses. If you're at an organization that has a three-day in-office policy, make sure your days are the ones when the people you need to see and *be seen by* are there, too.[41]

Be intentional about your time in the office. Schedule one-on-one time with your manager, and don't forget to plan time to catch up with colleagues, too. This is the moment to talk about any big ideas, promote your successes, and remind bosses of your particular talents. In-person conversations might seem intimidating, so, on your commute, write down a couple of points you want to make. The act of writing will both crystallize your thoughts and prime you to feel powerful when you engage with others.

It's not about you. Taking the "I" out of your route to power is a great all-around motto. If you tend to take things personally, now's a good time to let go and reframe your perspective. You're nervous about public speaking: so is everyone. You messed up that presentation: humans screw up—it's an annoying design flaw in the species. That male colleague steals your points and hogs the limelight: you're not the only one who sees it. Your peer gets an opportunity you wanted: good for them (power isn't zero-sum, remember). Now move on and find another way to contribute.

7

POTS AND PANS AND POWER

The room wasn't anything to get excited about. Barely a storage closet really, but it had a door that locked, and to Erin Zimmerman that made it perfect.

Erin had spent years working from the family's kitchen table in their home in southern Ontario—years pulled between the demands of young children, meals to be cooked, laundry to be done, housework that piled up, and never-ending interruptions that made quiet concentration on her own work almost impossible. All she wanted was space and quiet and time, so that her career could flourish. That storage closet was her secret to success, but it had taken global upheaval for her to stake her claim to it.

Erin has a PhD in plant sciences and hers is the story of millions of educated women. Women who would like to pursue their careers but are held back by the demands of family life, by children who need tending, and by husbands who still get first call on the job front. These are the women who need the flexibility we outlined in the previous chapter, but it's not just the workplace that doesn't work for them; their domestic setups don't, either.

Our home lives aren't keeping up with our roles in the outside world, and until we change that, we really can't change much else. As we dived deeper into this subject, we were shocked at how little has evolved at home, and how much this inertia holds women back.

Sure, some women have managed to get to the very top, by defying centuries of traditional, stubborn models to forge a path to power. But they are the exceptions. It's not a path open to most women because at the moment it requires one of two things: superhuman strength that allows those extraordinary women to work crazy hours and somehow also find time to run a household, or a partner who's happy to take on the lion's share of raising children. (The third way, which involves enough wealth to totally outsource childrearing doesn't seem ideal, for obvious reasons, even for those who can afford it. Typically, even when women have some help at home, they are still running the show as the primary parent.)

As we envision a working world that values women's multifaceted talents, we also need to reenvision the domestic sphere. It's impossible to have one without the other. As several smart people told us during our interviews, the biggest barrier to women getting power isn't, in fact, bosses—it's husbands. For the most part, research shows, it's in marriages between a man and a woman that these barriers continue to be the most immutable.[1] This chapter deals mostly with relationships between male and female partners—so-called heteronormative relationships—because it's those relationships that seem so stuck. (Relationships between women are free of some of those traditional expectations, though, as we write about later in this chapter, research suggests even same-sex marriages between women who have children haven't managed the transition to a fair distribution of child care totally smoothly.)[2, 3]

We don't usually write about marriages. Confidence, science, diversity, economic policy—we've tackled all that. But as we researched power, we realized we couldn't ignore what happens at home because it turns out women can't get power outside the home until it's more fairly distributed inside the home. In the same way that women experience the perfection paradox at work, so too it is at home, with expectations and demands placed on women (sometimes, it must be said, by themselves) that are unrealistic and limiting. *We can't do it all.* Or rather, we can and we do, but it's hugely stressful, unsustainable, and simply unfair. It shortchanges women's career potential, and it also shortchanges our partners and, perhaps, even our children, who end up perpetuating worn-out stereotypes in their own adult relationships as well. Of course, as we've mentioned, economics matter—wealthier couples, families, individuals are able to consider outside help, ease the burden in many ways. But that doesn't change the central fact that there is a massive gender imbalance in this realm, that cuts across income levels.

We need men—society needs men—to become equally and fairly invested in domestic life and in sharing the physical, emotional, and cognitive labor of raising children and running a household. This is a significant type of power we already exercise—it's just unheralded and undervalued. Recognizing this aspect of our formidable societal power—the caring for children, community, human connection—is part of a new power code. It will benefit men as much as women once it's shared and accounted for; it's a slice of power that contains considerable meaning and joy. It's part of the new power code that benefits women and men, too, as we explore in chapter 8.

It may seem like we've come a long way since the 1950s, but dig beneath the surface just a bit and you'll uncover a minefield of unspoken tensions, fears, and contradictions. And few subjects turn out to be more contentious than money—specifically, *who* earns it.

MONEY: "IT'S SIMPLE MATH"

After she got her doctorate, Erin Zimmerman worked for a few years in academic research, but the pay was poor and the hours were very long. When she had her second child, the situation was no longer tenable. "It was the same old push and pull," she tells us with an exasperated sigh, as if she's almost embarrassed to have found herself there. "I was never going to earn as much, but it was still a sixty-hour-a-week job. And we couldn't both have one of those, not as parents."

So, having hit that boring old brick wall of kids versus career, Erin gave up academia and started freelancing as a science journalist. Her trajectory is similar to what so many professional women experience. She enjoyed the work, and the flexibility suited her life as the mother of a two-year-old and a five-year-old. But it was sporadic, and the pay was still low, and she always felt that her work didn't matter as much as her husband's. There was also something about the geography of the house that worked to diminish the importance of Erin's work. It was almost as if working from the kitchen table was chipping away at her stature. (Remember, this was pre-Covid, when the world had yet to take kitchen table offices seriously.)

Erin's husband, Eric, had been in the same academic field but he switched careers to become an optometrist and joined a private medical practice, where the pay was higher. The income disparity between the two of them rapidly widened. It also led, almost imperceptibly at first, to a shift in their relationship and in the distribution of domestic labor between them. Erin still worked, but she was the one on call when child care issues came up, which forced her to limit her professional commitments. At the same time, because they had children's costs and their own college loans to pay off on top of his medical school fees, they had an incentive for Eric to maximize his earnings, which meant he worked even longer hours. "The numbers are unavoidable," she says. "It doesn't make sense for him to take time off, and in fact it gets financially untenable very fast." By Erin's account, Eric is one of the really good guys, genuinely interested in her writing and sympathetic to her situation, but they had gotten sucked into the vortex that is today's reality for so many couples.

When we spoke with Erin in the spring of 2020, she was despairing of a professional world that still hasn't figured out how to give mothers and fathers an equal shot at success. What she was experiencing at home was a direct reflection of how careers are structured. She knew he was working long and hard, so she didn't ask for more help. He didn't offer to help more because, well, he was working long and hard. What had started as the practical triaging of a hectic life with small children became something of an imbalance they couldn't seem to escape.

At least that's the way they were until Eric's private practice had to shut its doors because of the Covid-19 lockdown. Almost overnight, her freelance writing fees became the family's only source of income. Her salary mattered in a way it never had before, which meant her *work* mattered in a way it never had before—and she loved it. Suddenly she had both a room of her own (or at least a closet of her own) and reliable child care because her husband was home all the time. The shift was sudden and dramatic, and it affected everyone in the family.

For Erin, it meant freedom to work full-time, and a new place in the family's earning hierarchy. It wasn't that she stopped being a parent or stopped being involved in the home, but for the first time in a long time, she had a fully present, engaged domestic partner, and she discovered a better blend between the working and parenting parts of herself.

For her children, it meant seeing their mother in a new light. "Now they're actually seeing me sitting at a computer writing and they're being told that they can't interrupt me because I'm doing something important. And I think that has been really significant for them. Especially my five-year-old. I think she's really absorbing that her mother works and that it matters," she told us in the midst of the shutdown.

For her husband, it was an insight into her world. "I don't think he fully appreciated what it was like to be with them so much of the time. Normally he works a lot of weekends, so I spend long stretches of time caring for them alone. And I think he has been a bit surprised at how hard that is. Yes, it looks easier from the outside, they're great kids—but I mean . . ." In the yin and yang of relationships, she'd broadened her life, her range of experiences, and in fact, he'd done the same. After Covid we asked Erin whether Eric had enjoyed that time as the main parent, whether he'd gotten something out of it. She didn't think *enjoy* was the right word, but he had certainly gained a newfound empathy for how hard her juggle is. A window into different worlds had been opened for both of them.

In general, Covid was very tough on women. The coronavirus-induced downturn was dubbed the she-cession because for the first time in decades women lost more jobs than men.[4] In the early months of Covid, women lost 1.7 million more jobs than men.[5] Women of color, who fill a lot of service sector positions, were particularly hard hit.[6]

Erin Zimmerman had a different experience. She had gotten a taste of what things could be like if her professional priorities were given equal weight as her husband's. She even wrote an article titled "The Pandemic Has Reversed the Usual Gender Roles in My House and I Love It," which received widespread attention.[7]

When we first spoke to Erin from that tiny storage space in

the midst of the lockdown, wedged between the shut door and a pile of packing boxes, she was enjoying her new status in the family. We could hear it in her voice. Her story moved us because it illustrated not just the burn of frustration many women in her pre-Covid position felt, but also something rare—that sudden, magic-wand version of the opposite: the rush of satisfaction, joy, and pride that gaining a different degree of power, status, and help at home can bring on.

Erin was able to work more and get help from her husband, because she was the sole breadwinner during a global crisis that forced them all to stay at home in pandemic lockdown. Not something that happens every day or even every century. She knew even then that it might not last long. And indeed, it didn't. We caught up with Erin again after Covid and life had reverted to the old, frustrating norm. But she had glimpsed the world of being the primary breadwinner and seen its benefits. "It's simple math," she says.

WHAT WE LIE ABOUT (HINT: IT'S NOT SEX)

What makes Erin's story surprising is her willingness to talk openly about money and earning power at all. For most women, the math is not simple. Not at all.

In all our years researching women and work, we have never come across a subject about which so many women asked us not to use their real names. In the past, women have opened up to us about their children, housework, love, ambition, even sex, but when we asked them what it was like to earn more than their husbands, ooohhh no . . . that was too awkward. They suddenly grew skittish.

Earning power is an especially difficult topic to unpack because, as they say in academic-speak, it's a highly "gendered" subject—meaning we all have a lot of unconscious biases about how traditional marriages should work and what roles men and women should play in these partnerships. We're talking major gender expectation baggage.

In fact, one-third of American women now earn more than their husbands and the number grows every year.[8] But the ripple effects of that growing economic disparity within marriages are seismic—that is, if an earthquake can be silent.

That may be why Misty Heggeness first suspected people were covering up an important truth. Heggeness is an economist with the US Census Bureau. She has spent years crunching numbers to see whether the stories we tell about ourselves match reality. Think of it as psychology by statistics, a massive study of the nation's mindset based not on therapy, but on census data.

As Heggeness researched the income gap between Black and white men, another intriguing disparity showed up. She found that in couples where the woman earns more than the man, they lie about it on the US census form.[9] Yes, you read that right. They lie to make it look like the man is still the bigger earner (statisticians call it misreporting, but it sounds an awful lot like a lie to us). It's as if a wife earning more than a husband is an embarrassing secret, a threat to their marital bond.

When Heggeness uncovered the discrepancy, her statistician brain kicked in with a bunch of questions: Who was doing the misreporting? Was it husbands or wives? Were men inflating their own earnings? Or was it wives deflating theirs? And, most importantly, why? What on earth was going on in those marriages?

"My fellow researcher and I initially thought maybe only the men's earnings were getting misreported, getting inflated, to try to protect themselves," she says. "We were wrong." They found that the earnings of the husband were getting inflated *and*, at the same time, the earnings of the wife were getting deflated. So, effectively, the wife's earnings were taking a double hit—or, seen another way, the husband's earnings were getting a double boost. Then they looked to see if the results were any different if it was the husband or the wife who answered the survey. The short answer: no. Regardless of who was answering, the women's earnings were deflated and the men's earnings were inflated. "Again we had an assumption that it's just husbands doing this to protect their egos. Again we were wrong," she said.

It's almost instinctive, this need to protect the status quo, at least on the surface and for the public. It's as if both husband and wife, without even consulting each other, understand a deep need to preserve the appearance that theirs is a traditional marriage—where everything is "as it should be." Both parties are so keen to keep up this appearance that they will even lie about it on an official government form. Remember, this subterfuge is in an era when one in three women in America earn more than their husbands.

Heterosexual couples in America are not the only ones struggling with a shifting financial landscape. Using Swiss government labor data in 2020, economists Anja Roth and Michaela Slotwinski spotted a similar financial anomaly suggesting that an awful lot of Swiss women seem to have salaries just slightly below their husbands'. Or, at least they *say* they do. In fact, as in America, it's a case of massaging the truth to protect the husband's ego and perhaps the relationship's equanimity. The Swiss economists go further than their American counterparts in confirming what are pretty obviously the reasons behind the fairy tale.[10] "Individuals misreport both their own as well as their partner's income," Roth and Slotwinski conclude, "in order to adhere *to traditional gender norms* and place the couple *below the threshold where the woman would outearn her partner*."

Once you understand this phenomenon, it's hard not to notice it in everyday, seemingly trivial interactions. You've probably seen it among your friends; you may even collude yourself. For example, when a couple goes to a restaurant, how often does the check go to the woman? Rarely. If two couples are on a night out together, how often do the wives whip out their credit cards to pay the bill, even if the women are the higher earners? We've almost never seen that happen. We guess it would be too much of a blow to the husbands' pride.

Who gets the restaurant check may sound trivial, but it's symbolic of bigger fractures. In 2010, a Cornell University study showed that husbands who earn less than their wives were more likely to be unfaithful.[11] Then, in 2015, the University of Chicago depressed high-earning women even more with a study that shows marriages where the wife was the primary breadwinner were 50 percent more likely to end in divorce.[12] (We hated those studies. They felt like a personal affront.) Then along came the research Misty Heggeness was part of in 2018 and that Swiss census study from 2020 suggesting the fundamentals haven't changed.[13]

Maybe none of this would matter if it were just the internal workings of a single relationship. After all, marriages are complicated, and people do different things, make different compromises, to keep their relationships alive. But the social penalty suffered by an individual woman who is the main income earner has a knock-on effect for other women, too. It makes women reluctant to say openly that they care about money—in a world where that's already frowned on. We're certainly unlikely to publicize our financial achievements. It can even trigger our socialized reluctance to ask for bigger salaries in the first place. It also impacts public policy. If we're lying about the wages in our own household, do policy makers even know what the real wage gap is? Are they taking the right public-policy steps to support fathers who earn less, and women who earn more?

When women are spending this much time and energy holding up the status quo at home—while fighting for changes at work—you have to wonder whether part of the problem is that even when we're married, or at least married to a man, we're in it alone.

THE MARRIAGE TAX

Whether they earn more, the same, or less, something else keeps women all over the world from realizing their power and maximizing their impact (specifically, all women in relationships with men—we'll talk about what we can learn from lesbian couples in a bit): chores. Yes, chores! We know how incredibly pedantic and outmoded that sounds. But here we are, a couple of decades into the twenty-first century, and it turns out that in order to have power, women first need to get rid of the mountains of pots and pans that still stand in their way, literally and figuratively. The roles we play at home, the amount of time invested there, can be a huge impediment to having power. Women have achieved many brilliant things but we still haven't figured out how to fit more hours into a day and time on domestic work is time away from other activities. As Erin says, it's simple math.

Pots, pans, and money appear to have a complicated relationship. By way of illustration, and in the interests of throwing light on this weirdly secretive issue of who earns what, and who cleans what, we will come clean about our own struggles with money and equality. It's not something we've spoken about before, but, hey, this feels like the right moment.

Katty: In my family, I've been the primary breadwinner for several years. When it first happened, it caused some unspoken tension. My husband and I never sat down and talked about what it meant for us as a working couple or how to divide up the chores so that we could both do what we needed to do. Over the years, as his paid job became more part-time, my husband did take on more of the child care and household duties, and he was happy to do it. But when Covid hit, I realized something was still bugging me. We were a household of five people, all with full-time jobs or school work, living 24/7 at home, surrounded by a growing mountain of laundry, doorknobs that needed disinfecting, serious Covid cleaning that had to be done, meals to be made, a dog who needed walks, and cats whose poop needed scooping. We drew up a color-coordinated chart, assigning each person chores every day. My paid job was the most demanding. I was trying to put a live TV broadcast on-air every day from the basement—my pay was also twice anyone else's in the house. Periodically I'd get fed up that the floors hadn't been cleaned in weeks, and even if I was on cooking duty, I'd be the one who mopped the floors. When I complained to my husband that I was overstretched, he replied, rather irritated, that he was doing 50 percent of the chores, which was correct. The problem was, I secretly wanted him to do 60 percent or 70 percent because he has a part-time job that brings in significantly less of the family income than my very full-on job. Somehow, I realized, we had neglected to follow the formula that applies to men who make more than their wives and get let off doing their fair share of the housework. I wanted my husband to say to himself, even to our kids, "Hold on, this isn't fair. Mom's got a more time-consuming job; she should be let off some of her chores. She shouldn't have to be cleaning the floors." I couldn't shake the feeling that there seemed to be some historic injustice in it. Women have made so much professional progress, but we can never shake off our roles as caretakers. I don't like the way I felt at that moment. I'm embarrassed and I'm still not sure if I was right or wrong to equate income/workload with chore distribution. What I do know is that it would have been different if the roles were reversed.

You'd think the relationship between money and chores would be logical, that if the wife earns more, her job would take priority, with her work schedule and business trips dominating the couple's calendar. Isn't that how it was for men? It should be simple math, right?

In some cases, yes, it is something like that. Katty's husband, Tom, has indeed taken on more of the chores, and just as important, more of the parenting and household logistics. The school now has him as the first point of contact. He attends more parent-teacher conferences and back-to-school nights than she does, simply because he is around more. If she has to travel for work, he will arrange to stay home. But it took some difficult conversations to get to a more equitable division of labor, and she knows her situation has been an exception, not the rule. Here's the reality:

Around the world, women spend 100 percent to 1,000 percent more time on unpaid household work than men do.[14] *In Ethiopia, to take just one example, the number of women who spend time collecting water and firewood for the family is twice the number of men who do those tasks.*

Women's domestic workload hasn't changed in over a century. Economist Valerie Ramey found that in 1900, women spent twenty-seven hours a week on "home production," a catch-all phrase for cooking, cleaning, child care, and general unpaid household labor.[15] That number was exactly the same in 2008.

Working women in America do more housework than—wait for

it—*men who don't work*! Do we need to repeat that? Men who don't have jobs do less housework than women struggling to do both.[16] A US mother who has a job outside the home not only does more housework than a dad who doesn't; in fact, married men also have three more hours of leisure time than their wives.[17] (By the way, the only type of household work that men routinely do more of compared to women? Gardening and DIY jobs.[18] It's safe to assume that these domestic chores are deemed "okay" because they tend to reinforce stereotypes about men's masculinity and dexterity with power tools.)

Young American men aren't any better at sharing household duties than their dads or even their granddads! This shocked us. Men ages 18–34 may have thrown out traditional concepts of gender when it comes to same-sex marriage, pronouns, politics, or education, but they cling stubbornly to a very old-fashioned view of who should do the housework.[19] In other words, men are happy to have a female partner who has an education, a career, and a salary, but they're not happy to do more chores. Change in this area of life is glacial. Researchers at Oxford University estimate that at the current rate, we'll be halfway through this century before men are doing their fair share of cleaning.[20]

There's not much evidence of a big racial disparity when it comes to men and housework. One study suggests that Hispanic men in the US do the least, African American men do the most, and white and Asian men somewhere in the middle.[21] A British study did find significant differences between ethnic groups, with Black Caribbean men doing the most (more than seven hours of housework a week) compared to their white counterparts (just six hours).[22] Though let's not get too excited: British women are still doing an average of fourteen hours a week of cleaning.

How can we possibly find the energy to aspire to powerful positions and then change the very nature of how power is deployed, when we are spending all that time still doing so much more at home? (These distressing findings give a whole new meaning to the phrase "power vacuum.")

In July 2020, in the midst of yet another Covid surge, Jessica Valenti, a journalist who specializes in work-life issues, wrote a provocative column titled "The Pandemic Isn't Forcing Moms Out of the Workforce—Dads Are."[23] She'd hit on something big. During the Covid lockdown women picked up more of the household duties than their husbands, and as a result they cut back more of the paid work they did.[24, 25] (Interestingly, the men believed they were doing as much home care as their wives were. The wives, and the data from surveys, didn't agree!)[26]

But Covid was really just an extreme version of what is going on in normal times.

Lots of men say they are supportive husbands. They tell us earnestly that they are so proud of their wives. They make all the right noises about equality and women's rights. They claim they do as much around the house as their wives. Many even believe their own words. But the data (and believe us, we've shown you only a fraction of what's out there) show that husbands are not backing those words up with the action it would take to free their wives from the burden of household labor.

ALL THAT PLANNING YOU DO: IT HAS A NAME—AND A VALUE

Multiple global studies now show that women spend more time than men cleaning, cooking, and caring, but physical labor is just the start of it.

Allison Daminger, assistant professor of sociology at the University of Wisconsin, studies the invisible planning that goes into all those tasks, what she calls the cognitive labor.[27] Add that in and women's chore burden is even greater, even more time-consuming.

While Daminger was doing research at Harvard, she studied the work of sociologist Arlie Hochschild, who first coined the term *emotion work* in the 1970s.[28] She had laughed along at the famous French cartoon simply called *Fallait demander* ("You should have asked"), a hilarious graphic novel showing how household management inevitably falls to women.[29] It was then that Daminger realized that women's unpaid work goes far beyond the physical tasks or even the constant people-pleasing tasks that the term *emotion work* implies. What is so striking about Daminger's description of all the cognitive labor women do at home is that it is precisely the kind of skill set that the corporate world so values.

Daminger breaks cognitive labor into four separate phases.

Anticipation: The first stage is anticipating what the household will need. "It's sort of putting something on the collective radar for the couple," she explains. "It could be something like, 'We're going to need child care in six months.' Or it could be, 'Hey, what are we having for dinner tonight?' It's recognizing that there is this upcoming need."

Identification: The second stage is figuring out the options for meeting those needs. "So it could be, 'Hey, we need child care. Okay. Let me do some research on the costs and benefits of using a nanny or a nanny share versus a day care center.' Or it could be as simple as identifying what you have available in your fridge to see how to pull those ingredients together for dinner."

Deciding: Having done the research, the third stage is selecting from the various options.

Monitoring: The final stage is monitoring how that option is working out. In corporate terms, it's the follow-up. Let's take the child care example. So you anticipated the need for child care, researched the various options, decided on a child care center, and then you need to monitor how it's working out. Is this meeting what my hopes were? If not, should we start this process over again and look at new options. Here's a non-child-related example. "Let's say that you realized that there was something wrong with the showerhead and your spouse said he'd find a plumber," Daminger explains. "Monitoring would be the work of actually following up to make sure that the plumber was indeed called, and if the plumber actually came to fix the issue, or if there was more work that needs to be done. And if so, is that happening? It is sort of, I'm checking in to make sure that whatever was needed originally actually took place in a satisfactory way."

Cognitive labor is all unrecognized work. We bet you do it every day, perhaps without even noticing. And—to get in the weeds a bit, because we find this stuff fascinating—it's different from physical labor and emotional labor. Here's a useful way to sort out the distinctions. Imagine a family dinner—it takes various types of work to bring it into being. There's . . .

Physical labor: Going to the grocery store, chopping the vegetables, laying the table, clearing the dishes.

Cognitive labor: Figuring out what to have for dinner in the first place, confirming people's preferences, checking what ingredients you have on hand in the fridge, making a list of what you still need to buy.

Emotional labor: Let's say you feel stressed-out at work right now and a bit resentful that you're cooking dinner. But you understand that as a parent it's your responsibility. You want to try to create a convivial atmosphere and not let your own bad mood infect the others at the table, so, even though you aren't feeling very cheerful, you take the time to ask your kids and spouse about their day. That's the emotional-work side of the dinner.

For her research project on cognitive labor, Daminger interviewed thirty-five heteronormative couples with young children and found, no surprise, that the mothers did the vast majority of all this cognitive labor. But the interesting, more nuanced finding comes from digging down into those four different stages: *anticipating*, *identifying*, *deciding*, and *monitoring*.

Daminger found that anticipating and monitoring are all predominantly female-initiated activities. The one area of cognitive labor where men always get involved and often actually lead is the third one, the decision making, especially on big-ticket issues. The women do the leg work, but the men make the final decision.

Does that sound like every office situation you have ever known? Well, guess what? We are replicating it at home. The one big exception is finances. It's the one area of cognitive labor where men take charge of the whole process, and wives often check out. Many of the men in Daminger's survey group took charge of the long-term finances and investments of the family and compiled the annual tax return.

The curious thing is that the couples Daminger interviewed actually portrayed themselves to her as enlightened partnerships where the men were involved in keeping the family wheels turning. "It was the idea of partnership, that was the ethos they wanted: we decided together," Daminger notes. "It's a way of saying, 'Hey, my husband is involved. He's not an old-fashioned checked-out dude.'"

That narrative fits what they aspire to in a partnership. But dig into the process and it's not what's actually happening—especially in the critical area of decision making, where our husbands often still have the final say. We do the leg work; they decide.

Daminger argues that decision making is a form of power because you get to control outcomes. She says sometimes the female respondents would say that all the planning they did was a burden and they wished their partners would do more. But they'd also insist they wanted a say in the direction their family was taking. The wives wanted to be the person to figure out which summer camps are acceptable options. They'd even tell her, "I like being able to decide what choice we make." That might be fine, Daminger points out, except the wives are *not* actually the ones who are doing the deciding.

"The women would do all of the pre-work to get something to the decision stage. And then the men would come in at that stage and make the actual decision." Or put it in the context of power, we do the work, but we give away the power of decision making.

What struck Daminger was that the couples all said their ideal would be to split the cognitive labor fifty-fifty. When it was pointed out that they didn't actually do that, they treated the discrepancy as the quirk in their relationship—an exception to the rule they'd set out with.

To account for why they still did all that cognitive labor, the wives would explain that their husbands were just more laid-back about all that stuff, or they worked longer hours. The men would say that their wives just cared more about it all, or, least believable of all, they claimed that they would be happy to help plan stuff, but they weren't very good at it. These were surgeons, business executives, "people," says Daminger, "who clearly had the skills and even the temperament to do these things and get paid for that kind of work." One was even a senior project manager—someone who literally plans things for a living. "He told me, 'My wife is just much better at organizing all that stuff than I am.'" Daminger added, incredulous, "Really? You're a top project manager but you can't plan a child's birthday party?"

What is so striking, and so maddening, about Daminger's research is that all of these skills that she puts under the umbrella of cognitive labor are exactly the skills that should get valued and rewarded in the world of work. What company wouldn't want to hire someone who anticipates a need, researches the options, keeps on top of the follow-up, *and* even includes others in the decision? That sounds like a dream corporate leader. Throw in women's capacity for empathy and we've just described ideal leadership material.

The corporate world is looking at women's unpaid household work all wrong. Imagine if companies examined what it takes to run a household, and measured those skills in a neutral way—not as household skills but as the executive function skills they really are. Wouldn't companies, and women, be better off?

It's not just that women's cognitive labor isn't rewarded—it actually holds us back. All that thinking, planning, and doing at home is time *not* thinking, planning, and doing at work. In our ideal world, we've proposed that the two realms of effort—work and home—would be equally valued and would complement each other. But right now it's not, which may help explain why being a parent is bad for Mom's income, but good for Dad's.

DO IT FOR THE KIDS

If the argument that there's a power play in housework doesn't persuade you to hand over planning of summer camps, ask yourself what your children think as you notch up yet another hour of household duties more than your husband. Our girls—especially our teenage girls—may pretend to be dismissive of us and act as if we are species from a different planet with no relevance to their lives, but they watch and absorb everything we do. Our sons are equally susceptible to our influence. Do you want your boys growing up thinking, *Oh, in my house it was always Mom who organized dinner, so I guess I can leave it to my wife, too*?

In 2018, the British scouting group Girlguiding asked girls ages 7–10 how housework *should* be divided between men and women. Forty-five percent said men *should* share the work. That's up from 25 percent in 2009. So, there's progress in their aspirations. There was a similar change in views when it comes to child care. In 2009 only 57 percent of girls thought moms and dads *should* equally share the work of looking after children. In 2018 that was up to 65 percent. There was evidence, too, that today's girls also feel it's women's responsibility to take on more of the traditional male tasks, like dealing with the car and paying the bills.

But we italicize those *should*s for a reason. They are aspirations. Asked about the reality, girls have an altogether more pessimistic view of how things actually are. Forty-six percent of girls surveyed expected the task of housework to fall to women.[30] (Yes, that was down from 69 percent who were surveyed in 2009 but still—*almost half of girls assume they will do the lion's share of caring for the home.*)

Flip it all around—you aren't the only role model in the house. When girls watch their dads doing household chores, it has a positive impact on their own careers.[31] They develop broader career options than girls whose dads don't help around the house. Think about that: when your husband picks up the vacuum cleaner, he is helping your daughter's future career. It's a win-win. You get a clean house that someone else has vacuumed, and a daughter with a really healthy attitude toward her own professional advancement. Talk about a cheap, simple social fix.

DENTISTS, MUSTARD, AND OTHER THINGS THAT MATTER MORE THAN YOU THINK

You might initially believe that the occupant of this warm office, punctuated with bright, organized Post-it Notes, colorful books, and sheafs of paper, and whose hair is pulled back with flair, would be just the type to offer upbeat advice to women about reclaiming their lives. Until she opens her mouth.

"Claire, Claire, I *never* wanted to be an expert in the gender division of labor. It wasn't my fucking third-grade dream answer to 'what do you want to be when you grow up?'"

"But," she continues, words like a hail of precisely aimed bullets, laced with just the right amount of humor, "I now believe I understand why I exist on this earth—to make this clear: Power is time; it is control of our time. Historically, the best way for power structures to stay in place has been to control women's time with reproducing, raising kids, and running the home. And all of that, and our other ancillary work, is free labor."

Eve Rodsky is a Harvard-trained attorney, and more recently the author of the book *Fair Play*, and star of a documentary by the same name, which details the balance of work between men and women, or rather the appalling imbalance, especially at home. Incensed by her own experience, what she was witnessing around her, and her research into Alison Daminger's work, she's now on a crusade to accurately value the work women do that isn't measured. She happily calls everybody out.

"I don't just want to ask my partner to take out the trash. I can't use my time well until he is willing to step fully into the home, make decisions, be a transporter of children, anticipate and schedule, take them to doctors—all of it. That's why I say to men—fuck servant leadership. Fuck whatever the hell new radical candor is out there. . . . [A]ll you need to know as a male leader, if you care about being an ally and changing why women are not in power, the only thing you need to know is the name of your child's dentist."

Big pause for laughter. But she's not joking. At all.

"I've had a hundred men online, the top CEOs in the world, explain to me why they don't know that name, the name of their child's dentist. They're different, they say. They support women. But that question—just listen to the excuses it brings out."

What is most exhilarating in our journey, over the years, exploring women's leadership and confidence, and how to empower girls, is when we find fellow travelers. Women are energized at the prospect of communal power, and when we stumbled onto Rodsky's work, we became instant fans, though slightly bummed we hadn't seen her Fair Play card game (more on that at the end of the chapter) in time to get us through our own child-rearing years. What Rodsky has hit upon, in translating the domestic imbalance to the workplace imbalance, is what we've uncovered about power, from a different starting place: until men value the work that goes into letting society and families thrive with the same attentiveness they display at work, sharing power will remain difficult.

"Everything to me stems from that disconnect—women are the social safety net. We do the unpaid labor in society," she says. "And by the way, America has always been built on unpaid labor. And so why would we think that's any different now."

Rodsky offers some solutions by getting innovative, digging into the underlying details of what's going on at home, rather than just reassigning chores. Two personal breakdowns—one over blueberries her husband chastised her about, and another watching friends cancel a lunch date because their spouses all had too much to handle with the kids solo on a Saturday—set her to work documenting, in meticulous detail, a massive "shit I do" list.

"What I've been doing for ten years is really about time use.

And I have this giant spreadsheet of conception, planning, and execution of every single task. The 'shit I do' list that came from thousands of women. How much time did you spend thinking about your second son Johnny liking French's yellow mustard, and not spicy Dijon, and noticing exactly what he needed for his protein otherwise he would get light-headed? How much time did you spend getting stakeholder buy-in for the grocery list for everybody else in your house? And how much time did you actually spend going to the store? Because the problem is we're overreporting on execution and underreporting on cognitive labor, which is why we're all sick, why women are sick, and our stress responses are going haywire. We need to not be the only ones who notice our second son Johnny likes yellow mustard and we need partners not just bringing him spicy Dijon every fucking time."

Getting this balance right, mustard and all, is especially critical for working women who have children, because that's when the cost of all this unpaid labor really kicks in. When a man has children, his earnings go up (by an average of 6 percent). When a woman has children, her earnings go down (by an average of 4 percent per child). Childless, unmarried women earn 96 cents for every $1 a man earns, but get married and become a mother? Your earnings fall to just 76 cents for every dollar a guy earns. This mothering penalty is most extreme for those who can least afford it. Michelle Budig, a sociologist at the University of Massachusetts Amherst, has found that high-income men get the biggest pay boost from becoming fathers, while low-income women pay the biggest price for having children.[32] That's why psychologists such as Darcy Lockman regard division of labor in the home as one of the most important gender-equity issues of our time.[33]

For many couples, the division isn't really articulated—lives are busy, roles emerge, and they aren't always what either party might choose, with forethought, because they both represent losses. As the husband works more and more, he gets further and further removed from being able to participate fully in one of life's most rewarding experiences: raising children and caring for family. Meanwhile, all this unpaid "women's work" becomes more and more essential to keeping the wheels of a husband's career turning.

Claire: My ex is an unusual guy, by most standards. He didn't care about the fact that for years I outearned him, by a significant amount. I had a higher public profile, and he happily answered to "Mr. Shipman." He kind of loved it. And he has been an amazing dad. I hadn't thought much about how our roles would break down before kids—we had them late and were both busy working. I remember at one point, after our son was born, putting forth what I thought was a reasonable, although slightly utopian idea. Hey, what if we both work part-time and don't get any child care? I was struggling with the thought of returning to work after maternity leave and having to walk away every morning from this little being. Jay looked at me like I was from another planet. I like my career, he pointed out. I knew then we were experiencing different levels of inner turmoil. We got child care, and attempted for a while to share household duties. I'm pretty horrible at cooking and cleaning—we divided a lot of that. On the organizational labor front, though—planning the family's schedules and so forth—that fell my way. As time went on, I started working part-time and in a more flexible fashion, so more of that labor—child care, planning, and other things around the house—kept piling up on my to-do list. I wanted time with the kids, and my husband's career took a positive turn, which made his workdays longer and more unpredictable, so someone had to be around home more, working more flexibly. He was out earning me by a lot at that point. It was a logical, practical decision, but I didn't expect to become a stereotype. At certain moments or career pivot points, we might have rethought the balance, but by then, the time he'd invested professionally had made him more marketable than me. It seemed silly not to take advantage of that. A lot went without saying. Do we regret the choices? No. Might we have planned better, in hindsight? Likely yes.

We felt sure that some nations do it better than we do. Typically, we can count on Scandinavia to show us what the future can look like, so we turned north. But even in Sweden, one of the most gender-equal countries in the world, women still pay a higher personal price for their ambition than men. Economists Olle Folke and Johanna Rickne came to that conclusion after discovering that very successful women are twice as likely to get divorced as equally successful men (no wonder we struggle to find joy in having power). The pair studied thirty years of government records and found that women who ran in political races were more likely to get divorced than the men who won elections.[34] The same pattern applies to female doctors, police officers, and even members of the clergy.

Those findings may sadden us, but they probably don't come as much surprise to all the women who have busted their gut to get ahead and get promoted. We know the tension it creates with our partners. Perhaps we should make Folke and Rickne required reading in college—before we choose our life partner—because the Swedish pair found that there is a way around this penalty.

In their research, they divided marriages between men and women into those they designated "traditional" and "nontraditional," with a traditional marriage being one where the husband is at least four years older than the wife and the wife takes 90 percent or more of the parental leave. In nontraditional marriages, the wife and husband are closer in age and the couple splits the parental leave more evenly. What their data found is that promotion hits women in those traditional marriages harder than women in nontraditional marriages—largely because of personal expectations.

Younger wives may start out lower on the professional and income ladder than their husbands, who have already had more time to make progress in their careers. Then she starts to have professional successes, and that's what causes problems. When a marriage begins with one reality and then gets sideswiped by a change in circumstances, it makes the relationship shaky. Years of a well-established routine and implicit expectations have been upended, and it's a shock to the marital system.

But the shock, they found, is less dramatic if the marriage is not so traditional. A "nontraditional" marriage—one where the couple shares the parental leave equally—among other things, proves more resilient to the wife gaining professional success. That's because *nontraditional* isn't just an economist's stodgy label; it implies a whole different type of relationship, a different, more egalitarian mindset from both partners. It's a marriage where husband and wife can develop different facets of themselves, without her success harming the relationship. If you want the freedom and support to enjoy power, this sounds like a good way to start.

Companies would do well to hear these voices. They have spent millions of dollars on programs to keep women in the workforce in their child-rearing years. But perhaps they need to shift their focus. Where are the employee diversity programs targeting dads, encouraging them to share the burden? That's what would really increase the number of women in leadership ranks. Where are the TV shows and chat rooms that nurture a community where dads discuss changing diapers, doing laundry, and pureeing baby food? Those scenes are fodder for domestic comedies, but not much more. They don't exist because the expectation is that most men don't do these things. (Indeed, as you'll see in the next chapter, we've interviewed men who blog about being a good father. Who's their primary audience? Women.) Moreover, a broader embrace of the work that women are doing, of the time it really requires, of the societal values it represents, would force change at work.

Eve Rodsky remembers one top male executive who wanted to work with her team to bring her Fair Play concepts into the office. He regaled her with stories about how he's mentoring and supporting women, and that his organization does a lot in that regard. "I said, 'That's amazing, but I'm just curious. Tell me about your family structure.'" He told her that he and his wife had just moved to Connecticut, and they had decided it didn't make sense for his wife to go back to work, because he was traveling so much, and had a long commute. Then he added, as so many powerful men do, "I owe my career to my wife. And I couldn't do my job without her. We are partners." At that point Rodsky stopped him and reminded him that he'd just told her his goal was to get single mothers into positions of power. "'Aka your job,'" she told him. "'But then you say you couldn't do your job if you were single.' I never heard from him again. The reality is, even though he's a male ally, and talks about implicit bias and the rest, the structure he is part of doesn't allow single women to do his job."

This exchange is emblematic of that pernicious problem of greedy work that we talked about in chapter 6, and also the societal constraints that cordon men off from much of the work of nurturing. If that executive were really serious about supporting women, he would do more to help high-flying single mothers by working less himself and role-modeling a style of work that includes shouldering responsibilities in his home life, as opposed to simply touting his DEI programs at work.

SAME-SEX, SAME ISSUES?

One day, after we had complained, yet again, about the unfairness of having to rush between demanding jobs, school pickups, and late-night Safeway runs, we remembered a friend of ours saying with a wry smile, "Well, you could marry a woman." It turns out she had a point. Same-sex couples are indeed largely able to at least avoid the unequal-housework problem. Why? Lesbian and gay couples haven't inherited centuries of expectations about who should be the main breadwinner or the main home builder. Chores are just chores. It helps, too, that more same-sex partnerships are dual-income relationships. Research from 1997 by British sociologist Gillian Dunne suggests that lesbian couples may actually make a conscious decision that both women work so that neither woman becomes trapped in economic dependence—the kind of dependence that has traditionally come with the power imbalances of many heterosexual marriages.

Even back in the late 1990s, a more egalitarian approach to professional work and housework was evident, something Dunne believed heterosexual couples could learn from, if they could only shed all that gendered baggage. "The flexibility that lesbians experience is based on negotiation within a non-gender polarized context. Respondents who had lived with men, spoke of their relationships with women offering freedom from gender assumptions around the allocation of household tasks," Dunne wrote.

"There's no question, he felt inferior," confirms a friend of ours, Lisa, detailing an earlier relationship with a man. Lisa was already a partner in her top-tier consulting firm, and he wasn't secure in his job. "It was a real tension for us. It was definitely awkward."

Fast-forward several years, and she and her female partner have a teenage son they are raising. They also have busy professional lives. "We both love our work, and would never think of asking or expecting the other to give that up," Lisa says. They bring in different levels of income, but that hasn't created the same tension, helped, perhaps, by healthy salaries.

How about division of labor?

"We just split things really equally, compared to most heterosexual couples I see," says Lisa. "We're not stuck in roles. This morning, we both had work, but she'd been on the phone all day yesterday dealing with something from our son's school that I couldn't deal with, so this morning I handled the whole morning routine, getting him off to school and the dog. We give each other back and forth."

She adds that they try to thank each other. "That makes a big difference to feel appreciated. I shouldn't generalize, but I think women do that more than men."

Dozens of studies of gay and lesbian couples also show that they do, like Lisa and her partner, divide household chores more equitably than their different-sex peers.[35] Without gender assumptions pressing down on the relationship, perhaps they're freed from society's expectations. They have space to express their power to do what fulfills them in various ways, rather than a need to exert power over either the domestic sphere as a whole, or over their spouse by taking all that unpaid labor for granted.

"When your partner is the same gender as you, you don't have the one person that is necessarily going to think, *Oh it's my job as the woman to do more of the house care*, simply because your partner is a woman, too," says Melanie Brewster, a psychology professor at Columbia University who studies same-sex relationships. She thinks the social pressure that heterosexual women feel to be good caregivers, hosts, and nurturers has a different impact on lesbian women. "When you have a relationship with two women, they both look at each other and know that they are both feeling that pressure. In some ways that in itself is affirming. It's a situation you have to figure out together."

Claire: I am appearing in this chapter as a unique test case for the difference between heterosexual relationships and same-sex relationships—in terms of division of labor. Who knew this would be a new area of expertise for me!

A few years ago, after much love and mutual support, my husband and I decided to separate. It wasn't easy, but because we are still good friends, it's pretty awesome. We still hang out, travel together, speak all the time, and see the kids together with our new partners. Two years ago, I started dating a woman I'd met, by chance, at a conference hosted by the soccer team in which I'd invested. Not in my plans, but my daughter told me to go for it—to broaden my horizons! Still, it wasn't until my editor said, "Claire, um, you know you could offer fascinating insights in this chapter," that I thought, *Huh, true*.

I notice a few differences. I mean—there are two truths. First, shit still has to get done, and somebody has to do it. I still leave cupboard doors open, and I still hate to unload the dishwasher, and hope if I ignore it, Kati Jo will miraculously empty it. She does more shopping. I do more planning. She remembers to order dog food. In some ways, it's not that different from the arrangement I had with Jay. We both struggle about who decides on/prepares dinner, and our new plan is week on/week off. Of course, there's less chaos this time, because my children are away at school. But the whole setup feels less infused with the weight of history and stereotypes. It's lighter. Neither of us can fall back on traditional roles and expectations. It feels more like wide-open territory with a sense of constant exploration. Obviously this is all new to me, but I've also noticed something else I want to keep exploring. It does feel as though we have two cognitive labor experts on the scene now, and in particular two people turning high-EQ headlamps onto situations, which can be incredibly useful—a partner reminding me to thank the electrician or to stick some surprise in a kid's suitcase—but sometimes it can be intense if we're both worried about, let's say, a mutual friend. But this is for sure—after two years together, neither of us feels "stuck" playing a traditional housewifey role.

There's not much data on how power imbalances play out in same-sex couples over time. By and large, psychologists agree that same-sex relationships are similar to heterosexual relationships, with the same stresses and triumphs. But in the US, same-sex marriages tend to be wealthier on average than different-sex couples; they also live in areas of the country considered more liberal, more educated, and more affluent. Proportionally fewer same-sex couples have children, which increases the couple's disposable income and, critically, decreases the amount of household chores there are to fight over.

The division of labor can become less egalitarian once same-sex couples have children. Although that hasn't been the case for Lisa and her partner, arrangements can start to resemble those made by heterosexual parents, with one taking on more responsibility for earning a salary and the other taking on more responsibility for child care and housework. "Once you have children, it starts to almost pressure the couple into this kind of division of labor, and we're seeing this now even in same-sex couples," Professor Robert-Jay Green, of the California School of Professional Psychology, told the *New York Times*. "Circumstances conspire on every level to get you to fall back in this traditional role."[36]

Housewife or househusband—same-sex or opposite sex—the

1950s model of marriage was already outdated in the 1950s, and stereotypical roles can confine. It felt freeing to hear about the more even balance Lisa has found. As Elizabeth, the young political media worker we told you about in chapter 4, puts it, "I don't want somebody to put more stuff in my wagon, to slow me down. I just want someone to run with and build a relationship with that's almost like a business relationship, but in a personal life." It doesn't sound like too much to demand.

MIND WHAT'S MEASURED

As Eve Rodsky has pointed out, along with many others, all of this could have been avoided, or at least mitigated, if policy makers had kept up with the times and implemented sensible programs that would have nudged us as a society to value domestic work. As the old adage goes, what gets measured gets managed. If suddenly domestic work earned a salary, you can bet that it would have been valued more and then more evenly distributed between the sexes. Shockingly, that almost happened.

In 1941, a young economist named Phyllis Deane was sent off to the British colonies in Africa to test out a new way of measuring economic output that today we call gross domestic product, or GDP. Created by her two (male) bosses in the United Kingdom, economists James Meade and Richard Stone, GDP determines a country's wealth by the amount of goods and services that are bought and sold, with everything else not counting as economic activity. On the ground, in what was then called Northern Rhodesia (now Zambia), Deane realized the system was flawed. As she went from village to village, she observed women walking for hours to get water or collect firewood, activity that clearly contributed to the economy. She concluded, quite rightly, that the only reason all this unpaid labor was left out was that it was traditionally performed by women.[37]

A few decades later, left-wing Italian economist Silvia Federici also made the argument that male economic production is impossible without women's uncompensated labor. Federici took Deane's observation and made it into a radical policy proposal, arguing that women should be paid for housework. Her 1975 treatise "Wages Against Housework" opened with a caustic swipe: "They say it is love.[38] We say it is unwaged work."

Despite Deane's and Federici's best efforts, it still hasn't happened yet, perhaps because economics is still a male-dominated profession. As we know from chapter 1, when female researchers started looking into the nature of power, they started to change our understanding of the subject, simply because their lens is different. The same might eventually become the case in the field of economics. Perhaps it just requires more and more female economists, looking in this direction, in order to gain traction.

Because it's blindingly obvious that household work has value. The IMF estimates that if housework and child care were given an economic value, it would add anywhere from 10 percent to 60 percent of a country's GDP.

Says Rodsky, "A male economist told me recently, 'The reason why your work is so challenging is that the underlying assumption of economics is that we can optimize our time, that we are rational actors.' I've told him for women, he's wrong. My time is not optimized; my time is chosen for me by society. Every hour of the working day is either as a parent, partner, or professional, and it has been predetermined for me by society because God forbid I try to do anything outside of those realms, or ask that it get fairly valued."

This should be obvious, but as long as the GDP doesn't include women's unpaid labor, that same labor will not be considered important when it comes to making government policies. Politicians would respond very differently to issues like child care, elder care, and housework if we put a monetary price on those tasks. With financial value comes a degree of power. And if those tasks were seen as valuable, and therefore accrued power and political attention, wouldn't men be more willing to share in them, too?

LOVE, SEX, AND LAUNDRY

As the chore distribution shifted in Katty's household, she found herself more observant of other families and she noticed that in most couples it is still the mother who gets the routine email about sleepovers, or school logistics. In a bid to shift the needle, she now makes a point of including the dads in the message chains about birthday parties etc., going into the school directory to find the father's email address (which is quite often missing, she notices) to make sure the men are included. It's a bit time-consuming and tedious, and she sometimes feels a bit awkward doing it. The dads rarely expect it, nor do the moms, honestly. She's conscious of being a bit of a gender police officer. But without that extra step, how will things ever change? How will dads be pushed to take on the household load if they aren't even asked to?

It is an issue that, by and large, needs to be solved in each woman's home. We hate laying this on women—it's annoying, even angering. But just to be real, we all know that it will fall to us to get a conversation started. And then to get labor—physical, emotional, and cognitive—actually shared, we'll have to keep pushing.

One starting point—caring less.

Here's more irritating data to make the inequity point. In a 2019 study, researchers showed a group of some six hundred people, men and women, photographs of a messy room.[39] There were dirty dishes left on countertops, clothes strewn about the place, a cluttered coffee table. They were also shown photos of the same room when it was tidied up. Both men and women in the control group deemed the messy room equally messy—which debunks the myth that men simply don't see mess.

But then things got more complicated. Participants were told that the rooms belonged either to a woman, Jennifer, or to a man, John. The tidy room, when it belonged to Jennifer, wasn't tidy enough. But when the exact same room belonged to John, it was just fine.

The researchers then asked the participants to assess how much the owner might be judged negatively by an unexpected visitor—say, if the neighbors dropped by for a coffee. Again, Jennifer was held to a higher standard. The neighbor would be more likely to disapprove of Jennifer's messy room than John's, they felt. His untidiness was met with an "oh well, boys will be boys" type of shrug.

Finally, the participants were asked who had more responsibility for keeping the room tidy. They were told that John and Jennifer were both full-time working parents with a spouse. In that scenario, and by a significant margin, the participants felt it was Jennifer's responsibility to pick up those clothes, clean those dishes, and declutter that coffee table.

No surprise, right? But. There was no distinction between the reactions of men and women among the participants. *Women* judged Jennifer just as harshly as men did.

Is the dirty secret—fair or unfair—of this uneven distribution of labor that women insist on higher standards for ourselves and for other women, too? Are we perhaps trying to retain some kind of control or even supremacy in a domain we have long been judged in? We hear the screams of outrage. But think about it. For centuries the domestic sphere was our *only* source of power. So, just as men are reluctant to give up power at work, it would be understandable that we don't want to give it up at home, leading us perhaps to subconsciously deter our husbands from becoming more involved by criticizing their efforts.

Katty: In a bid to make my home as perfect as possible, I was guilty of just that. I realized the balance was off during an election campaign when I had to travel a lot to follow the candidates. Before I left for a reporting trip, I would fill the fridge with extra food, lay on extra babysitting, and leave my husband long, quite obnoxious lists of household tasks: "Poppy has a dentist appointment. Jude needs to practice his piano. Maya has a math test." After a while I got resentful. When Tom left on work trips he never did any of that. So one day I confronted him. "It's so unfair," I said. "I'm working hard, traveling a lot, and doing all this extra stuff as well." "You're right," he replied. "But I never asked you to." And he was right. It was my choice. The next trip I decided not to do any of those extra things, and, of course, everything was fine. Except, Tom did go shopping and bought ten pounds of cod for six people, so we had a lot of frozen fish.

For years I'd tell that story in speeches at women's networking events as a way of showing how important it is to cede control and not to try to do everything perfectly. The women in the crowd would smile knowingly. At the end I would pause for the inevitable laugh about the big fish purchase. "You see," the chuckles seemed to say, "we knew he'd screw it up somehow." But I grew increasingly uneasy with milking that joke. I was belittling Tom's efforts, which was bad enough, and beyond that I was undermining my own success in shifting power in our home. By making myself sound like the competent adult in the home, and my husband sound like the partner who couldn't quite keep the household together, I was perpetuating a trope that was not much better than all those "here's another smiling wife with detergent" ads I so hated.

So. One step in the process may be caring less, or lowering standards, both for ourselves and other women.

But that only gets us so far. Melanie Brewster, the couples therapist, offers other ways to address the imbalance, without shouting matches over the dishes. Who does more housework and child care is a universal source of tension, so no, you are not alone. Often, she says, the husbands aren't even aware that they are doing less; again, you are not alone.

To resolve the tension, her technique is to get the couple to fill out a log of their daily chores. Once the man sees the disparity in black and white, the couple can start the conversation to rebalance their efforts. If men can reframe doing chores as acts of love and service, as something that makes their partner unhappy when they don't do their share, then things can change. She tries to talk about it in the language of love and point out the emotional consequences. "When it's done in a more removed, clinical way, like a worksheet, I do think that can be motivating," Brewster says. There is no magic formula for producing more housework, she admits. She has tried tips like getting husbands to set an alarm on their phones, for example, to remind them to take out the trash once a week, or having a chart on the fridge with separate lists of chores. But it's not, she says, as if a lightbulb suddenly turns on: "It takes months to change these habits." It has to start with deliberate communication.

Again, women can have some agency here, really examining why they consistently shoulder the burden. "When I have female clients who are feeling really overwhelmed by it all, I ask why is it that a clean house or being the one that shows up smiling at soccer practice is some sort of indicator of your worth, or how good you are at mothering?" says Brewster. She believes we need to move to a place where mothers feel less pressure to be so full-on, but she rarely gets a sense that women themselves are actually prepared to scale back. "Most people," she says, "are not very receptive to that. As a psychologist I wish I could think what's going to break the pattern, but [this social pressure] has a really tight grasp. It's kind of disheartening."

That explains why American mothers are more likely to say they are exhausted than American dads are. They are doing so much. Too much. Maybe it feels retro to keep going on, and on, and on about housework and child care, but it remains a major barrier between us and power. Let's remember: American women do almost 40 percent more household work than men.[40] Something has to give.

If the men in your lives are still resistant, then ask them to consider this. Opposite-sex couples are happier when husbands do a fair share of household chores. Indeed, a survey of German couples found there's even more sex in marriages when men do their fair share.[41] Matt Johnson, professor of family ecology at the University of Alberta, conducted the survey of German relationships and said it's pretty obvious: when husbands pitch in, their wives like them better. "Completing housework may or may not be enjoyable, but knowing that a partner is pulling his weight prevents anger and bitterness, creating more fertile ground in which a satisfying sexual encounter may occur," he says. It's an intriguing selling point: more vacuuming equals more good sex.

THE OTHER F-WORD

Um. This is hard to talk about, but we would be remiss if we did not mention:

Fun.

One of our interviewees, an academic whose focus is on men and women, bias and negotiations, talked about this with us in hushed tones, because she feels it's politically incorrect to say it. But we are all about being real in this book. So here it is.

> *One of the big gender divides I hear from men, and sometimes from women in the field, is that women are just too intense. We are not fun.*

Ouch.

Are we just less fun than men? Do we kill the atmosphere? Does our intense focus on getting shit done preclude a good time?

We felt defensive, but we also recognized a bit of truth here. (By the way, there is a big difference between fun and joy—which we've been in pursuit of with our new power code. Fun is typically active. You have it doing something. Laughter is often involved. It's usually a shared experience. Joy can be more internal, in our thoughts, a silent sense of transformative peace or a lingering wash of positive emotion. We clearly want some of both!)

Our stealth expert put it this way—that the workplace used to be where men would go to play. "They'd be on the floor of the stock exchange with silly games involving saltine crackers, or at the office shooting hoops. And then women come to work and say, 'I want to get things done.' And suddenly the workplace is not where you are going to be playing hoops."

Of course, what used to be considered "fun"—dirty jokes, inappropriate advances, and worse—is just . . . sexual harassment or assault. But there's lots of other fun and we get that, whether banter, games, dinners with colleagues, etc. That's all important for connection as well, so it ought to be in our wheelhouse.

Our source also noted, "Power to men is a game. In negotiations, men will do all sorts of things to 'win' because they gamify everything. Women want to add value; it's less about winning."

Okay. Maybe there is something we can learn here. We would like to have fun, too. But the fact is, we need time to have fun. Could it be that we are less able to have fun at work because our work life isn't protected? We have, typically, two jobs?

Still. This really struck us, and we're filing it away for future study. We don't want to be the boring bad cops. A few women leaders have mentioned how critical humor is. We've heard that.

So, men. Duly noted. We hear you, too. A bargain—let's share the life load, and we will get our fun game on.

GEN Z—REALISM REINS

With all of this research on the discrepancies in housework, the sensitivities around income, the irritations around child care duties, you'd be forgiven for thinking younger, unmarried women might have no interest in having either a partner or kids. Not necessarily true, although more than it used to be, as we discovered with Marianna in chapter 6. What younger women have in common is that they seem to approach the entire enterprise with a more astute view of what they want, and the fact that something may have to give.

Take Cole Kendall, whom you met in chapter 4. A full-time TV journalist, there is no doubting her ambition. But she also knows she wants a family, and she's already eying the ladder as to how to get to a place in her career that will allow her time off and perhaps flexibility after they are born. "My close friends who don't want kids are much more willing to take chances with jobs, or quit when they don't get a raise, for example." I feel like I'm on a path, and then in a certain number of years I'll be able to count on time off for family. I feel like I have to amass a certain amount of achievement before I can have kids and have the balance I want."

Initially her deliberations sounded similar to our thought process at her age, that search for balance. But whereas we assumed we'd have kids, assumed (erroneously it turned out) that our husbands would do half the child rearing, assumed we'd relentlessly keep busting a gut to get the next promotion, all at the same time—this generation have their eyes wide open. They survey the landscape, with its myriad family and career and power options, and make choices that fit their individual needs.

Cole's not a Pollyanna; she knows it's not easy to combine children with work; she's seen her mother go through exactly the same juggle, but she is clear that she won't let the lure of career prestige derail her plans for a family. "Spending time cultivating a family and being close with them is more important to me than achieving X, Y, or Z in the power hierarchy at work." She imagines her partner may be more focused on work than she is, and that's fine, she says. Here's what else makes Cole different from us in our twenties. She doesn't want to quit her career and stay home 24/7, that's not what she's talking about—she wants an interesting, fulfilling professional life, and she believes she can have it, but she doesn't need to keeping climbing anybody's ladder.

Alexandra (not her real name) is just as clear about what she values and expects. She's ambitious. At the age of twenty-three she already has a successful job as a financial advisor in a New York bank. She's on the fast track in a world still dominated by men. But she's never let the lack of women in her profession deter her. She says she isn't put off either by the twelve-to-fourteen-hour days, and she fully intends to keep going and reach the top. Like Cole, she is clear that she wants children, but she can't imagine stepping back from her career once she has them. And, if we were posting job specs, what Alexandra wants in a life partner is someone who will match her drive. She just wouldn't be attracted, she says, to a man who wasn't as ambitious as she is, even if that were to make the home-life balance easier.

She says did have a boyfriend who wasn't a classically motivated professional, an Italian who worked as a ski instructor in the winter and hung out with her in New York in the summer. She liked him a lot, but he wasn't quite what she imagined as a husband, and she kept coming back to his lack of drive as part of the problem.

"Maybe it's because I'm Hispanic," she says with a laugh, "and we have a pretty conservative view of relationships. In my culture, our view of what real men should be hasn't changed much." Alexandra is intensely self aware—she knows even as she says it that she's perpetuating an ethnic stereotype, but for her, it is what it is.

We hope that Alexandra, Cole, and their peers, and the women who follow them, can benefit from being more aware of what they want, professionally and domestically. At the moment, most women find our professional plans heavily affected by our domestic setup in ways we didn't anticipate. We would also argue that a broader definition of power, and heavier value placed on the domestic by men and women, is the best gift we can give to future generations, to the younger women and the men. The benefits of a richer emotional life for men, with more ties to the domestic, is something we focus on in the next chapter. To us, the impact of the current domestic imbalance is blindingly obvious—we need some of our time back to implement our power code. Our worlds outside of work matter to us, and yes, we want to blend them seamlessly into healthier work-lives, but we really truly can't do it all. Placing an economic value on domestic labor would be the gold standard—short of that, we'd take a fair distribution of the many aspects of work on the home front.

YOUR POWER CODE

Another homework assignment? Another item on the heaving to-do list? We hesitate to suggest it, especially now that we're seen as fun-killers, but, yes, there's more we can do, and we're going to have to break a few glasses if we really want to rewire the power code at home.

Time codes. As several marriage therapists have suggested, until you and your partner can agree on how much more labor (of every type) you are doing, you won't be able to have a productive conversation about how to change the imbalance so that you can gain more time for work outside the home. So sit down with your spouse, agree on the parameters of different household and child-related tasks, including the cognitive labor of anticipation and planning, and spend one week each making a careful note of everything you do every day. Once you both have a written list, you can get to work on distributing the labor more fairly. Remember: "make dinner" isn't just cooking the food; it's planning, checking the pantry, and shopping, too. Oh, and now mindful of the fun of fun, perhaps add some "fun time" planning as a category as well. If we aren't doing it, we should be!

Make it a clean handoff. Rather than try to share the labor of all the different household tasks, which means you'll probably fall into doing most of the planning, Alison Daminger suggests you divide up whole areas of responsibility. So, for example, hand the entire area of laundry over to your partner. That includes:

checking if there's enough detergent
buying more if needed
planning which day to do the washing

remembering when was the last time the sheets were changed
keeping on top of towels being cleaned regularly
emptying the kids' laundry baskets, too
if you dry clothes outside, keeping an eye on the weather forecast
folding the clothes
putting them away
knowing when the kids need what

Suddenly he is in charge of all the thinking that goes into "laundry"—not just loading the machine and folding clothes from the dryer. If it doesn't get done, the responsibility is his. Laundry is a good area to start with because it will be pretty clear quite quickly if no one has clean clothes. Monitor your own response to this exercise. Are you tempted to step in and sort it out when the towels haven't been washed for a couple of weeks? Resist. Dirty towels are a small price to pay for a bit of power redistribution.

Buy a deck of cards. We mentioned Eve Rodsky's Fair Play card game. Order it immediately. These cards represent her years of research, the synthesis of her "shit we do" list, and they are an incredibly concrete and powerful behavioral change agent. Partners are meant to use the one hundred cards detailing household labor to decide what matters to them, and agree to a weekly division of tasks. Cards range from shopping for gifts or doing the dishes to bedtime duty—you name it. Here's what we love: on the back of each card are details about how to *assess*, *plan*, and execute. Cognitive labor for dummies.

Delegate, don't diss. Whatever chores your partner chooses, let's say the laundry, remember this: if you criticize the way the towels are folded, you're just undermining their efforts. There's a difference between useful input and being unnecessarily picky. As you transition to a more equitable distribution of labor, some things won't get done the way you might like. Your job is to live with that and cede control. If you have kids or are starting a family, get into this habit from day one. Your husband prepares the bottle, changes his first diaper, makes the baby food. Excellent. Telling him he's doing it all wrong is the best way to stop him from doing it next time. You're just setting yourself up for more work. Think of it in corporate terms: if you delegate a job to a team member, then you need to let them get on with it. It's a form of respect. Sure, you can review the process, but you won't get very far as a manager if you endlessly critique and micromanage someone's work.

Become the CFO of your household. Leaving your partner to run the household finances can be disempowering. We may control consumer purchases, but a lot of women, including a lot of well-educated, professional women, have surprisingly little involvement in their own finances. That needs to change. Start with this reality check.

Do you know what your partner earns?
Do you know how and where your savings are invested?
Are you involved in drawing up your family's tax return?
Do you know how much life insurance you have?
Are you involved in managing your retirement fund?

You'd be surprised how many women answer no to those questions (even women who are their families' primary breadwinner). So you're not alone. Patricia Astley, managing director at Julius Baer, a wealth management company, had this advice: before having the conversation with your partner, have it with your female friends. Treat it like a book club.[42] You can learn from each other, support each other, and then have a more informed conversation with your spouse. However you tackle it, the important thing is to get informed and get involved. Being chief operating officer is great, but you'll exercise more of your power as an equal partner in managing your finances, too.

Tackle the money tension head-on. For the millions of American women who outearn their husbands, this is a particularly tricky and particularly important issue. Left alone, these tensions will fester. But every couple has financial stresses. Here are a few ways you can ease them no matter the balance.

Talk about it. This seems obvious but is surprisingly hard. Try humor and acknowledge that it's awkward. Add some love and appreciation to get the conversation going. Remember, there can be substantial guilt and shame involved on both sides.

Budget. Understand your current relationship dynamics. Are you contributing equally to bills? That may or may not make sense. Same accounts or separate? The important outcome isn't the system but the open communication and shared financial goals.

Take stock of work that doesn't earn an income. Yes, salaries are important—especially for women who may not have much history of valuing their earning power. But, as we all know, what you bring in financially is far from the only thing that makes a family thrive. Your spouse may do the tax returns or chase those health insurance payments, handle child care, act as the family COO. That's worth a good deal. It takes a lot of time, literally saves your family money, and frees you up for other pursuits. Acknowledging this, in clear financial terms, might help men who earn less especially feel more comfortable with any disparity. (It goes without saying that women would benefit from this appreciation of their unpaid labor as well.)

More money doesn't necessarily mean fewer chores. When both partners have equally demanding hours, it helps defuse tensions to acknowledge that each career is important, and then share the load at home.

Pioneering attitude. If you are a woman outearning your male partner, understand this is new terrain culturally, and go easy on each other. Think of yourselves as adventurers homesteading a new land.

8

MEN'S WORK

Clint Edwards writes *No Idea What I'm Doing: A Daddy Blog.* It's a funny, honest, and touching chronicle of being a full-time, stay-at-home parent—a role both he and his wife, Melody, have taken turns at. Clint's experience of early fatherhood didn't prepare him for hands-on parenting. His father became addicted to painkillers at the hands of a doctor in the early days of the opioid crisis and was in and out of Clint's life. Eventually he ended up in jail. (Ironically, Clint now says, that was probably the best time in their relationship. "At least I knew where to find him and I knew when his visiting hours were.")

From the age of fourteen, Clint was raised by his mother and his grandmother. "I didn't have much of a script for being a father," he says. "I was very worried I was going to mess it up. I was going to do what he did. And one of the biggest arguments that we had was over having children." Clint was so concerned that he'd screw it up that he really wasn't sure he wanted to have children at all.

Melody persuaded him that he did, and when their son was born he realized that the giant task of inventing his own road map was also an oddly freeing experience. He could, and did, do things differently. "Because I didn't have that script, I just said we're going to have to figure this out. I wanted to look at our strengths and what we were good at." Here's where Clint became evangelical. "I like to think of it as we're in this egalitarian relationship where I really don't want to look at gender. I was raised with this idea of what the father *ought* to be doing and what the mother *ought* to be doing. We just kind of want to strip all that away and parent with our own skills. Of course, not everything works out equally, but we certainly give it an honest effort."

Clint hopes that by him writing openly about his "nontraditional" fathering, other men will see that they, too, can access those parts of themselves without wounding their egos. He believes men can embrace a new model of fatherhood that, in some ways, mirrors women's march to a fuller expression of themselves. Men can draw on their domestic power, in the same way women can express their professional power. It's not just men playacting at motherhood. It's something new and distinctive, and more satisfying. It's uniquely male, but also fully engaged.

Clint's path offers a different way forward, an escape hatch from the rigid box of stereotypes that have trapped men as much as they have trapped women. And, yes, we do realize this may sound heretical—calling out the woes of men—especially since we've spent years (and many pages in this book) explaining how the playing field is tilted against *women*. We've shown how business and society are skewed against us, how we don't get a fair shot in a system built by and for white men. We still believe all that. But two things can be true at the same time.

Some of Clint's more pointed blog posts have gained him a degree of fame, like the one titled "I blamed my wife for our messy house, I was wrong for many reasons." He has appeared on the morning TV shows talking about his commitment to making his marriage ever more egalitarian. He's written a book, *Father-ish: Laugh-Out-Loud Tales from a Dad Trying Not to Ruin His Kids' Lives.* He has a self-deprecating candor that his audience seems to love. Or rather, that his female audience seems to love. "Eighty-five percent of my readers are women," he told us. "I've got, what, 450,000 followers at the moment and it's eighty-five percent women. I'm probably the most hated man in America. I have basically all these women out there saying to their husbands, 'Why can't you be more like Clint?'"

Change—transformation—is uncomfortable to confront. It can feel like a loss. What Clint is discovering, despite his own impressive strides, is that this is an especially difficult journey for men. Indeed, men might not even recognize a journey is needed. As we've argued throughout the book and will discuss further in this chapter, more often than not, men see women gaining power as synonymous with their loss of it. "I know there are a lot of women that obviously think that my message would be good for their husbands, but the men won't read it," Clint tells us. "It's frustrating."

Men—their roles in our lives, our careers, our power—have been a constant presence in our research. Several times we've been asked to write a book just about men but we never felt it was our expertise. Researching this topic, it soon became clear that men needed their own chapter—and, more specifically, straight, cisgender men in different-sex partnerships. This chapter is about them. But it is for all the women and everyone else reading this who have those men in their worlds.

NOBODY LIKES TO LOSE

On this, the science is very clear: humans, of all genders, hate loss. The scientific term is *loss aversion theory.* It's painful to confront loss of almost any sort, big or small, whether it's the loss of a sweater we may have left at a theater, the loss of a house, a job, or a relationship. The suffering and regrets linger. That's why we fight so hard to keep what we have—or to get back what we've lost.

We are taking a scientific detour here because to really understand the problem we face in our power imbalance—and maybe more importantly, the problem men *themselves* face in their current situation—we have to step back and see things from both sides. The two of us found that these examinations of human behavior allowed us a much broader perspective. We found some empathy to add to our long-simmering frustration and determination. What we had always thought of as willful male bias we now see is laced with considerable anguish.

In 1979, behavioral scientists Daniel Kahneman and Amos Tversky conducted groundbreaking studies that clarified loss aversion theory, finding that the pain of losing is literally twice as powerful, psychologically, as the pleasure of gaining.[1] Evolutionary psychologists think these tendencies go back to the Stone Age; we've been hardwired for thousands of years to avoid loss when things feel good, and to cause chaos when our present situation is threatened. That means people are willing to go to extraordinary lengths—take risks, even behave dishonestly—in order to hang on to something they have.

In this case, we're talking about a deep, primal loss—the loss of status and the legacy of power that men, in particular, feel is at stake. It's the very measure of what they feel a successful and meaningful life looks like. No wonder they try so hard to bar the door to the old boys' club.

Loss aversion is a condition that affects all of us, but when we talk about reimagining the workplace and the home front, we can't underestimate how deeply men are feeling it, and if we don't take it into account, the changes we want to effect, both for women and for men, will not come easily, or perhaps at all. As Laura Kray, the UC Berkeley professor, reminds us, men view power as a zero-sum enterprise. And because men don't often define themselves by much more than their professional status, and aren't willing to listen to the Pied Pipers like Clint, the change we're advocating feels especially risky to them and definitely affects their behavior.

Jennifer Jordan, the organizational psychologist we met in chapter 3, points out that when you threaten to take away people's power, they become more "risky in their behavior, more reckless." "They're more likely to be stingy, to kind of hold on to or hoard their power," she says. "They become paranoid and lose trust in people around them—they're more likely to be suspicious."

If loss aversion theory isn't enough of a hurdle, throw in *status quo bias*. This is the idea that change of any sort is frightening because we tend to see it as a loss. Economists William Samuelson and Richard Zeckhauser discovered the bias and found it to be true even when our current situation isn't that great, when, objectively speaking, the status quo sucks.[2]

What to make of the impact of both of these theories? One broad conclusion is that men won't embrace change or loss; in other words, they won't give up power easily. This echoes what we heard from Ndéye Lucie Cissé about her experience with the Senegalese men. Of course it's obvious on the face of it, but understanding that this reaction is part of a general human bias depersonalizes it and helps us reframe some of the iciness between men and women on questions of power. It means we don't have to cast men as selfish or power-hungry troglodytes. It means we can connect with men, not oppose them, understand their human fear of loss, and perhaps make the rewards of change appealing to everyone. How very "power-to" of us, right?

Kray confirmed this thought process. "It's not just a matter of if we have more women in positions of power, then the world will be better," she told us. "It's also that we need to get men comfortable in the subordinate position. Because if they're not, then they're going to behave in ways that make that experience for women in power all the more unpleasant." Change, she explained, is a threat to men's egos, pure and simple. The backlash going on right now is the result of that. It is men digging their heels in to, as she puts it, "neutralize the threat."

As we reimagine what comes next, Kray suggests we need to "figure out ways in which men's inherent worth can be affirmed even when they're not at the top of the totem pole." (We can't help but note, with a sigh, that the "we" here is likely women. That this too is some version of the emotional, cognitive labor that usually lands in our laps. At least we have the Clints of the world to help us.)

IT'S NOT THEIR FATHER'S WORLD ANYMORE

There's a joke we sometimes repeat when we speak to women's groups, and which always prompts a chuckle.

> *White men have been the recipients of the best-ever affirmative action program in the history of the world—it's called the history of the world.*

When there are men in the room, it's met with awkward silence. And we get it: Loss aversion is real, remember?

For the past two thousand years or so, men could assume an elevated place in society, just by virtue of being born male. Heterosexual and cisgender white men, specifically, benefited from this built-in advantage. Being born into that elite club was a virtual guarantee of success. Historically, even poor white men were better off than many women, and better off than all people of color.

If you were white, male, and even a little educated, that job in a bank, a management consultancy, a hospital, the government was pretty much yours for the taking. The only competition was other white men. Even if you weren't particularly smart or hardworking or good at your job, you could still rise and get access to power.

Times have changed. Now white men have to compete for success with millions of women and people of color, even with people who live on the other side of the world. Having more diversity in organizations is proven to make them work better. Numerous studies show that companies with more diversity in leadership perform better than their competitors, so it's easy to make the economic case for including different groups.[3,4] It's a bottom-line issue. With more profits, those companies then grow, providing more jobs and a bigger return for everyone to share. There is a win-win here.

But even with that good news, it would be Pollyannaish to suggest there is room for everyone at the top. There isn't. Of course not. And some men resent the writing on the wall, to an extreme extent.

The reality is, at the moment, there's not much Clint-influenced behavior on public display. Rather, vivid loss aversion tactics are rampant in the workplace. Recall Clara Green, the Regions Banks diversity officer. Her job is basically to distribute power more equitably, and as we spoke with her about how some white men are losing out as power shifts in society, Green, who is one of the more diplomatic and nonjudgmental people we've met, became uncharacteristically sharp. "Power is shifting, and I know that makes those accustomed to having power uncomfortable, and so there is a natural tendency to hold on to it as best they can. Unfortunately, that delays progress and can make for very tense work environments." Or as another executive told us more bluntly, a small group of white men are making life miserable for everybody else. "Sometimes their presence feels enormous because of the antics they carry out," she said.

Stefanie Johnson, the professor at the University of Colorado Boulder who spent years studying sexual harassment in the workplace, is now studying men's reaction to the power shifts taking place at work. She says she hears a lot of hostility, with complaints such as "the boss is being inclusive, but that means I am experiencing discrimination, or I'm less comfortable, or I have fewer opportunities."

As we said in chapter 4, this perception doesn't always reflect what's actually happening. "In reality," Johnson says, "it's probably just slightly more equal than it used to be. But the perception or the fear is that it's going to be unfair for men." Men tell Johnson that they feel they have no say in this new world; their companies just come to them and say they are changing the status quo, and the men can get on board or get off the ship.

Some professional men are even trying to use the courts and the court of public opinion to plead their case. For instance, at Google, engineer James Damore filed a lawsuit alleging workplace discrimination against white men with perceived socially conservative views.[5] At Yahoo, Greg Anderson, an editorial director, alleged that he was fired because he was a man. He claimed the company's female managers "intentionally hire and promote women because of their gender, while terminating, demoting, or laying off male employees because of their gender." Also at Yahoo, Scott Ard sued the company for gender discrimination after he was fired. (One has to wonder whether it's just a coincidence that all three of these examples come from the tech world, with its reputation for being a boiler room for bro culture.)[6]

These examples may seem like outliers, but then we remember how many times we've heard white men, our colleagues, even some of our friends say to us, "Of course, I can't get a column published in a newspaper anymore—they only want women." Or "Normally I'd be in line for a seat on a board, but they only want diverse candidates." Or "If you're white and male, there's no point even applying for (fill in the blank with any lofty, high-paying position)." Or the more insidious version: "I'm all in favor of diversity, but they keep promoting people who aren't ready." One high-ranking reporter at the *Washington Post* pulled one of us aside to tell us about the mood of men in the newsroom. "Not happy," he told us. Many of the top men there were openly grumbling that they'd been shut out of the power sweepstakes when it was announced that the new editor in chief was a woman. "A kind of affirmative action," as he put it, casually taking a broad swipe at her qualifications.

This notion of reverse discrimination, of men, and white men in particular, feeling hard-done-by as companies try to diversify, produces a lot of fuzzy thinking. Look at the raw numbers: the demographic group that still dominates the senior ranks of almost every corporation *and* industry *and* government in the world? Men. And in the West, white men. It's not even close.

Yet, "white men believe they face an uphill battle in corporate America."[7] That notion came from a 2018 study, surprise, surprise, that found white men who ask for a raise are 25 percent more likely to get it than people of color.[8] Managers still routinely recommend lower wage increases—almost 6 percentage points lower—for women than for identically qualified men.[9]

"Men have a tendency to believe that decreasing bias against women is associated with increasing bias against men," explains Clara Wilkins, a professor at Wesleyan University who studies the psychology behind reverse discrimination. She adds, "So if things are better for women, things are worse for men." There it is again, that zero-sum view of power and success that is so limiting. It's an attitude that even infects life at home, sadly. While we've noticed, over the years, that so many professional men are ardently committed to the success of their daughters, it turns out they are threatened by the success of their female partners.

When University of Florida psychology professor Kate Ratliff first came across this phenomenon, she told us she wasn't even looking for a gender story; she just wanted to examine how people in general respond to other people's success. Specifically, she was doing research on how someone else's success affects our own sense of self. How do we feel when someone close to us has a triumph? But as she was conducting her study, she couldn't ignore the gender difference that emerged: "Success really seemed to affect men differently from women."

Ratliff and her colleague, Shigehiro Oishi, studied a group of almost one thousand students in both the US and the Netherlands.[10] They went across the Atlantic because they wanted to make sure their findings didn't reflect the cultural bias of just one country. The test was designed to find out how we feel specifically about a romantic partner's success. Critically, the test was designed to find out how we *really* feel, not how we *say* we feel, or even how we think we *should* feel. In other words, it was striving for emotional honesty.

In some experiments, students were asked to write about episodes in which a romantic partner succeeded or failed. Then they were given a cognitive test with word associations designed to get at how their self-esteem was doing. It's what psychologists call an implicit association test. That's important because obviously no one wants to be a jerk and say, "Oh, I hate it when my girlfriend does well." Or "Wow, I feel so much better when my wife screws up."

But Ratliff's rather depressing finding suggests that's exactly what many men may be feeling, even if they don't want to fess up to it. And, she told us, it really didn't make any difference what kind of success the female partner was having. Personal, professional, academic triumphs—they all made the guys feel equally shitty about themselves.

Men, Ratliff believes, are more likely to see success as a limited commodity. Women, she has found, don't measure it that way. They see a partner's success as a boost most often. It's not so much that men are bad people, it's that they see success as finite—and that in turn leads them to act ungenerously. "It's a zero-sum game," she says, making her yet another person to use this phrase when we ask about men and power. For a man, seeing a partner be successful somehow implies he is a failure because, if the supply of success is finite, they can't both be winners. She's taken a slice of the pie, which leaves less of it for him.

"Where's the arrangement my father had, and my father's father had?" That's the question many men ask, says University of Virginia sociology professor Allison Pugh.

Pugh has been investigating the impact of job insecurity on couples' relationships, and she is particularly focused on working-class men. The poorer men are, she has found, the harder it is to deviate from the norm. Society has a narrow view of what it means to be a man in the upper echelons, but it's even more vise-like for low-income men.

Pugh has done in-depth research with working-class couples.[11] What she found was that men feel that the payoff for their decades of hard work ought to be returned with deference at home, and they aren't getting it. The men in her survey were angry. But they weren't angry at their employers who had let them down; they were angry at their wives.

Pugh was surprised by how tolerant the men were of the corporations who had fired them, or had not paid them enough. They somehow excused their bosses, citing the "profit margins," and "new technologies" their companies had to contend with. But there was no such tolerance for their wives. "Every small fault at home was seen as a betrayal," Pugh says. The men had a "brittle inflexibility" when it came to the way they talked about their homes.

Interestingly, the women she interviewed were angry, too, but in a different way. She described them as "defiant," even "triumphant." It wasn't that anyone in her research project was well-off financially, but the women felt a freedom their men didn't. Many still had jobs, in health care, hospitality, or retail, and, as Erin Zimmerman found, money gave them power to choose. They didn't feel they had to stay with men who were grumbling dead weights. Pugh described them as having moxie—life was by no means perfect or even easy, but they felt they had more options than the men she interviewed.

But Pugh understands that men are also victims of centuries of societal norms (not to mention economic upheaval caused by automation, downsizing, and globalization). They are living out the legacy of their fathers and grandfathers, while many women have forged a new reality. "There's a great sense of loss among men," she believes. "It's really a modern-day tragedy."

Clearly, men are uncomfortable, perhaps grumbling at home and at work, and throwing up roadblocks. That's the most common experience. But then there are those who feel boxed out and act out violently—channeling their fear and insecurities in a frightening fashion. While we were researching this book, we spent a weird and unsettling few weeks diving into the dark world of angry white men who feel spurned, threatened, and victimized by female empowerment. At their most extreme they are a violent threat to society. There is no dearth of horrifying stories here in the US, and we can't explore them all. But they range from the self-described misogynist who drove more than a hundred miles to execute a carefully planned attack on a yoga studio, killing two women and injuring four more in a shooting spree, to the cold-blooded murder of eight people who worked in massage parlors (six of whom were women of Asian descent) in Atlanta in 2021 by a man who claimed he was motivated to kill because of his sex addiction.

Among mass shooters in the US, anger at women has emerged as one of the most common personality traits. The number of male mass shooters with a background of abusing women is astonishing—and underreported. In 2018, the Southern Poverty Law Center classified male supremacy as a hate crime in America.[12]

These are extreme examples, but a sense of thwarted entitlement is leading to behavior that can be dangerously violent, and threatening to society as a whole.

LESS EGO

As feminist icon Gloria Steinem famously observed, "I'm glad we've begun to raise our daughters more like our sons, but it will never work until we raise our sons more like our daughters." The extension of Steinem's thinking is that we need to give boys (or men) the opportunities we give girls (or women). They need access to all the things in life that we have—in order for us to have access to all the things in life that they have. As we explored in the last chapter, just as we need more holistic, blended lives, so do they. Actually, many of them want it. They want the joy that can come from having a blend of power, life, community, and values. Who wouldn't?

"I may just be getting a bit old and cranky, but there are a lot of careers that require people to work really, really, really hard, and it's just because that's the way it's always happened," Rady Johnson, an executive at Pfizer, told us. "For a lot of people, that comes with potential consequences. We just need a better model."

Johnson has worked his way up through the ranks of law firms, accounting firms, and now corporate America. He characterizes himself as an imposter in a world of workaholics. "I'm a type B, hiding in a type A world." He describes that as a good thing. He believes that spending time taking care of the house, being on the PTA, and making family dinners makes him happier than many of his male colleagues who don't do those chores. For him, the routines of home care provide a much-needed mental break from work, a mental break that actually makes him better at his day job. But it's not something many of his male peers feel able to emulate, much less express.

"Men get sucked into their careers and the demands of their jobs. They find it really difficult to say no, or make the decision that they've had enough. I know big partners in law firms, they're still there because they don't know what else to do, to be honest. They don't really love it," Johnson told us. They don't love it, but they don't know how to get out of it because there's no road map for doing things differently.

By comparison, in some ways the road map for women has expanded considerably in the past few decades. Think about it. Women can be married or single. Women can have children or not have them. Women can pursue careers or not pursue them. We can be badass superheroes, Navy SEALs, teachers, or lawyers. Society is fine with us working full-time, part-time, or no-time. All of those options are now socially acceptable, and still "feminine."

"Femininity is often perceived as natural because of its connection to child bearing," says Harvard sociology professor Alexandra Killewald, who has made studying the balance of power between men and women her life's work.

According to Killewald, women are seen as feminine just by virtue of being able to have children. But masculinity, she argues, is more difficult to define and harder to come by. "It's an achieved status that you get by acting in a certain way, by doing certain things," she says. In other words, men aren't manly by birthright; they have to work at it. It's a constant effort and often a source of anxiety. This helps explain why men are stuck with a 1950s view of what it means to be a man. It might also explain why both women and men underreport men's earnings on the US Census. And why men still pick up the check for dinner even when their wife's salary is funding the outing. "There's a kind of rigidity of what it means to be a respectable husband or father that hasn't really changed in the same way that we have seen an expansion of appropriate roles for women," says Killewald.

Men who do try to deviate from the norm often struggle under the weight of society's judgment, which puts their egos under pressure. "There's a kind of shame," Jon Malesic tells us. "Even if I'm not actually meeting people who say, 'You're not a real man because you don't do a job,' there's still that voice in my head."

Jon Malesic left his job as a college professor because he burned out. He says it was a relief to quit, and he knows he was lucky to be able to do so. His wife got a promotion that, with some belt tightening, allowed him to leave full-time employment. But he paid a price socially. "The self-recrimination was that I had a job and I didn't do it. I failed at the one thing I was supposed to have done," he says.

At the one thing I was supposed to have done. There is something deeply sad and limiting about that phrase. There was only one thing he felt he was supposed to have done—not a cornucopia of life's many options and parts. His life list had only one thing on it: having a paid job. Malesic has now made a study of our workaholic culture and its impact on men. He's particularly interested in how men burn out, and he, too, has come to the conclusion that even as gender roles seem increasingly flexible, men are still straitjacketed by traditional expectations. Malesic, who is soft-spoken and prepared to be vulnerable, is an exception because he is willing to talk publicly about his situation. He's written for the *Guardian* and the

New York Times about his experiences, exposing the shame he felt at quitting his job.

He's come to the conclusion that what makes the culture of masculinity so hard to change is the "breadwinner ethos." For centuries men have been expected to be the sole or, more recently, at least the primary breadwinner in the family. It is their identity, the thing that gives them that status Killewald refers to. And that ethos is remarkably tenacious. "Younger men, men under forty-five, thought we were over this model. We thought our marriages would be equal partnerships, that it wouldn't matter who is earning more and who is doing more at home." They were wrong, Malesic says. "The paradigm is still with us. It has a lot of power, and, think about it, why wouldn't it. It's been in place for decades, for centuries. It doesn't go away overnight." Indeed, as work has become ever more demanding, ever more greedy, the burden of their breadwinner role has become heavier, the walls of their box thicker.

Here's the twist. For all his own unusual openness, even Malesic doesn't talk about this power shift with his male friends. When he moved to Dallas, without a job, to follow his wife's career, the first friend he made was in a similar situation. His friend's wife also earned the family income. Two men in a sea of breadwinners.

The two husbands hung out together. But did they talk about their unusual situation? Did they trade advice on how to handle the voices in their heads, their fear of social disapproval? No. Even Jon, who is in touch with his feelings, and courageously honest, kept his situation to himself. Almost as if it were a dirty secret. At least women can talk to their girlfriends and get support. But Jon couldn't get guidance or comfort from someone who was in exactly the same position, who was, presumably, going through some of the same struggles. That cone of silence is yet one more thing working to keep men boxed in.

Indeed, perhaps one of the most tragic elements of modern

manhood is a rather alarming discovery by Killewald. The single biggest factor contributing to modern divorce, she found, is not substance abuse, empty nests, physical abuse, or even cultural differences. The single biggest predictor of divorce is whether the husband has a full-time job or not. (This sounds like the flip side of that research in chapter 7 showing that women who get promoted are more likely than men to get divorced.)

Killewald studied 6,300 heterosexual couples and found that, all other factors being equal, marriages where the man was not working full-time were 33 percent more likely to end in divorce.[13] The reason is simple: "Contemporary husbands face higher risk of divorce when they do not fulfill the stereotypical breadwinner role," Killewald told an interviewer at *Time*.

Once we got over being depressed by this research, we were fascinated by the why of it. Is it because men themselves become depressed if they're not fulfilling the male stereotype—and, as the research in chapter 7 suggests, do they become annoying because they stop helping around the house? In the give-and-take of relationships, are they less givers, and more takers?

Or, perhaps more insidiously, is it because their wives don't like the fact that their husbands aren't the breadwinner? Do women in fact have less respect for men who don't behave in a traditionally masculine way?

Killewald doesn't resolve the "why." She's just reporting the data. But, as a sociologist, she does have her own theory. "I think it's consistent with the idea that we expect men to work and when men aren't working it's disruptive to how we *all* think about what it means to be a competent husband," she told us.

Killewald's research is not great news for our quest for a society where men and women split child care and housework evenly. How can we chart the path when we want men to share equally but also expect them to be the primary breadwinner?

It's that equation that has to change. Not just for us, but for men's sake, too. As Rady Johnson and Jon Malesic show us, men are missing out on the intense gratification and satisfaction to be found in hanging out with their children, cooking dinner, organizing the household, volunteering in their community, sharing emotions with friends. That's the deepest joy we can tap, but because manhood is still seen as fairly one-dimensional, men are denied a full, satisfying life. That's why we'd love to see new economic models that would take into account the value of unpaid, domestic work. It would be good for women, but it would also be good for men, because it would give this kind of work, no matter who's doing it, respect and status.

Certainly women face hurdles men don't hit as they tread the route to power. But men face hurdles women don't experience when they try to lead a blended, less work-centric, more nurturing life. A more "power to" life, in fact. Unless we fix the latter, we can't fix the former.

ENDANGERED SPECIES: STAY-AT-HOME DADS

As young, optimistic students starting out in our careers and hoping one day to have children of our own, we had an idealistic view of sharing parental responsibilities. We believed we were entering a world where men would soon, inevitably, feel just as comfortable as women in choosing to stay home with their children.

Playgrounds around the world would be as full of fathers as they were of mothers. At 11 a.m., we imagined, you'd find as much testosterone as estrogen in the aisles of a supermarket, and school pickup lines would be populated by Malik as often as by Monique. We were wrong. Wildly wrong. About our own husbands, and about the world.

By now, given all the research we've presented about the vise grip of masculinity, you probably won't be surprised to learn that the stay-at-home dad is still a remarkably rare breed. Ultimately, we still believe that turning this around is essential to making our society better for everyone. But before we make the case for why this should be our challenge, we need to look at the data.

The reality is this: according to 2020 US census data, men make up only 5 percent of all US families with a stay-at-home parent. A broader definition of stay-at-home dads by PEW research, one that includes same-sex fathers and gives wider reasons for staying home, puts the number at 18 percent of all stay-at-home parents in 2021. (Even with those bigger numbers, less than a quarter of all stay-at-home dads, straight or gay, say the main reason they left the labor force was to look after children—most often stay-at-home dads fall into being full-time parents after being laid off.)

And honestly even PEW's 18 percent is pretty paltry.

The United Kingdom is little different. In 2019, the number of fathers choosing to stay at home with their children fell to its lowest level in five years. Reports in the British press cited experts who suggested that dads had "grown tired" of the thankless task of raising children.[14] In Finland, the only country in the world where fathers spend more time with their children than mothers do (only eight minutes more, it has to be said), dads are also reporting burnout due to stress.[15] "Parenting is a black hole filled with inadequacy and it has ruined my life," said one dad interviewed for a psychological study of Finnish fatherhood. Tell us what you really think!

Why is it that dads are stressed out at such high levels the world over? Belgian sociologist Isabelle Roskam's 2020 study suggests that mothers are simply more flexible in their expectations of what it means to be both a parent and a worker, and that makes them less likely to burn out.[16] Women are better prepared for the disruption their lives will inevitably experience from having children.

"In our study, we assumed that mothers' higher exposure to parenting stress would result in higher parental burnout in comparison with fathers." Roskam wrote, but it wasn't the case. "Women are more prepared to cope with demands in the context of childcare and education than men are."

But Roskam's explanation for this phenomenon actually gives us some hope. It turns out that women aren't simply better, naturally, at handling stress and exhaustion, although it often feels that way. She believes that from a young age, "girls learn, through imitation, how to behave as women, and boys how to behave as men." And because parenthood "is still conceived along the heterosexual gender binary, equating women with mothers and men with fathers, girls also learn how to behave as a mother and boys as a father." Roskam writes that boys/men are particularly resistant to imitating behavior not typical to their gender, so it has made it even harder for them to break out of traditional views of what it means to be a man and a dad. But, what is learned can be unlearned, or relearned, or learned differently. As gender roles are acknowledged as more fluid, that learning process should become less rigid, too.

The key, Roskam agrees, is to give boys more chances to see themselves as fully engaged dads. "Any measure that would help to instill in young boys the parenting behaviors that they will have to adopt later as fathers would be useful in preventing parental burnout among men," she wrote.

We often hear the phrase "our daughters can do anything." Indeed, we've both used it about our own girls. But we never hear the converse. We've honestly never heard a parent say, "I'm excited because my son can one day be a stay-at-home dad, or a full-time homemaker, or run a part-time business. He can change diapers, organize playdates, cook dinner, and join a book club with his stay-at-home dad friends." And if it's not being said publicly, then it's not being broadcast to our boys that it's a viable possibility. Which also means that their sisters aren't getting the message that being a full-time dad is something their big brother (or their eventual spouse) could be proud to do. Moreover, until this message is spreading at home more easily, it's almost impossible to imagine Cynt-like workplace where male senior executives are comfortable not only sharing emotion, but being the parent who leaves the meeting because of a sick child, or who limits long hours to spend time with family. And kind of workplace is what we really need for a better power.

All the research we've sifted through, the interviews we've conducted, point to the idea that our boys' lives need to be broadened, too; men need to feel as though spending more time on household work, or even being a full-time stay-at-home dad, is a good option, and that women need to see men who do this as stronger, not weaker. How many more studies will we have to read pointing out that in the seemingly evolved twenty-first century, boys in the United States still feel that character traits such as strength and toughness are what society wants from them? Plan International USA polled teenage boys and found that three-quarters of them still felt pressure to be physically strong and play sports. Large numbers of young boys still said they believed society expected them to respond to anger with either aggression or silence. When they felt scared, the boys believed society wanted them to either hide those feelings or act tough. Fully 82 percent of the boys in the survey said they had heard someone criticize a boy for "acting like a girl." And yes, the girls in the survey were more likely to say they could cry, yell, or talk about their emotions.[17]

Actually, we did meet a parent, an educator in Scotland, Maggie Rait, who told us she'd be thrilled for her twelve-year-old Beau to be able to be authentically himself when he grows up, staying at home to raise a family, or working, depending on the needs of his partnbership. Maggie's husband spends as much time running the house and caring for the kids as she does, and she herself employs a very *new power* ethos at work. "If you want a short-term solution, use hierarchy and aggression. If you want a long-term solution, use patience and lead from within." Still, she's concerned about the modeling her son sees in the world.

"What worries me about boys, at the moment, is whether we are giving them permission to be all of who they are in all of the spheres of life—to be everything, the way girls can be, the way I hope my daughter Gracie feels she can be. Some boys aren't comfortable in every space, in more emotional spaces, but perhaps their parents might not be that comfortable, either."

Ultimately, the tyranny of low expectations for men and for boys, on the social-emotional-domestic spectrum, coupled with the lack of alternative role-modeling, is a tremendous loss for all of us, and is, perhaps, the best starting point for broadening their possibilities, and broadening minds—theirs and ours. Supporting a fuller existence for boys and men is critical in order for our new power code to thrive, but, more importantly, it's essential for their happiness.

MORE MAN MOMENTS

There are men who are becoming standard-bearers for a new model of manhood, fatherhood, and partnerhood. Look no further than Clint Edwards, whose blog breathes fresh air into stale rooms stained with male stereotypes, Jon Malesic, who has escaped breadwinner burnout by choosing to leave his full-time job, and Rady Johnson who was willing to speak openly to us about his ambivalence. Like the women who are making change, it will require some men to brave the uncomfortable future, and we can learn from them. Kenny Marshall, husband to Cynt Marshall, the powerhouse CEO of the NBA's Dallas Mavericks, whom we introduced in chapter 2, has a lot to teach us all.

Kenny has been a stay-at-home dad for two decades, raising four children, while his extremely successful wife, Cynt, has followed her career. As he puts it, "I've always had a job, raising the kids. My wife has always had a career." (By the way, we love that framing, for men and for women.)

We talked to Kenny and Cynt by Zoom from her home office for the Mavericks. Kenny had temporarily taken her big office chair for our call, while Cynt stood behind him, her hand on his shoulder. We ask Kenny a few questions, but Cynt can't help herself—she jumps in to join our interview. Cynt "the Sprint" Marshall is a bundle of infectious energy. Kenny's more laid-back; he talks more slowly—and more deliberatively.

"But how do you handle those man moments? That's what they're asking," Cynt interjects. As she does so, she rubs his shoulder affectionately.

"Man moments," according to Kenny, are those times when he feels he isn't being heard or when he worries that he doesn't get enough social recognition. When they come, he walks around the house "soft" talking to himself to get his head into a different place. "It's fleeting," he says. "It's grief or anger."

When we ask him why he deals with them this way, he tells us about his own troubled childhood, how his parents' marriage wasn't happy. When he married Cynt, he says, they decided to be real partners. So when he gets angry, he takes responsibility for managing those emotions. In Kenny's telling, it wasn't a difficult decision to give up his own career to stay with the children. The couple had experienced real problems getting a family at all, having experienced several late-term miscarriages and, tragically, losing a baby girl six months after she was born. They eventually decided to adopt children from the foster system, two boys and two girls. At the time, both Kenny and Cynt were working.

One evening, when Kenny and Cynt were both tied up with work commitments, they were late to get to the child care center. In Cynt's telling, her young son, having been rescued from a foster care system that had failed him too often, looked at her in terror when she finally arrived to pick him up. Was he about to be fed back into the social welfare system and abandoned once again?

That moment convinced Kenny and Cynt that one of them needed to be there to look after their children, and in Kenny's words, the salaries spoke for themselves: "My wife was earning thirty percent more than me. Most of my income went to child care costs. The child care opens and closes at set hours. Those people had to get home to their families, too."

So the decision was made. It was 2002 when Kenny Marshall became a full-time house husband and father. He was an original unicorn. Even among Black men, who are more likely than white men to be stay-at-home dads, his decision was rare. The lack of hesitation or angst that accompanied his choice was hard for us to absorb. "It was a simple equation," he says.

Cynt jumps in, again. "He says it's simple. I tell you, it's not." Given how few men have ever made that decision, let alone twenty years ago, we have to agree with Cynt here.

Kenny is modest. He doesn't think he did anything exceptional, even though Cynt is adamant that she could never have risen through the ranks as she did if he had not stayed home with the children. A ton of men wouldn't have done what you did, we say. "A ton of men probably didn't have my family challenges," he replies.

Which is when he admits to the occasional man moment.

Beyond giving himself a talking-to, it seems to us that the way Kenny deals with those moments is with a huge, generous heart. The concept of zero-sum doesn't apply to Kenny. "I've given a lot.

But she's given a lot, too. It's fifty-fifty." The key is that he doesn't feel competitive with his high-achieving wife. He really respects her talents and what she does. "There's never been a time in our working lives where I could say I can do what she can do, because I can't. She's smarter than me. She's more disciplined. She is more steadfast. I'm more emotional." It's not that he is intimidated by Cynt, or lacks confidence. Indeed he has enough confidence in himself to enjoy their respective strengths and recognize her ability. He enjoys what their life together has given him and doesn't harbor regrets about what could have been if he'd pursued his own career.

Kenny's clarity and generosity are remarkable, and, yes, even inspiring. Cynt clearly feels it, too. Could she have done what she's done without him? we ask. "Not for a second, not for a second," she says. Kenny supports her emotionally and practically. When they need to move house, he'll contact the realtor, see a bunch of properties, and then call her up and say, "I've found six for you to see. Can you meet us during your lunch hour?"

Kenny has upended society's expectations and even come to relish the unconventional role of supporting husband. He values the close relationship he has with his kids, his role in nurturing them, in creating the family life. That's a gift, and he's aware it's not one many men get to experience. Somehow, men need to see what they are missing, and help to create change. In the early days Kenny would get questions about what he did, what his job was, and it would bother him a bit. They nearly always came from other men, he says. Now he doesn't even notice it. It's all projection, he believes: "It's a social constraint."

These days he is amused by the disquiet and confusion his role seems to incite in others. When Kenny and Cynt go to one of her work events, he's often probed about what he does for a living. He tells them, "I'm just with her," nodding in his wife's direction.

YOUR POWER CODE

This is a complicated section to write. We're tempted to say something like, just get the men in your life to read this chapter—that's your power code, and theirs. But there are clearly things we can do to encourage and support men in a world of new power structures. Indeed, we wrestled with whether we were writing for you or for the men in your life. In the end we realized there's not much distinction. We are trying to get our husbands and partners to step up, but we're also trying to help them shed the limitations of centuries of training. We're offering some broad ideas based on what we've seen that can help you and your partners, or future partners. Most critically, we all have to know that to get there, we need to do more than understand where those restrictions come from—we need to empathize.

Start at the very beginning. Before we even start with men, we need to start with boys. If you have sons, or boys in your life, make an inventory of how you talk to them and what kind of role models you hold up for them. Are you perpetuating stereotypes? Make a point of suggesting to your son that *not* being the breadwinner is fine. Tell him that looking after children is as valuable and rewarding as having a career. If your son has younger siblings, remember to include him in the nurturing of that child—there is no reason your son can't mix a bottle, change a diaper, and read bedtime stories.

Welcome dads. A friend of ours recently moved to a new city where his wife had taken a very big job. He also worked, but since his work was more flexible, he took on the lion's share of child care. One morning he took his daughter to the local park to meet some other kids and parents from her school. Those parents were all moms, and although they had suggested he come along, once he got there it was awkward. He felt like he was intruding on their comfortable social routine. They made him feel kind of unwelcome, and he didn't bother joining them again. That story made us sad, and not just for our friend and his daughter, but for all of us. It made us realize how important it is to make dads feel welcome. If you're at a birthday party, parent-teacher event, or just in the park, and you see a dad alone with their kids, go up and talk to them. It's really important they don't feel lonely in that role. Stick with the conversation, ask about their kids, their work, their hobbies—anything. Then make a plan to include them again in your next kid-focused social engagement.

Convert, don't cut out. Take a page from Ndéye Lucie Cissé's playbook in dealing with the Senegalese men. Her breakthrough came when she focused on equality rather than women gaining power "over" men. If men are afraid of loss, help them see the win. Of course we can't sugarcoat everything, and at times someone will lose out, but look for opportunities to convert men into allies by helping them understand what's in it for them, rather than cutting them out altogether.

Show them what they're missing. This is one concrete way to embrace the conversion mindset. In chapter 7 we talked about ceding control of areas of responsibility of domestic life, and getting full buy-in. The work of opening up the complicated but rewarding world of emotional connection, can be slow going—but the payoff can be huge.

Eve Rodsky gave us a terrific example of how she worked with one couple to help them foster a deeper, more meaningful change.

The wife in question nervously handed over a high-stakes assignment to her hard-charging CEO husband. Her son had drawn a Secret Santa recipient who had been bullied at school, so she felt that an extra level of care was needed in crafting a gift, which, by the way, was supposed to be handmade. She also felt that the project would be an opportunity for her own son to practice empathy, kindness, and generosity toward others. All in all, it was a potentially fraught emotional and cognitive labor situation. She worried that her husband would forget about it and buy something mass-produced and impersonal at the last minute. So she explained to her husband *why the endeavor mattered—with no judgment or criticism.* That conversation, she reported, helped him engage, without feeling micromanaged or judged. With no further input from her, the father and son spent a full day building a Popsicle stick jewelry box. Because he'd committed to owning the task, her husband was invested in the outcome and willing to spend the day on the floor with glue and glitter, talking about what it would mean to the recipient. This same man has taken that experience into his workplace and now tries to bring a more empathetic approach to his leadership. He also admits that, up until this event, he had pretty much been on autopilot at home—the exact opposite of the can-do attitude he'd taken at work. Most importantly, his wife says, that day on the floor helped him feel the joy of spending time with his son, time that might have seemed tedious or unnecessary previously, but is the essential conduit for building connection. He'd seen, the wife related, a glimpse of what he's been missing.

9

MAXIMUM IMPACT

We know we need a new power hierarchy, a different system that can not only fit the way women operate, but can better promote a healthy society. We also know deep in our beings that the world already understands and feels our capacity for leadership.

Deepa Purushothaman, the leadership expert we met in the introduction, described this state of limbo, this moment of cultural regrouping and examination in which we currently sit in a way that resonated with us. In her speeches, when she asks people, both men and women, to visualize a leader, it's still often a particular archetype, typically a male, who comes to mind. But visualize whom they admire? It's women. Mother Teresa, a mother, a grandmother. "It's the male leadership model we still uphold, versus what we really want to be like," she told us. "There's something there, in that gap."

That gap. It's the limbo in which we currently exist. It's the gray space between where we've been, and where we want to go. Who do we really want to be, as women with power? Accessing that, is, of course, the essence of our power code, a code that allows power to thrive, that is packed with authenticity, respect, a fuller range of our values, and, in the end, therefore, offers less ego, more joy, and maximum impact.

We're going to be blunt here—authentic and egoless—part of the code, remember? We don't have a foolproof map to hand out at this point, with which to send you happily on your way. Yes, we've offered many concrete tips and thoughts at the end of each chapter. But, in fact, the most useful information we can give you is something we've tried to impart more generally, throughout the book. It's the radical idea that the way we, and you, want to use power, the way you envision it, instinctively, is legitimate. We don't have to remake ourselves. Understand that, and much will follow. Deepa's recommendation in this moment of flux is to encourage women to focus on different brands of power—both the personal and the collective. She believes we need this period, this time in the gap, for deep examination. "We haven't been given permission yet to reimagine, to think about the fact that we can actually remake structures." The power to make change, in other words, rests with us. People change structures. We don't have to accept the status quo.

As we've also noted along the way, the two of us are believers in questioning, in reimagining, but also in changing the system from within. We want to think and conceive radically, but we also don't really want all women to walk away from the levers of power we do hold at such a critical juncture. We'd point back to the transformations Zanny Minton Beddoes makes by reordering meetings and listening. To the concrete achievements, like toilets and electricity, of Lucie Cisse, as part of the establishment in Senegal, or to Cynt Marshall, opening up her corner of the male-dominated sports industrial complex to emotional connection.

We'd also list Kristalina Georgieva on taming egos, Jeannine for teaching us to say "let me finish," and Amaya for subversively handing work back to her male colleague. All of that matters. Our minds have been opened on this journey by science and statistics and big ideas—but most critically by the stories from women, and the examples they've given us about what they do to innovate, to make things work. That's the stuff that can motivate all of us to more creativity as we reflect, and move ahead. In that vein, in this chapter, we want to also offer you a slice of inspiration in terms of innovations on an organizational level. These are macro-level attempts at systemic change. It's not a comprehensive survey of all that is new and potentially effective in the workplace. But these methods and experiments, we hope, can frame thinking and nurture debate, as we all attempt to reimagine, on a larger, more revolutionary scale, how power should be used. (We know, by the way, that discussing systemic change doesn't always [or ever, perhaps] sound radical, exciting, or sexy. But if these methods lead to greater numbers of women in power—that's sexy enough for us.)

When we think about a woman who embodies the new power code—a vision for using it differently, proudly, and authentically, within the system, creating change as she goes—it's Christine Lagarde.

Today she is the first female president of the European Central Bank. When she took over at the IMF in 2011, she was the first woman to run that institution, and was the subject of countless newspaper articles and TV documentaries that analyzed everything from her yoga regime to her love of shopping in French markets.

Almost overnight she became a role model for literally millions of women around the world, and she's been an inspiring guide to us over the years.

Lagarde combines empathy with a steeliness of purpose. She is committed to giving more women around the globe access to power. No small challenge. She has long believed that to get there, we cannot force ourselves into uncomfortable, inauthentic, more masculine styles of the sort demanded by the existing hierarchy.

That just makes us less effective as leaders, she contends. Lagarde helped us see that confidence, for example, doesn't have to be *Mad Men*–style—always interrupting people, operating with swagger, throwing one's ego around the room. Her style of leadership—the way she carries herself, the way she listens and acts with purpose—is very much her own, but also shows other women what's possible. She's a model of a woman with maximum impact.

Having run two big financial institutions, and exercised power on both sides of the Atlantic for more than a decade now, she offers, with a laugh and a sigh, this worldly-wise take on power: "The bloody financial world is still very male." But the new power code will be different: "Power as I see it," she continues, "is inclusive. The ability to take others in a direction that is good for the group." She adds, "When you have power, you can say no and not fear the consequences." She doesn't mean the ability to say no to mundane things you don't want to do, but rather the ability to reject being party to policies or practices we don't believe in. That's the new power code talking.

"Power over," for Lagarde, is flawed, and must evolve. "The way men hold power—it needs to change," she adds. "But it takes a lot of intruders. We can't count on men to change. It can't be a string of men, followed by one woman. Then another string of men, charging on."

What we also admire about Lagarde is that she's always been a doer. She's helped us see that in order to make change, you have to be willing to innovate, boldly. Her choice of words—calling those who confront the current power code "intruders"—is telling. At the same time, her innovations are practical. We'll never forget her badass habit for combating the lazy sexism she has routinely encountered from the most powerful men in the world. So often they've told her that they really, really want to find women to serve on their boards or in their C-suites, but that they just didn't know any who are qualified. That's the moment she hands them a list of "qualified" women that she keeps with her.

On the issue of power, she told us, she's trying something similarly groundbreaking. For years she had noted the hidden obstacles that hold women back from promotions—especially the demands of child-rearing. As a mother herself, and then watching her son and daughter-in-law parent, she realized "that skill set is perfectly suited to the workplace. It's crisis management. It's something all primary parents do."

The skill "of maternity, of multitasking, of nurturing kids, and all that it entails as management, is extraordinary." She reasoned that four or five years of doing that kind of work might be just the right training program for the demands of the financial workplace and equally effective as time spent running a business operation in another country. This is a conclusion we had come to, and discuss in chapter 7, but hearing this validation of the painstaking, often thankless and invisible work mothers do from a high-flying woman like Lagarde was revolutionary.

She is redefining the "soft" work of parenting as practical leadership skills. Lagarde told her board of directors, almost all men, that henceforth, time at home raising children would count as acceptable experience on the leadership ladder. That's not the only experience, clearly, that qualified applicants would need. But now it counts as legitimate experience, whereas in the past it would have been an awkward gap on a résumé, good for nothing but brushing under the rug. "It takes a woman to suggest that. That's the beauty of power. I can say it, and they listen and act." She adds, with a wry grin, "Let's see how recruiting goes."

Lagarde's innovation forces everyone to take a fresh look at assets that have been there all along (like mothering) but haven't been valued in a tangible way. We want her willingness to intrude on the status quo to serve as an exemplar, or a call to action—for the kind of creative thinking in the workplace that is necessary to banish those pernicious, murky hurdles we face. In addition to embracing the radical idea that your instincts about power are valid, here is the other key bit of wisdom we want you to remember as you contemplate change: Disruption, essentially, is what works. Below are some tried-and-tested practices, along with some state-of-the-art experiments, for inspiration.

WHAT GETS MEASURED MATTERS

Christine Lagarde, by the way, is also highly disciplined about data and results. She was uncompromisingly clear that there is an essential baseline to change: targets, quotas, and other established metrics of inclusion and diversity are still necessary. "Without those," she says, "nothing will change."

Research proves her point. Companies that set targets for diversification and then track representation by monitoring things like promotions and hiring outcomes have better success in building more diverse workforces. But oddly, not enough companies do it. Only 65 percent of companies track promotion rates by gender, and only 35 percent track promotions specifically for women of color.[1] How can they possibly know if they are getting more women to the top if they don't even monitor who's getting promoted?

Kweilin Ellingrud, a senior partner at McKinsey and director of the McKinsey Global Institute, who has been leading gender research there, describes what her firm has found when producing their annual Women and the Workplace survey, one of the most extensive examinations of US trends as regards gender. "There should be clear, qualitative aspirations. What is the goal? That goal needs to cascade across the organization, not just be attached to a few areas like IT."

Sticks, and carrots, are essential, says Ellingrud. "Most successful companies tie these goals to incentives, or offer compensation based on results. Sometimes it can be a straight number, or sometimes it might be one of five things that matters for your bonus. But accountability matters." Many companies do hold leaders accountable at a senior level, but fewer than a third hold middle managers accountable, and those middle managers matter because they control the talent pipeline.

Ellingrud also confirms what diversity experts have said for decades: for true diversity at the top, women must be considered for C-suite jobs that are in direct business lines, positions with profit-and-loss responsibility that visibly affect the company's profitability. The recent increase of women in C-suite jobs has often been in important support areas, roles such as head of HR or the general counsel, but if a woman wants any shot at being CEO she typically needs a line leadership role first.

While you're monitoring representation, you need to ensure that time spent on DEI work (and, we believe, all that NPT work, too) is properly considered when it comes to leadership roles and promotions. Seventy percent of companies say DEI work is essential for managers. But only 25 percent of companies make it part of managers' performance reviews and the metrics for promotion.[2] Forty percent of women leaders say their DEI work isn't acknowledged at all in terms of performance, and women shoulder roughly double that burden of that work.[3]

BREAKING THE MOLD

Addressing bias may seem like an intractable problem because, as we discussed in chapter 5, it's subjective and hard to pin down.

Our biases reflect deep-rooted perceptions—what does a leader look like, how do they act, what personality traits do they exhibit? Bias is what feeds that focus on performance instead of promise. It fuels that perfect woman syndrome, and even that rigid, outdated checklist. And the fact that we come to the table thinking about and using power differently, more broadly, with a desire for different outcomes, contributes to the sense of us as "others."

"I could give you the same résumé, same font size, with every detail the same," sighs Ellingrud. "And even women like us, who are open-minded about leadership and study these issues, would ascribe greater leadership on average to this imaginary man and [give him] higher future potential." In person, of course, eliminating bias can be even tougher, given the persistent typecasting of leaders as tall, white males who speak with a deep voice.

We mentioned earlier Yale professor Kelly Shue, and her research on promotions, and in particular, her analysis of promotions at a large retail chain. The results were depressing and stunning. Women at the company routinely got higher performance ratings than men, but they were constantly and wrongly seen as having less leadership potential. Even though entry-level workers were 56 percent women, department managers were only 48 percent women. It got worse the higher up they looked: store managers were only 35 percent women, and district managers a dismal 14 percent.[4]

A deeper look at the process that led to this result is illustrative, as we think about change. It turns out that managers used an evaluation grid with nine boxes, intended to measure candidates on two dimensions: performance and potential. Employees with high scores in both categories would get promoted. Performance is arguably a more objective measure—either you did the job or you didn't. But "potential" is an abstract and subjective construct—meaning it's highly susceptible to biased decision making. Specifically, the characteristics used for measuring potential were also very much in the eye of the beholder. Things like assertiveness, charisma, leadership, ambition—all are attributes typically associated with male leaders. It's not a surprise that women got lower ratings on those dimensions. The real kicker is that managers' judgments were literally wrong and not predictive of potential because at the next evaluation period, those same women once again *performed* better than the men in their cohort.

What we found most revealing about this study is that it highlights two concrete solutions for companies: bias training and rewriting the evaluation checklist.

Done well, bias training helps evaluators understand that qualities like charisma, leadership, and ambition might be expressed differently in candidates who don't fit the white male mold. Not surprisingly, companies that have made the greatest strides in women's representation are more likely to have robust practices in place to train against bias on a regular basis.[5] Alas, the positive effects of bias training don't last very long, so we need repeated training to avoid its creep back into performance and promotion reviews. And beware the one-size-fits-all workshop. "The two-hour training in a large conference room, it's a nice gesture, but I think we're fooling ourselves if we think it's going to change any outcomes," says Ellingrud.

So what does work? We got a terrific example from a female leader at a large consulting company. She was determined to force change and took over how her office was dealing with its performance reviews. Three steps created dramatically different outcomes:

- Unconscious bias observers
- A bias cheat sheet
- Deep, honest discussions that excavated underlying issues and helped to redefine leadership

The unconscious-bias observer was not an outsider, but a company employee trained in best practices and regularly rotated with other employees trained in this manner. What would those observers notice or raise? Things such as: Would we have said the same thing if Katty weren't just back from maternity leave? Would we have called her aggressive at problem solving if she were a man? Or sunflower bias: When everyone in the interviewing group is turning their heads to follow one person, typically a man, who has somehow been deemed the leader. Or affinity bias: When we find something in common with someone, something we like, and stop accurately judging them. The addition of this observer to the discussions served as both a reminder to everyone in the room about the seriousness of the effort, and as a neutral guardrail to ensure the process stayed as objective as possible.

The cheat sheet, offered to the observer and everyone at the firm, outlined the most common bias traps, and was created with an external expert to include biases that might be particularly prevalent in their specific industry. A few examples: "She doesn't fill the room. She doesn't have 'great presence.'" That is code for: she doesn't look like an alpha male. The cheat sheet also reminded everyone that describing the company as a "meritocracy," and thus devoid of bias, was in itself a shield that needed to be challenged by the group.

Finally, these efforts triggered honest and thoughtful conversations in the room of people responsible for decision making, which served to build a new model of leadership. The team got used to having to pause, consider, and reflect rather than rely on first impressions. Instead of assessing whether the candidate could "fill a room," the focus moved to "client outcomes and impact on the team, even though she doesn't take, you know, sixty percent of the airtime like some of the other folks that we're talking about today." The efforts, she told us, resulted in substantial upward movement of female and other diverse candidates.

"We're opening the aperture on what leadership styles are acceptable, effective," explained the executive, "and we dig underneath to understand what really matters here, as opposed to falling back on a very narrow set of leadership styles that we've almost been conditioned to think work."

An obvious fix for that warped nine-box grid system, and a fix that would help every company—expanding the so-called checklist. In this case, it would mean expanding the list of attributes used to measure high potential. We're talking about adding: empathy, listening, problem solving, and other prosocial behaviors that tend to be women's strengths—and that organizations need more of.

There are other ways to challenge the checklist. Christine Lagarde did it when she added mothering children to the list of relevant job experience for banking, and Ellingrud uncovered an innovative example of rewriting checklists at a large regional bank. Executives there were studying promotion rates from branch manager to regional manager, and wondered why they weren't finding enough women, when so many of their excellent branch managers were women. What they discovered was that promotions tended to be contingent on the candidate moving to a different part of the state or a different state entirely, which just happened to coincide with the time when women candidates were creating families or might be part of a dual-career couple, making relocation more difficult.

Instead of simply shrugging shoulders and sticking to the old trope that regional experience is essential, these executives got creative. They asked questions like:

What is the actual underlying skill and capability we are looking for in regional managers? Are there different ways that we can kind of test and develop those same skills that are more gender neutral than asking the family to relocate? Would this help men as well? The bank was able to think more expansively about the skills they wanted high-potential employees to develop, and then find alternative paths to give their promising women those skills without an immediate move. Later, when the time was right for them personally, they would be ready to make a leap.

Ellingrud notes that while some companies may be reluctant to change their long-established checklists—particularly this stubborn idea that leadership ability is formed through foreign assignments or multiple relocations—inflexibility on this issue won't attract the best talent, especially in a tight market. Not everyone can or will move globally across business units, especially with a dual-career family—not only the women, but increasingly the men, too.

Zanny Minton Beddoes, the *Economist* editor, thinks companies and leaders should be asking a few critical questions: Are they just doing things because that is the way things have always been done? Are they just asking for the same old résumé they've always asked for? Can they rethink what skills someone actually needs for a job, as opposed to the skills white men have always had? Can they put time and effort into training people who come to jobs with less formal education?

Minton Beddoes isn't suggesting that organizations compromise on expectations, which is a common complaint against diversity and affirmative action programs. "That's not doing women any favors." Diversity doesn't mean lower standards. Remember Josipa Petrunic's comment about how many mediocre men have made it just fine through the career gauntlet while women are expected to jump through invisible hoops without a hair out of place? No one we talked to implied that standards should be lowered or softened for women and other groups—but actually that hardly ever happens anyway. Rather, standards are unfairly raised for people who are different from the norm. Standards simply ought to reflect the wide range of experiences and talents that are worthy of an organization's recognition and rewards. "Taking risks and being creative about how you bring people along" is the point, says Minton Beddoes, and being willing to move people quickly is important. "You just have to think differently about how people can get there."

Another concrete measure is for companies to mandate a diverse slate of candidates for promotions or open positions—at least two, if not more.[6] When there are multiple diverse candidates, they tend to be judged not for their differences but for their talents and on a level playing field. Why? First, the odds are better for the diverse candidates. But when you are looking, for example, at two women out of six candidates, the woman doesn't read as much like an "other." Much of the unconscious bias we may be layering on candidates tends to disappear. You start to see women and other diverse candidates as individuals instead of as generic representatives of their gender or race, for example.

There are two points in the continuum of a woman's career in which a company's sustained focus on de-biasing the promotion process can maximize her impact. The first is quite early in her career, that so-called broken rung in the ladder at the very first level of promotion. "Seventy to eighty percent of all workers, including women, are at that entry level," explains Ellingrud. "We can't forget that. And if we don't fix that rung at the first promotion to manager, where for every one hundred men who are promoted, only eighty-six women are promoted, there is nothing that we can do in the rest of the talent pipeline to catch up."[7]

It's pipeline development, but that has to be deliberate. One leader told us, "I don't want the same three women on everybody's pipeline. That's not helpful, right? I tell my team—I need you to say, who are the three people who don't look like you? What are you doing to proactively support their careers and create the rotational opportunities, two to three steps before the C-suite, that are actually going to make the difference so that we have a broader and deeper pipeline?"

Equally compelling is a focus on the top positions, for a few reasons. Promotions at that level are even more vulnerable to unconscious, or even conscious, bias, which is why some of the techniques we've described above are ripe for the picking when it comes to the C-suite. Additionally, a woman added to top management can swing the numbers in a big way, percentage-wise, but most importantly, the effects of that choice, of adding diversity of management style, can flow down throughout the organization in multiple ways. It's an argument, backed by data, that we've been talking about for decades and Ellingrud and her team have been studying almost as long.

"We've looked at thousands of publicly traded companies around the world, in Europe, Asia, Africa, and of course, the US," she says. "And what we see is that companies that are in the top quartile of gender diversity of their management teams are about twenty to twenty-one percent more likely to outperform economically, in terms of total returns to shareholders. Companies that are in the top quartile of ethnic diversity, or racial diversity, are thirty-six percent more likely to outperform, so that's controlling for industry, geography, etc."

Most essentially, women do more to support their teams and advance diversity, equity, and inclusion efforts.[8] That means, ultimately, more women. Female leaders are also more likely than men to practice allyship. The higher they go, the more that matters. Senior women leaders sponsor, on average, more women, more women of color, and more men of color. "Their sponsorship load is just much higher," explains Ellingrud. That's good for everyone. This work is often, as we have discussed, unrecognized and unrewarded; nonetheless, it means that getting women to the top has a huge multiplier effect, in terms of more diversity. Then, we'd like to think, it's only a matter of time before this vital work gets measured and rewarded. And, ideally, shared.

RADICAL AUTHENTICITY

Just as Christine Lagarde shifted our mindset about breaking down obstacles, Cynt Marshall opened our thinking to something we are calling radical authenticity in the workplace. It's the idea that work can be a place in which our individuality is valued, our problems and vulnerabilities are acknowledged, and our differences are celebrated. This, in turn, creates more connection, more teamwork, and more joy for everyone. Companies have to get this culture piece right because nobody is going back to the days of monolithic company men. Employees, particularly younger ones, now want to be seen for who they are. They want to bring their whole, unique beings to work. They want to live a life, not just work to live. Or as the millennial generation put it, YOLO.

Embracing some version of authenticity, of "whole self" management, a more human and humane workplace, requires careful stewardship and a clear definition of corporate values. Those values will vary, but it's essential that leadership is willing to define and defend them.

Gwen, whom we met in chapter 4, is a global HR professional, the head of people at a billion-dollar financial institution. She explained that although her organization had already been creating affinity groups—what are known as employee resource groups, or ERGs—and encouraging support for employees in myriad ways, George Floyd's death in 2020 was a watershed moment. It opened the floodgates in terms of what employees needed, and, because the societal reckoning was so great, the company was able to link its values to employee needs in an immediate and direct way.

The firm expanded their ERGs and labeled them business resource groups (BRGs) to make it plain to everyone that they view cultural issues and issues of inclusivity as part of the business mission. The list of groups is in the dozens, and it includes groups for LGBTQ, Hispanic, Black, Asian, transgender, and women employees, to name just a few. The BRGs are open to everyone, and widely advertised. Allies are actively encouraged to attend, and employees typically invite bosses to participate. "People come," she says, "they love it. We went from three hundred people before George Floyd in our BRG for Black employees to over three thousand, from all backgrounds." The topics are distinct with each group but have covered everything from raising transgender kids, to freezing eggs, to family therapy. The meetings serve multiple purposes: they encourage allyship among colleagues, afford leaders the opportunity to model the inclusive and empathetic culture the organization is trying to promote, and elevate the company mission, tying it to purpose, meaning, and radical authenticity—values at the heart of the "power to" code, we must point out.

Gwen acknowledges that encouraging employees to bring their "whole selves" to work can occasionally provoke a vitriolic or uncivil response from a participant, but when that does happen, the company quickly takes a stand, and did so most recently on its home page, reminding people of the community's standards.

Regions Bank is another organization undergoing an internal transformation. It is headquartered in Birmingham, Alabama. John Turner, the CEO, is a middle-aged white man running a powerful regional bank, which makes him an unusual case for sharing power, reckoning with long-standing traditions and beliefs, and practicing radical authenticity. The irony isn't lost on him.

Turner acknowledges that the civil rights atrocities that were committed in his hometown don't make it the obvious place to run an organization that's committed to diversity, equity, and inclusion or to employ techniques of openness necessary to get there. Or perhaps it's the ideal place. The bank has branches all over the South and Midwest and often, Turner says, it will be the most inclusive organization in the area.

Clara Green, whom we introduced in chapter 4, was hired to launch the bank's diversity program, and initially Turner wanted just what you'd expect: goals, targets, results. He wanted to measure things. But Green had other ideas. For at least the first year, she told him, there would be no goals. She just wanted people to talk. She wanted the bank to have a company-wide conversation about inclusion and belonging. She wanted the bank's leadership to listen, and encourage authentic dialogue. She understood the impact that could have.

At first leaders were nervous about saying the wrong thing, but they overcame their anxiety through positive affirmations, and "grace" from their team, who welcomed their efforts.

"During our conversations, we talked about a lot of issues and sometimes the conversations were emotional and hard," Turner says. "What it means to be a gay man, what it means to be a Black male, what it means to be Hispanic, and even what it means to be a straight white male, too."

Those same white men were encouraged to be vulnerable themselves. This struck us as essential, especially given that white men aren't likely to have an affinity group at work these days, although, in fact, they might really need one. (We know, we know—the world is their affinity group! Or the golf course, etc. But the fact is, empathy toward men, about this massive societal change, is essential.) The added advantage of this company-wide conversation was that it helped minimize the backlash and cynicism that change can produce. If you start by *only* setting goals and filling quotas, you meet resistance, Turner believes. But by starting with an honest discussion—by enabling authenticity and awareness—you build understanding and connection. People are more cognizant of the benefits of diversity and less likely to kick back against the notion that you win, I lose.

There is, however, a limit to radical authenticity. Oversharing is a real thing. The fact is, while women have been adept managing their emotions and caring for the emotional lives of others, some men may need guidance on this issue. A funny/not funny article in the *New York Times* caught our attention recently as an example of what TMI looks like. It featured one instance of a boss admitting in a large Monday meeting that he had a massive fight with his wife over the weekend. Another example featured a boss posting a picture of himself crying after laying off two employees. Enough said. No, really: enough said.

Is your struggle at home affecting your work? Then it may be okay to let a few close colleagues and perhaps even your boss know what you're dealing with. But be judicious; oversharing is a burden, not a route to better connection. Be patient with yourself and generous with others who are also trying to figure out the boundaries of radical authenticity. As the Regions Bank team put it, extend grace to yourself and others. A sincere "thanks for trying" may be just the opening needed to make a radically authentic connection.

A MORE JOYFUL BLEND

A key to company culture today, to providing that more fulfilling, more manageable Blend, is getting the benefit of flexibility right. Hybrid work, embracing flexible hours, according to HR experts, is one of the most effective ways to support employee well-being. It's working, and is hugely popular. Research on employee satisfaction shows that in companies offering significant flexibility, and the ability to work from home at least a few days a week, employees feel heard and are less likely to feel burned-out.[9] In the past, flextime was mostly deemed a "woman's problem," but today it's a talent-retention problem across the gender-generational spectrum.

Two issues threaten the obvious benefits of flexibility. First, overwork is rampant. We described greedy work in chapter 6, and flexibility has given many enterprises an insatiable appetite for productivity. Even more so now, when employees aren't necessarily seen doing their work, they feel the need to be always on, constantly available. It remains a particular challenge for women. Forty-three percent of women leaders are burned-out, compared to 31 percent of men at their level, and almost 40 percent have considered leaving the workforce or downshifting their careers.[10]

Healthy companies are establishing work norms to combat burnout, such as encouraging employees to take a few days off and reminding them when they have too many unused vacation days. Increasingly, leaders are setting email etiquette guidelines to spell out expectations for appropriate response times and finding ways to acknowledge employees who practice anti-burnout behaviors. Most important of all these initiatives is when leaders set those boundaries for themselves and model the changes they want to see in their organizations.

The other drawback to all the now baked-in flexibility is that men are spending more time back in the office than women. We mentioned in chapter 6 how that imbalance, and the lack of comparative face time, can hurt women's career prospects. It's true, and women should keep that in mind. But we want to encourage something different as well.

On the organizational level, new policies will help—paternity leave, family leave, and the like. And on the individual level, explicit rules of engagement—such as scheduling in-person meetings on fixed days in the office and holding critical sessions on those days only—are a good start.

But we're asking for something much bigger. We're looking for a few truly exceptional role models, for top leaders who will take a different approach to work and life. Think back to the men we met in chapter 8. When men hear their bosses talking about the benefits of flexibility—taking their kid to the doctor in the middle of the day; working in the office three days a week and the other two at home; discussing how less time spent commuting has given them a chance to handle bedtime routines or to care for an elderly parent—that will drive change. The new way of working gives men something they've been too afraid to ask for: permission to live a better life, too. It only stands to follow that if more leaders are living fuller, better lives—with more connections to their employees through radical authenticity and with more time with their families and friends through flexible work—the world will have better leaders and organizations with better values.

Lest you think we are too optimistic, let us put it in more practical terms. Gen Z is going to head this way no matter what. Jeannine, that top-level finance executive we introduced in chapter 4, brought this home for us when she told us that her very traditional firm finally instituted generous paternity leave. She was with a group of senior partners, all male, who declared no men would take it. And if they did, they'd be "marked down." "I told them they were wrong, that these guys are different," she said. "Sure enough, a year later, men are all taking the leave. We have to have a diverse power style to deal with the next generation. They are not the old guys."

So perhaps it will be an invasion of Gen Zers, marching with a horde of women "intruders" who force the power shift most people want, even if half of the population is afraid, at least for now, to admit it.

YOUR POWER, TOO

We've offered vision from phenomenal leaders and innovative companies, but most of us don't work for the most inclusive employers, and many of us might not know how to start on a journey to get some of the good stuff that is "power to." That's why we've given you a personal tool kit at the end of each chapter, so that you can make change at any level, for yourself, and others. Yes, we need to push for big changes, systemic and institutional changes, but that doesn't mean you can't practice a bit of everyday disruption yourself. Interrupt the ordinary practice of power, and it begins to change shape.

Take some inspiration from our friend Amaya, who admitted that, at first, she was disheartened by what was going on at her company, which was still chanting the shareholder value mantra instead of focusing on diversity. She told us, "We don't do anything innovative. I think it's at the bottom of the list of what we value." But then she realized—after she told that male partner on Zoom to handle his own follow-up task and then four young women thanked her for doing it—that she had already started to remake the hierarchy without any official, corporate support.

Or take some advice from Jeannine, who encourages women colleagues to start using phrases and asking questions like this:

- Don't interrupt her.
- Let her finish.
- Give her that job.

- Why not her?
- Why is that woman the lowest-paid person at the firm?

We do have the *power to* make change on our own. It's the power Cynt Marshall showed us, to bring your whole self to work. It's the power Claire felt in that meeting when she rose up in support of a female colleague with "I don't think Kate got to finish her point." It's the power Katty felt when she quickly walked away from a situation that was against her values. It's the power to say, we don't do things that way. It's the power to care for others. The power to gather together and lift up new voices. It's the power to reevaluate what leadership looks like and then set new standards. It's also the power, when we are in charge, despite our desire for consensus, to make hard decisions that might leave some people unhappy.

Women can do hard work. We don't tend to shy away from it, as the research in chapter 6 makes perfectly clear. And there is enormous satisfaction to be found in reaching for that next level of power, in putting that power to good use, and in redefining it. *In the doing.* We have always had to be innovative and shrewd. We've always had to stitch things together to create a whole piece of cloth. As Camille, the professor, puts it, "It's almost refreshing to know this space you are in was not built for you." That recognition liberates us to recreate.

Give it your own twist, as Lagarde does: "Power is best with humor and the ability not to take yourself so seriously. It's best when you use it without imposing it. It's less selfish and more gratifying."

Less ego. More joy.

We've offered you a broad view of a changing power landscape, a clash of styles in which one, we believe, is far superior to the other. That's unfolding out against a chaotic workplace backdrop—which we can use to our advantage. We face ridiculous barriers that still need dismantling—but now that we see them, we can call them out, again and again if necessary. We have a distinct time and pressure crunch from employers and partners, who expect too much and for whom we can set some limits. Men aren't bought in yet, but they really really need this change, too.

The centerpiece of all this, we hope though, appears gleaming, pristine, approachable. A new power code, with huge promise.

More Joy, fueled by authenticity, action, the ability to actually exercise our will, access to our broader values.

Less Ego, a result of influence versus *power over*, of respect, empathy, a non–zero-sum game attitude.

Maximum Impact, because we say *Power to*, and ask why.

All of these pillars of power operate in tandem, mutually reinforcing each other, a virtuous circle of action. (Women are more immune to power's ego inflation, but let's just keep an eye on that as we power up.)

With this formula, and all of the new ideas being wielded by women and creative leaders we've highlighted in these pages, we want you to see yourself as an ambassador for this new form of power—as the source code for a new operating system for all parts of your life. We're hoping that giving you this new vision, this new understanding of power, *is* the radical move. As we said at the start of the book, it's hard to unsee something once you've seen it. We hope you see clearly that your power can activate more power, and that women seem to handle it with more empathy. We hope you know now, if you didn't already, that we do a lot of vital work that needs to be valued—and that you now feel empowered to say so and to ask someone else to plan the damn holiday party. We hope you can talk to partners and spouses openly about balance at home—and that you can let go a little and just see what happens. And we do hope we can all muster empathy for those who are facing a lot of changes, and aren't always equipped emotionally, historically, to deal with them.

We told you we were going to offer you a different story about power. It's not simply a redefinition; it's a recognition of something that already exists, and now needs to be seen, valued, and fully employed. It's what has been, what is, and what is possible. Let's just say it: it is a better way. For all of us.

That better way, for all of us, is what inspired our opening image, that reimagined "ascent of woman." Let's pick up where we left off. She is setting off in a different direction, with zig and zags, in a variety of guises. She is not alone, but surrounded by friends, colleagues, partners, kids; she is listening, laughing, thinking, deciding, offering wisdom, conveying approachable connection, enjoying the journey. (By the way, she/her might be a he/him or a they/them. Everyone is welcome.) Confident, and powerful, she emerges, in charge of her own path.

ACKNOWLEDGMENTS

This book has been a few years in the making and along the way dozens of people have been kind enough to share their stories, research, editing skills, and advice. We are grateful to all of them.

Several women leaders were particularly generous with their time and experiences. Lucie Cissé inspired us in Dakar, Senegal, with a glimpse into what politics can look like when women walk in. Zanny Minton Beddoes clarified the exercise of power in language worthy of her magazine. Kristalina Georgieva walked us through the halls of the International Monetary Fund to explain the importance of power without fear. And Cynt Marshall really is the queen of our castle, and we'd be happy if her husband, Kenny Marshall, were king of everything. Christine Lagarde has always been our North Star, we thank her again for her work, her ideas, and her warmth.

Thank you too to Erin Zimmerman for her insight and honesty during the stressful months of lockdown; to Mariana Atencio, who cheered us up with her energy and candor and humor; to Clara Green, John Turner, and the team at Regions Bank for all the important work they do and the generosity with which they do it. Josipa Petrunic helped us rip apart the perfect woman syndrome with a memorable notion—mediocre has always been good enough for many men, after all—why not for women?

Power turns out to be a sensitive topic and many, many of the women we spoke to chose to remain anonymous—either because of formal work restrictions, or, more often, because of the simple fact that they want to keep their positions and they can't afford to piss off bosses or colleagues. Things are changing—but full-frontal honesty? Still too much. Others were protecting sensitivities at home, which can be even more acute. Gwen, Susan, Jeannine, Elisabeth, Louise, Alexandra, Sally, Camille, Cole, and Amaya . . . and all of the others who informed our ideas but didn't even want a pseudonym—you know who you are, and we could not have finished this book without your candid, blunt, sometimes shocking, sometimes laugh-out-loud, sometimes maddening tales, and your analysis and advice. You are helping the cause immeasurably. And thank you to our friends Maggie Rait, and also Lisa, both of whom talked about sensitive topics with us with candor and incredible insight.

Several men contributed to our research and were candid with their own experiences. We know it isn't easy talking about this power shift and we are especially grateful to the many men who took the time to explain their point of view. In particular we'd like to thank David Leonard at McCarthy Tetrault, Jonathan Lavine, Jon Malesic, Clint Edwards, and Rady Johnson.

Our work relies on the work of experts and we want to thank the academics who spend years producing great research, and are then kind enough to distill it all in interviews with us. A few in particular have been especially helpful.

Alison Wood Brooks was one of the very first academics we interviewed—her startling discovery that women don't really want power was one of the intriguing things that led us to write this book. Misty Heggeness gave us an awareness that power isn't just about workplaces, it's about our home lives, too, and what we do to shield our husbands from any perceived loss of power. Allison Daminger patiently explained the different stages of cognitive labor and in so doing changed how we see our own households. Alexandra Killewald's work on the rigidity of men's roles helped us understand the box the men in our lives are often in. Stefanie Johnson was researching sexual harassment in workplaces even before #Metoo and then followed up after the movement, and generously shared her findings with us. Eve Rodsky took time, in the midst of her own busy book tour, to explain the finer points of fair play. Olle Falke showed us that even in admirable Sweden women still face a penalty for their success. Kate Ratliff helped us see that we can't even count on our spouses to root for us, even though we root for them.

Melanie Brewser had great advice, for all of us, on how to reduce inequality at home. Heejung Chung stayed up late in Kent, England, to warn us of the futility of overwork. Jennifer Jordan gave us a fascinating overview of the effects of power on people's behavior. Kweilin Ellingrud gave us a thorough understanding of best practices, as they currently exist.

Allison Pugh enriched our understanding of the dislocation felt by some men. Laura Kray led us to the invaluable distinction between power *over* and power *to*. Sonya Mishra expanded our understanding of that concept with her useful work on status. David Winter was generous with his time in our early exploration into what power is and isn't and with his brilliant mug analogy clarified the notion of power as a force for change. Joe Magee extended that concept to explain how power involves a relationship. Deborah Gruenfeld showed us how important it is for women to be involved in the very study of power. Dachner Keltner walked us through the importance of cookies and power. Yes, there is a relationship, you'll discover it in chapter 3. Sukhvinder Obhi patiently explained and then re-explained how power affects our brains. Adam Galinsky's work on power and perspective has been invaluable, not to mention his substantial time pressure testing our subject and sending us to multiple experts who helped inform our work.

At HarperCollins, we'd like to thank Hollis Heimbouch, our

incomparable, brilliant editor, who believed in this project, and us, and kept the faith. Whenever we're stuck or confused, we turn to Hollis, whose impeccable editorial instincts provide clarity and inspiration. Indeed, even when we don't think we're confused, Hollis will offer us such novel insights, with such enthusiasm, that we emerge reoriented and reinvigorated. She's hands on in the best sense—happy to get in the weeds with us when needed, or to muse philosophically, or to give us an old-fashioned push. A true partner in our work; it's not an overstatement to say we write books in part to get another chance to work with each other, and also to work with Hollis. We'd also like to thank our publicist, the talented and incisive Leslie Cohen, who's worked with us patiently over the years, and also much gratitude to Kirby Sandmeyer, James Neidhardt, Lydia Weaver, Robin Bilardello.

Christy Fletcher, our ingenious literary agent, also championed this idea from the start, and understood the power of taking on power, for us, and for women. Ever talented and creative, she cast her sharp eye over the manuscript and came up with innovative solutions when we were stuck on everything from titles to book covers to ideas. Sarah Fuentes, Melissa Chinchillo, and Yona Levin at Fletcher and Company have been stalwarts on this project over the years.

Along the way two people were especially generous with their time in reading the manuscript and giving us detailed notes. We'd like to thank Emily Graff at HarperCollins, and Deepa Purushothaman, author of *The First, The Few, The Only*, for their invaluable feedback. This book is better and, we hope, more inclusive, because of their insights. Novelist Sofia Groopman gave us some luminous, elegant help and insights in a few really sticky places. We are ever grateful. Thanks too to Melanie Rehak who stepped in at short notice to help us wrestle the research and ideas into shape, and whose help was invaluable. Sue Carswell and Beatrice Hogan did an amazing job with footnotes and fact checking, offering other wisdom as they went. We had an assist from two formidable research assistants: Alliemarie Schapp, whose talents were essential in the early stages of this book, and Tanya White, who stepped in to help us with everything from complicated scientific research to hard-to-track-down academics to quote-pulling to deadline crunch footnoting—thank you. We're grateful to Liane Bolduc, our intern extraordinaire, for employing top-notch research skills on our behalf. And thanks too to Sarah Convissor for all your help keeping us on the rails.

As ever our families are our rocks, and our sources of joy.

Katty: Thank you Tom and Poppy for all the adventures in Senegal where the very first interviews for this book were done. Tom, you pushed me to go, and you were so right. Our time there was very special—who knew we'd ever learn to surf? Thank you for reading the manuscript. You are my best editor; this book is better for the time you spent reading it. My children are my joy. Poppy, your growing confidence and independence are a pleasure to watch. I'm so impressed that you threw yourself into north Yorkshire and made it work so brilliantly. Thank you, Maya, you somehow make a PhD in astrophysics look simple, while baking beautiful cakes, and being there at the end of the phone whenever I need you (which is often). Felix, you supported me and kept me company during the long hours of working from the basement during Covid. I literally couldn't have done it without you and I loved that time we spent together in the early hours, half asleep, trying to make sense of the scary world outside. And Jude, your love of adventure is a constant source of inspiration and smiles. I'm not sure where you get your powerful sense of self but those around you are happier for it. Zainab, you arrived in our lives from a country in chaos. We're amazed by your courage, grateful that you've kept us company and let us share your journey here.

Claire: Kati Jo—thank you, for the inspiration and comfort, spark and safe harbor. Your smile is everything. I love you. Della and Hugo—thank you for your constant sense of palpable pride in your mother's book writing. It may be more that you are amazed, observing the process, that the project ever gets finished. Still, it sustains, and I love you both so much. Hugo—watching you expand your world, grow ever more wise, find serious purpose, and also joy in your studies, in your singing, in new friendships and relationships—all while keeping that kind heart—it gives me such pleasure. Your creativity is boundless. Della—I'm in awe of your audacity at moving across the ocean at sixteen, excelling academically, making deep new friendships, taking on challenging roles, pushing yourself at every turn, even when it's hard. You are one of the strongest, kindest, most radiant women I know—with a secret weapon: that devastating sense of humor. You are a true explorer. Jay—you've encouraged me, always, in this pursuit, and I'm extraordinarily grateful for our love and friendship. Susannah—you've always supported me no matter what, and your love is so grounding. Janet—nothing works without you and your fabulous energy—you are a force.

AUTHORS' NOTE

Power is an extremely complex and political subject—it affects everyone in the world in one way or another. As we dug into the subject it was clear there were so many ways we could examine it, so many different experiences and stories and struggles we could portray, centuries of history we could layer in. We have chosen only one slice of this enormous field—women's relationship with power today, primarily as it affects us at work and at home. But even in attempting to examine that narrow slice, we're well aware that power's other labyrinthine tendrils are critical, and part of a larger power story. We thought it useful to offer this note about what we did and did not take on.

In writing this book we have drawn on our own experiences as two white women who have spent many years working in the media industry. We are aware that our own lives by no means represent the lives of all or even a majority of women. We have used our own stories in this book in a number of places, but this is, by and large, a reported book. We've relied on our backgrounds and skills as journalists to offer a much broader view than our own.

Over the years, we've interviewed hundreds of women who come from different generations, races, sexual orientations, countries, industries, and backgrounds, and their views and information heavily inform what is in this work, which is mainly a book about power and gender. Any book on power must recognize the inequities created by discrimination based on race and sexual orientation as well as gender. While we have included some reporting, research, and stories on issues beyond gender, it would be wrong to pretend that this is a book primarily about race and power or LGBTQ+ communities and power—important topics that deserve and require book-length discussions of their own. We also do not claim to provide comprehensive solutions to the disparities in access to power that women of color, particularly Black women and LGBTQ+ communities, experience. Fortunately, many other journalists and academics are exploring these topics, and we are eager to learn more from them. And we do hope, certainly, that our more general findings offer a broad path forward for us all.

As we've done in previous work, we have relied heavily on both social science and neuroscience. Sometimes the academic research makes a point of including women of color, or women of different sexual orientations. But not all the academic research in this field addresses the specific problems encountered by different groups and there is clearly more work to be done in that area.

We have also not focused heavily on the issue of class and power. In the United States that tends to mean money and access to financial resources. Obviously poor women have even less opportunity to exercise power than professional and or wealthy women. We cannot do justice to their struggles within the pages of this book. As income disparities grow, and non-college-educated women disproportionately feel the brunt of recessions and pandemics, there is clearly more advocacy to be done to close the equality gap.

Finally, many different women were generous enough to share their experiences, and quite often those women asked us not to identify them by their real names, either because they were worried about blowback from their employers or they didn't want to cause upheavals at home. We have never written about a subject where so many women asked us to use a pseudonym. Our relationship with power is complicated and often shrouded in silence, embarrassment, or frustration. That alone underlines the need for this book.

NOTES

INTRODUCTION

1. Juliana Menase Horowitz and Janell Fetterolf, "Worldwide Optimism About Future of Gender Equality, Even as Many See Advantages for Men," Pew Research Center, April 30, 2020, https://www.pewresearch.org/global/2020/04/30/worldwide-optimism-about-future-of-gender-equality-even-as-many-see-advantages-for-men/.
2. Siobhán O'Grady, "New Zealand's Ardern Names 'Incredibly Diverse' Cabinet, Including First Indigenous Woman as Top Diplomat," *Washington Post*, November 2, 2020, https://www.washingtonpost.com/world/2020/11/02/new-zealand-ardern-cabinet-diversity/.
3. Katie Bishop, "How We Work: Women Breadwinners: Why High-Earners Compensate at Home," BBC, April 6, 2022, https://www.bbc.com/worklife/article/20220406-women-breadwinners-why-high-earners-compensate-at-home.

CHAPTER 1: POWER SHIFT

1. It's of course obvious, but worth mentioning, that not only are all of these great musers men—those who have garnered the most attention are white European men. A more representative group might include Menicius, the ancient Chinese philosopher, who emphasized the basic goodness of human nature. Chanaakya, an Indian philosopher in the fourth century BCE, preached that wise rulers use power gently. Zeraa Yabob, a seventh-century Ethiopian philosopher who lived in a cave for years, was clearly a man ahead of his time. He developed a philosophy of espousing the supremacy of reason, and the radical notion that all humans, men and women, are created equal. (Even worldwide, thoughts considered worth recording still came from mostly men.)
2. Naomi Stanford, *The Economist Guide to Organisation Design,* 2nd ed. (London: Economist, 2015).
3. Lord Acton, Letter to Archbishop Mandell Creighton, April 5, 1887,

Online Library of Liberty, https://history.hanover.edu/courses/excerpts/165acton.html.

4. Ashley Crossman, "The History of Sociology Is Rooted in Ancient Times," ThoughtCo, August 28, 2020, thoughtco.com/history-of-sociology, https://www.thoughtco.com/sociology-of-work-3026289.
5. Ashley Crossman, "Biography of Auguste Comte," ThoughtCo, February 16, 2021, https://www.thoughtco.com/auguste-comte-3026485.
6. Bertrand Russell, *Power: A New Social Analysis* (London: Allen & Unwin, 1938).
7. Catherine Brennan, *Max Weber on Power and Social Stratification: An Interpretation and Critique* (London: Routledge, 2020).
8. R. A. Dahl, J. March, and D. Nauatir, "Influence Ranking in the United States Senate," read at the annual meeting of the American Political Science Association, Washington, DC, September 1956, https://fbaum.unc.edu/teaching/articles/Dahl_Power_1957.pdf.
9. John F. Gaski, "On Contemporary Misdefinition of Power and the Importance of Definitional Fidelity," *Cogent Psychology* 7, no. 1 (2020), doi:10.1080/23311908.2020.1772647.
10. L. J. Kray and L. Thompson, "Gender Stereotypes and Negotiation Performance: An Examination of Theory and Research," in R. Kramer and B. Staw, eds., *An Annual Series of Analytical Essays and Critical Reviews, Research in Organizational Behavior* 26 (2004): 103–82, https://www.scholars.northwestern.edu/en/publications/gender-stereotypes-and-negotiation-performance-an-examination-of-.
11. Alison Wood Brooks, "Get Excited: Reappraising Pre-Performance Anxiety as Excitement," *Journal of Experimental Psychology* 143, no. 3 (2013): 1144–58; F. Gino, C. A. Wilmuth, and A. W. Brooks, "Compared to Men, Women View Professional Advancement as Equally Attainable, but Less Desirable," *Proceedings of the National Academy of Sciences* 112, no. 40 (2015): 12354–59, https://gap.hks.harvard.edu/compared-men-women-view-professional-advancement-equally-attainable-less-desirable.
12. Francesca Gino, Caroline Ashley Wilmuth, and Alison Wood Brooks, "Investors Prefer Entrepreneurial Ventures Pitched by Attractive Men," *Proceedings of the National Academy of Sciences* 112, no. 40 (October 2015): 12354–59, https://www.pnas.org/doi/10.1073/pnas.1321202111.
13. Christine Kuehner, "Why Is Depression More Common Among Women Than Among Men?" *Lancet Psychiatry* 4, no. 2 (2017):146–58, doi:10.1016/S2215-0366(16)30263-2.
14. Tetyana Pudrovska and Amelia Karraker, "Gender, Job Authority, and

Depression," *Journal of Health and Social Behavior* 55, no. 4 (2014): 424–41.

15. Mary Beard, "Women in Power," *London Review of Books*, March 16, 2017, https://www.lrb.co.uk/the-paper/v39/n06/mary-beard/women-in-power.
16. Krystie M. Davis, "20 Facts and Figures to Know When Marketing to Women," *Forbes*, May 13, 2019, https://www.forbes.com/sites/forbescontentmarketing/2019/05/13/20-facts-and-figures-to-know-when-marketing-to-women/?sh=2f7d4de51297.
17. Jonathan Barnes, ed., *The Complete Works of Aristotle*, vol. 2, Revised Oxford Translation (Princeton, NJ: Princeton University Press, 1984), 2015.
18. Beard, "Women in Power."
19. Cora Lewis, "Steinem Headlines Talk About Feminism," *Yale Daily News*, February 1, 2010, https://yaledailynews.com/blog/2010/02/01/steinem-headlines-talk-about-feminism/.

CHAPTER 2: THE POWER (AND JOY) OF HAVING POWER

1. Afua Hirsch, "Has Senegal's Gender Parity Law for MPs Helped Women?" *Guardian*, November 12, 2012, https://www.theguardian.com/global-development/2012/nov/15/senegal-gender-parity-law-mps-women.
2. CIA, *The World Factbook*, Senegal, https://www.cia.gov/the-world-factbook/countries/senegal/.
3. UN Women, "Following Elections, Proportion of Senegal's Female Parliamentarians Almost Doubles," July 12, 2012, https://www.unwomen.org/en/news/stories/2012/7/following-elections-proportion-of-senegal-s-female-parliamentarians-almost-doubles.
4. Supriya Garikipati and Uma Kambhampati, "Leading the Fight Against the Pandemic: Does Gender 'Really' Matter?" June 3, 2020, https://ssrn.com/abstract=3617953.
5. Marianne Tøraasen, "Gender Parity and the Symbolic Representation of Women in Senegal," *Journal of Modern African Studies* 57, no. 3 (2019): 459–81, https://ssrn.com/abstract=3648090.
6. UN High Commissioner for Refugees, "Preventing and Reducing Statelessness: Good Practices in Promoting and Adopting Gender Equality in Nationality Laws," UN Refugee Agency, March 7, 2014, https://www.unhcr.org/531a001c9.pdf.
7. Institute for Human Rights and Development in Africa, law no. 2020-05 of January 10, 2020, modifying law no. 65-60 of July 21, 1965, on the Penal Code, https://sgbv-ihrda.uwazi.io/en/entity/7xur2iqdfr.
8. Global Progress Report on Water, Sanitation and Hygiene in Health

Care Facilities: Fundamentals First, Geneva, World Health Organization, 2020.

9. Belinda Luscombe, "Cancer, Discrimination, and Toxic Culture: How the Dallas Mavericks CEO Beat Them All," *Time*, September 11, 2022, https://time.com/6212470/dallas-mavericks-ceo-cynt-marshall-interview/.
10. Natalie Maher, "Why Should Women Have to 'Act Like Men' to Get Ahead in Design?" *Design Week*, March 7, 2019, https://www.designweek.co.uk/issues/4–10-march-2019/why-should-women-have-to-act-like-men-to-get-ahead-in-design/.
11. Leading Effectively staff, "The Importance of Empathy in the Workplace," Center for Creative Leadership, June 28, 2022, https://www.ccl.org/articles/leading-effectively-articles/empathy-in-the-workplace-a-tool-for-effective-leadership/.
12. Y. Kifer, D. Heller, W. Q. E. Perunovic, and A. D. Galinsky, "The Good Life of the Powerful: The Experience of Power and Authenticity Enhances Subjective Well-Being," *Psychological Science* 24, no. 3 (2013): 280–88, https://doi.org/10.1177/0956797612450891.
13. S. Wu, D. M. H. Kee, D. Li, and D. Ni, "Thanks for Your Recognition, Boss! A Study of How and When Voice Endorsement Promotes Job Performance and Voice," *Front Psychology* 12 (2021), doi:10.3389/fpsyg.2021.706501, https://www.ncbi.nlm.nih.gov/pmc/articles/PMC8329334/.

CHAPTER 3: YOUR BRAIN ON POWER

1. Dacher Keltner, Deborah H. Gruenfeld, and Cameron Anderson, "Power, Approach, and Inhibition," *Psychological Review* 110, no. 2 (2003): 265–84, https://doi.org/10.1037/0033-295x.110.2.265.
2. Melissa Dahl, "Powerful People Are Messier Eaters, Maybe," The Cut, January 13, 2015, https://www.thecut.com/2015/01/powerful-people-are-messy-eaters-maybe.html.
3. Adam D. Galinsky, "Losing Touch," Kellogg Insight, August 1, 2019, https://insight.kellogg.northwestern.edu/article/losing-touch.
4. Deborah Gruenfeld, Ena Inesi, Joe Magee, and Adam Galinsky, "Power and the Objectification of Social Targets," *Journal of Personality and Social Psychology* 95 (2005): 111–27, https://www.researchgate.net/publication/5246875_Power_and_the_Objectification_of_Social_Targets.
5. Marius van Dijke, David De Cremer, Gerben Langendijk, and Cameron Anderson, "Ranking Low, Feeling High: How Hierarchical Position and Experienced Power Promote Prosocial Behavior in Response to Procedural

Justice," *Journal of Applied Psychology* 103, no. 2 (2018): 164–81, https://doi.org/10.1037/apl0000260.

6. Dacher Kelter, "Don't Let Power Corrupt You," *Harvard Business Review*, October 2016, https://hbr.org/2016/10/dont-let-power-corrupt-you.
7. (Batson et al., 1996; Gault & Sabini, 2000; Lennon & Eisenberg, 1987; Macaskill et al., 2002; Schieman & Van Gundy, 2000).
8. Klein & Hodges, 2001).
9. Nicole Abi-Esber, Sapna Cheryan, and Matthew Asher Lawson, "New Insights on the Obstacles, Opportunities, and Outcomes on Women's Path to Leadership," *Academy of Management Proceedings* 2021, no. 1 (2021): 10479, https://doi.org/10.5465/ambpp.2021.10479symposium.
10. Oliver Genschow, Sophie Klomfar, Ine d'Haene, and Marcel Brass, "Mimicking and Anticipating Others' Actions Is Linked to Social Information Processing," *PLOS ONE* 13, no. 3 (2018), https://doi.org/10.1371/journal.pone.0193743.
11. J. M. Kilner and R. N. Lemon, "What We Know Currently about Mirror Neurons," *Current Biology* 23, no. 23 (2013), https://doi.org/10.1016/j.cub.2013.10.051.
12. J. Hogeveen, M. Inzlicht, and S. S. Obhi, "Power Changes How the Brain Responds to Others," *Journal of Experimental Psychology: General* 143, no. 2 (2014): 755–62, https://doi.org/10.1037/a0033477.
13. P. Smith and Adam Galinsky, "The Nonconscious Nature of Power: Cues and Consequences," *Social and Personality Psychology Compass* 4 (2010): 918–38.
14. Sumeet Farwaha and Sukhvinder S. Obhi, "The Effects of Socioeconomic Status and Situational Power on Self-Other Processing in the Automatic Imitation Task," *Experimental Brain Research* 239 (2021): 2519–28, https://doi.org/10.1007/s00221-021-06152-2.
15. A. D. Galinsky, D. H. Gruenfeld, and J. C. Magee, "From Power to Action," *Journal of Personality and Social Psychology* 85, no. 3 (2003): 453–66, https://doi.org/10.1037/0022-3514.85.3.453.
16. Nathanael J. Fast, Deborah H. Gruenfeld, Niro Sivanathan, and Adam D. Galinsky, "Illusory Control," *Psychological Science* 20, no. 4 (2009): 502–8, https://doi.org/10.1111/j.1467-9280.2009.02311.x.
17. Bogdan Wojciszke, "Power Influences Self-Esteem," *Social Cognition* 25, no. 4 (2007): 472–94.
18. J. Filson, E. Ulloa, C. Runfola, and A. Hokoda, "Does Powerlessness Explain the Relationship Between Intimate Partner Violence and Depression?" *Journal of Interpersonal Violence* 25, no. 3 (2010): 400–15, doi:10.1177/0886260509334401.

19. Warren D. TenHouten, "The Emotions of Powerlessness," *Journal of Political Power* 9, no. 1 (2016): 83–121, doi:10.1080/2158379X.2016.11 49308.
20. Brian Middleton Goldman and Michael H. Kernis, "The Role of Authenticity in Healthy Psychological Functioning and Subjective Well-Being," *Annals of the American Psychotherapy Association* 5, no. 6 (2002): 18–20.
21. Kennon M. Sheldon, Richard M. Ryan, Laird J. Rawsthorne, and Barbara Ilardi, "Trait Self and True Self: Cross-Role Variation in the Big-Five Personality Traits and Its Relations with Psychological Authenticity and Subjective Well-Being," *Journal of Personality and Social Psychology* 73, no. 6 (1997): 1380–93, https://doi.org/10.1037/0022-3514.73.6.1380.
22. Alex Liu, "Making Joy a Priority at Work," *Harvard Business Review*, July 17, 2019, https://hbr.org/2019/07/making-joy-a-priority-at-work.
23. Joris Lammers, David Dubois, Derek Rucker, and Adam Galinsky, "Power Gets the Job: Priming Power Improves Interview Outcomes," *Journal of Experimental Social Psychology* 49 (2013): 776–79.
24. Brynne C. DiMenichi, Ahmet O. Ceceli, Jamil P. Bhanji, and Elizabeth Tricomi, "Effects of Expressive Writing on Neural Processing during Learning," *Frontiers in Human Neuroscience* 13 (2019), https://doi.org/10.33 89/fnhum.2019.00389.
25. Kitty Klein and Adriel Boals, "Expressive Writing Can Increase Working Memory Capacity," *Journal of Experimental Psychology: General* 130, no. 3 (2001): 520–33, https://doi.org/10.1037/0096-3445.130.3.520.
26. Zoe Andres, "Psychologically Speaking: Your Brain on Writing," Writing and Communication Centre, University of Waterloo, August 4, 2022, https://uwaterloo.ca/writing-and-communication-centre/blog/psycholog ically-speaking-your-brain-writing.
27. Keita Umejima, Takuya Ibaraki, Takahiro Yamazaki, and Kuniyoshi L. Sakai, "Paper Notebooks vs. Mobile Devices: Brain Activation Differences During Memory Retrieval," *Frontiers in Behavioral Neuroscience* 15 (2021), doi:10.3389/fnbeh.2021.634158.
28. Adam D. Galinsky, Deborah H. Gruenfeld, and Joe C. Magee, "From Power to Action," *Journal of Personality and Social Psychology* 85, no. 3 (2003): 453–66, https://doi.org/10.1037/0022-3514.85.3.453.
29. Adam D. Galinsky and Gavin Kilduff, "Be Seen as a Leader," *Harvard Business Review*, December 2013, https://hbr.org/2013/12/be-seen-as-a-leader.
30. Pamela Smith, Nils Jostmann, Adam Galinsky, and Wilco van Dijk, "Lacking Power Impairs Executive Functions," *Psychological Science* 19 (2008): 441–47, 10.1111/j.1467–9280.2008.02107.x.

CHAPTER 4: WHAT HAPPENS WHEN EVERYONE'S FED UP AT WORK

1. Women in the Workplace 2021, McKinsey & Company, 2021, https://www.mckinsey.com/featured-insights/diversity-and-inclusion/women-in-the-workplace.
2. Stephanie K. Johnson, Ksenia Keplinger, Jessica F. Kirk, and Liza Barnes, "Has Sexual Harassment at Work Decreased since #MeToo?" *Harvard Business Review*, August 27, 2021, https://hbr.org/2019/07/has-sexual-harassment-at-work-decreased-since-metoo.
3. Ksenia Keplinger, Stefanie K. Johnson, Jessica F. Kirk, and Liza Y. Barnes, "Women at Work: Changes in Sexual Harassment Between September 2016 and September 2018," *PLOS ONE* 14, no. 7 (2019), https://doi.org/10.1371/journal.pone.0218313.
4. Leanne E. Atwater, Allison M. Tringale, Rachel E. Sturm, Scott N. Taylor, and Phillip W. Braddy, "Looking Ahead," *Organizational Dynamics* 48, no. 4 (2019): 100677, https://doi.org/10.1016/j.orgdyn.2018.08.008.
5. "Corporate Donations to Black Lives Matter Total $67 Billion," Creative Investment Research, accessed October 3, 2022, https://www.prlog.org/12874879-corporate-donations-to-black-lives-matter-total-67-billion.html.
6. "Corporate Pledges to Black Lives Matter," Creative Investment Research, Black Lives Matter (BLM) Donation Tracker, accessed October 3, 2022, https://www.blacklivesmattercorporatepledges.com/.
7. Women in the Labor Force: A Databook 2012 Edition, US Bureau of Labor Statistics, accessed October 3, 2022, https://www.bls.gov/cps/wlf-databook-2012.pdf.
8. David A. Cotter, Joan M. Hermsen, and Reeve Vanneman, "The End of the Gender Revolution? Gender Role Attitudes from 1977 to 2008," *American Journal of Sociology* 117 (July 2011): 259–89.
9. Francine D. Blau, Mary C. Brinton, and David B. Grusky, *The Declining Significance of Gender?* (New York: Russell Sage Foundation, 2006).
10. "The State of the Gender Pay Gap," Obama White House Archives, accessed October 3, 2022, https://obamawhitehouse.archives.gov/sites/default/files/page/files/20160614_gender_pay_gap_issue_brief_cea.pdf.
11. Claudia Buchmann and Thomas A. DiPrete, *The Rise of Women: The Growing Gender Gap in Education and What It Means for American Schools* (New York: Russell Sage Foundation, 2013), xviii, 277.
12. Claudia Goldin, Lawrence F. Katz, and Ilyana Kuziemko, "The Homecoming of American College Women: The Reversal of the College Gender Gap,"

Journal of Economic Perspectives 20, no. 4 (2006): 133–56, doi:10.1257/jep.20.4.133.
13. Francine Blau and Lawrence Kahn, "The Gender Wage Gap: Extent, Trends, and Explanations," NBER Working Paper No. w21913, January 2016, https://doi.org/10.3386/w21913.
14. David G. Smith, Judith E. Rosenstein, and Margaret C. Nikolov, "The Different Words We Use to Describe Male and Female Leaders," *Harvard Business Review*, January 20, 2021, https://hbr.org/2018/05/the-different-words-we-use-to-describe-male-and-female-leaders.
15. 2020 McKinsey study How the LGBTQ+ community fares in the workplace. Diana Ellsworth, Ana Mendy, Gavin Sullivan. https://www.mckinsey.com/featured-insights/diversity-and-inclusion/how-the-lgbtq-plus-community-fares-in-the-workplace.

CHAPTER 5: POINTLESS PERFECTION AND OTHER BURDENSOME BIASES

1. Boris Kingma and Wouter van Marken Lichtenbelt, "Energy Consumption in Buildings and Female Thermal Demand," *Nature Climate Change* 5, no. 12 (2015): 1054–56, https://doi.org/10.1038/nclimate2741.
2. "Is Expectant Mothers' Parking Expected?" Curcio Enterprises, February 20, 2019, https://curcioenterprises.com/2019/02/25/is-expectant-mothers-parking-expected/.
3. Beth Tauke, Korydon H. Smith, and Charles L. Davis, *Diversity and Design: Understanding Hidden Consequences* (New York: Routledge, 2016).
4. "Injury Vulnerability, and Effectiveness of Occupant Protection Technologies for Older Occupants and Women," US Department of Transportation, National Highway Traffic Safety Administration, accessed October 4, 2022, https://crashstats.nhtsa.dot.gov/Api/Public/ViewPublication/811766.
5. R. Aldred, R. Johnson, C. Jackson, et al., "How Does Mode of Travel Affect Risks Posed to Other Road Users? An Analysis of English Road Fatality Data, Incorporating Gender and Road Type," *Injury Prevention* 27 (2021): 71–76.
6. Pavi Dinamani and Rich Shibley, "Why Aren't Smartphones Designed for a Woman's Hand Size?" Digital Trends, October 15, 2020, https://www.digitaltrends.com/mobile/smartphone-size-design-for-woman-hand/.
7. Women in the Workplace 2022, McKinsey & Company, 2022, https://leanin.org/women-in-the-workplace/2022/the-importance-of-managers.

8. "Burnout, Leadership, and Hope: A Year-and-a-Half into the Pandemic, Looking at Women in the Workplace," McKinsey & Company, September 27, 2021, https://www.mckinsey.com/about-us/new-at-mckinsey-blog/one-year-into-the-pandemic-what-does-our-women-in-the-workplace-report-say.
9. Thomas Bradford Bitterly, Alison Wood Brooks, Li Huang, and Kai Chi Yam, "New Insights on Moral Underpinnings of Humor, Consequences of Aggressive Humor, and Who Laugh More," *Academy of Management Proceedings*, no. 1 (2018): 10387, https://doi.org/10.5465/ambpp.2018.10387symposium.
10. Linda Babcock, Brenda Peyser, Lise Vesterlund, and Laurie Weingart, *The No Club: Putting a Stop to Women's Dead-End Work* (New York: Simon & Schuster, 2022).
11. Timothy A. Judge, Beth A. Livingston, and Charlice Hurst, "Do Nice Guys—and Gals—Really Finish Last? The Joint Effects of Sex and Agreeableness on Income," *Journal of Personality and Social Psychology* 102, no. 2 (2012): 390–407, https://doi.org/10.1037/a0026021.
12. Linda Babcock, Maria P. Recalde, Lise Vesterlund, and Laurie Weingart, "Gender Differences in Accepting and Receiving Requests for Tasks with Low Promotability," *American Economic Review* 107, no. 3 (2017): 714–47, https://doi.org/10.1257/aer.20141734.
13. Women in the Workplace 2021, McKinsey & Company, 2021, https://www.mckinsey.com/featured-insights/diversity-and-inclusion/women-in-the-workplace.
14. Andrew O'Connell, "Emotional Labor Doesn't Pay," *Harvard Business Review*, July 23, 2014, https://hbr.org/2010/09/why-is-it-that-we.
15. Michelle King, *The Fix: Overcome the Invisible Barriers That Are Holding Women Back at Work* (New York: Atria Books, 2020).
16. "Women Aren't Promoted Because Managers Underestimate Their Potential," *Yale Insights*, September 17, 2021, https://insights.som.yale.edu/insights/women-arent-promoted-because-managers-underestimate-their-potential.
17. Jill E. Yavorsky, Lisa A. Keister, Yue Qian, and Michael Nau, "Women in the One Percent: Gender Dynamics in Top Income Positions," *American Sociological Review* 84, no. 1 (2019): 54–81, https://doi.org/10.1177/0003122418820702.
18. Christopher A. Littlefield, "A Better Way to Recognize Your Employees," *Harvard Business Review*, October 25, 2022, https://hbr.org/2022/10/a-better-way-to-recognize-your-employees.

CHAPTER 6: THE BLEND

1. Katie Abouzahr, "Why Women-Owned Startups Are a Better Bet," Boston Consulting Group, June 6, 2018, https://www.bcg.com/publications/2018/why-women-owned-startups-are-better-bet.
2. M. K. Sumra, "Masculinity, Femininity, and Leadership: Taking a Closer Look at the Alpha Female," *PLoS One* 14, no. 4 (April 2019), doi:10.1371/journal.pone.0215181, https://journals.plos.org/plosone/article/authors?id=10.1371/journal.pone.0215181.
3. Claire Shipman and Katherine Kay, *Womenomics: Work Less, Achieve More, Live Better* (New York: HarperCollins, 2010).
4. George Anders, "So Stressed! Women Report Bigger Burdens but See a Lot More Escapes," LinkedIn Workforce Confidence, August 25, 2021, https://www.linkedin.com/pulse/so-stressed-women-report-bigger-burdens-see-lot-more-escapes-anders/.
5. Josie Cox, "Why Women Are More Burned Out Than Men," BBC, October 3, 2021, https://www.bbc.com/worklife/article/20210928-why-women-are-more-burned-out-than-men.
6. Kayleigh Bateman, "Birth Rates Are Shrinking in Japan —and It's Part of a Worldwide Trend," Center for New Economy and Safety, World Economic Forum, January, 31, 2022, https://www.weforum.org/agenda/2022/01/japan-global-birth-rate-decline/.
7. Abigail Friedman, "Boosting Japan's Workforce (and Womenomics) Through Immigration," Center for Strategic and International Studies, December 15, 2016, https://www.csis.org/analysis/boosting-japans-workforce-and-womenomics-through-immigration.
8. Tiffany Burns, Jess Huang, Alexis Krivkovich, et al., Women in the Workplace 2021, McKinsey & Company, September 27, 2021, https://womenintheworkplace.com/.
9. *OECD Part-Time and Partly Equal: Gender and Work in the Netherlands, Gender Equality at Work* (Paris: OECD Publishing, 2019), https://www.oecd-ilibrary.org/sites/204235cf-en/index.html?itemId=/content/publication/204235cf-en.
10. Marieke De Ruiter, "Part Time Workers Won't Get the Top Jobs—and Most Dutch Women Work Part Time," Dutch News, June 25, 2020, https://www.dutchnews.nl/news/2020/06/part-time-workers-wont-get-the-top-jobs-and-most-dutch-women-work-part-time/.
11. Vicky McKeever, "Goldman Sachs CEO Solomon Calls Working from Home an 'Aberration,'" CNBC, February 25, 2021, https://www.cnbc

.com/2021/02/25/goldman-sachs-ceo-solomon-calls-working-from-home-an-aberration-.html.

12. Elizabeth Dilts Marshall, "Working from Home 'Doesn't Work for Those Who Want to Hustle': JPMorgan CEO," Reuters, May 4, 2021, https://www.reuters.com/article/us-jp-morgan-ceo/working-from-home-doesnt-work-for-those-who-want-to-hustle-jpmorgan-ceo-idUSKBN2CL1HQ.
13. Morgan Smith, "Twitter, Reddit and 8 Other Companies Offering Permanent Remote or Hybrid Work—and Hiring Right Now," CNBC, April 13, 2022, https://www.cnbc.com/2022/04/13/10-companies-that-switched-to-permanent-hybrid-or-remote-work-and-hiring-right-now.html.
14. Rebecca Stropoli, "Are We Really More Productive Working from Home?" *Chicago Booth Review*, August 18, 2021, https://www.chicagobooth.edu/review/are-we-really-more-productive-working-home.
15. Jose Maria Barrero, Nicholas Bloom, and Steven J. Davis, "Why Working from Home Will Stick," National Bureau of Economic Research Working Paper 28731, 2021, https://wfhresearch.com/.
16. Jose Maria Barrero, Nicholas Bloom, and Steve J. Davis, "60 Million Fewer Commuting Hours per Day: How Americans Use Time Saved by Working from Home," Centre for Economic Policy Research, September 23, 2020, https://cepr.org/voxeu/columns/60-million-fewer-commuting-hours-day-how-americans-use-time-saved-working-home.
17. Barrero, Bloom, and Davis.
18. Rachel Peita, "Survey: Men & Women Experience Remote Work Differently," FlexJobs, November 2021, https://www.flexjobs.com/blog/post/men-women-experience-remote-work-survey/.
19. "Understanding the Pandemic's Impact on Working Women," Deloitte Global, October 28, 2020, https://www2.deloitte.com/content/dam/Deloitte/global/Documents/About-Deloitte/gx-about-deloitte-understanding-the-pandemic-s-impact-on-working-women.pdf.
20. Yvonne Lott and Anja Abendroth, "Reasons for Not Working from Home in an Ideal Worker Culture: Why Women Perceive More Cultural Barriers," Hans-Böckler-Stiftung, November 2019, https://www.boeckler.de/pdf/p_wsi_wp_211.pdf.
21. Women in the Workplace, McKinsey & Company, September 30, 2020, https://wiw-report.s3.amazonaws.com/Women_in_the_Workplace_2020.pdf.
22. "Women's Economic Empowerment and Inclusive Global Economic

Growth: COVID-19 and Beyond," keynote speech by Chief Economist Gita Gopinath at the Inaugural Dr. Hansa Mehta Lecture, March 8, 2021, https://www.imf.org/en/News/Articles/2021/03/08/sp030821-gita-gopinath-inaugural-dr-hansa-mehta-lecture.

23. Future Forum team, "What Is Proximity Bias?" Future Forum, September 7, 2022, https://futureforum.com/2022/09/07/what-is-proximity-bias/.
24. Sian Beilock, "Why I Worry Remote Schedules Could Mean Fewer Women in the Office," *Washington Post*, March 3, 2021, https://www.washingtonpost.com/opinions/2021/03/03/remote-work-women-office-equity/.
25. Mark Mortensen and Martina Haas, "Making the Hybrid Workplace Fair," *Harvard Business Review*, February 24, 2021, https://hbr.org/2021/02/making-the-hybrid-workplace-fair.
26. Claire Cain Miller, "Women Did Everything Right. Then Work Got 'Greedy,'" *New York Times*, April 26, 2019, https://www.nytimes.com/2019/04/26/upshot/women-long-hours-greedy-professions.html.
27. John Pencavel, "The Productivity of Working Hours," Stanford University Discussion Paper, Institute for the Study of Labor, IZA, Bonn, No. 8129, April 2014, https://docs.iza.org/dp8129.pdf.
28. Erling Barth, Claudia Goldin, Sari Pekkala Kerr, and Olivia Olivetti, Olivia, "Average Mid-Forties Male College Graduate Earns 55 Percent More Than His Female Counterparts," *Harvard Business Review*, June 12, 2017, https://hbr.org/2017/06/the-average-mid-forties-male-college-graduate-earns-55-more-than-his-female-counterparts.
29. Derek Thompson, "Workism Is Making Americans Miserable," *Atlantic*, February 24, 2019, https://www.theatlantic.com/ideas/archive/2019/02/religion-workism-making-americans-miserable/583441/.
30. World Health Organization, "Long Working Hours Increasing Deaths from Heart Disease and Stroke: WHO, ILO," May 17, 2021, https://www.who.int/news/item/17-05-2021-long-working-hours-increasing-deaths-from-heart-disease-and-stroke-who-ilo.
31. Hye-Eun Lee, Nam-Hee Kim, Tae-Won Jang, and Ichiro Kawachi, "Impact of Long Working Hours and Shift Work on Perceived Unmet Dental Need: A Panel Study," *International Journal of Environmental Research and Public Health* 18, no. 6 (2021), 2939, https://doi.org/10.3390/ijerph18062939.
32. https://www.ft.com/content/54379f02-7db1-11e8-bc55-50daf11b720d.
33. World Population Review, "Average Workweek by Country 2023,"https://worldpopulationreview.com/country-rankings/average-work-week-by-country.

34. Andreas Kössel, "Working Time," Lutz Abel, June 1, 2021,https://www.lutzabel.com/en/employment-law-in-germany/20220601-working-time.
35. https://www.ft.com/content/e7f0490e-0b1c-11e8-8eb7-42f857ea9f09.
36. Organisation for Economic Co-operation and Development, "Hours Worked," 2023, https://data.oecd.org/emp/hours-worked.htm.
37. Glen Stansbury, "Why Germans Have Longer Vacation Times and More Productivity," *Business Class*, September 28, 2010, https://www.americanexpress.com/en-us/business/trends-and-insights/articles/why-germans-have-longer-vacation-times-and-more-productivity-1/.
38. Jenny Gross, "4-Day Workweek Brings No Loss of Productivity, Companies in Experiment Say," *New York Times*, September 22, 2022, https://www.nytimes.com/2022/09/22/business/four-day-work-week-uk.html.
39. Jack Kelly, "Could the Four-Day Workweek Become the New Global Standard?" *Forbes*, September 22, 2022, https://www.forbes.com/sites/jackkelly/2022/09/22/could-the-four-day-workweek-become-the-new-global-standard/?sh=32c3ffb05639.
40. Lindsay Ellis and Angela Young, "If Your Co-Workers Are 'Quiet Quitting,' Here's What That Means," *Wall Street Journal*, August 12, 2022, https://www.wsj.com/articles/if-your-gen-z-co-workers-are-quiet-quitting-heres-what-that-means-11660260608.
41. Joe Du Bey, "How to Mitigate Proximity Bias and Create a More Inclusive Workplace Culture," *Forbes*, April 4, 2022, https://www.forbes.com/sites/forbestechcouncil/2022/04/04/how-to-mitigate-proximity-bias-and-create-a-more-inclusive-workplace-culture/?sh=5387528727fa.

CHAPTER 7: POTS AND PANS AND POWER

1. Amanda Barroso, "For American Couples, Gender Gaps in Sharing Household Responsibilities Persist amid Pandemic," Pew Research Center, January 25, 2021, https://www.pewresearch.org/fact-tank/2021/01/25/for-american-couples-gender-gaps-in-sharing-household-responsibilities-persist-amid-pandemic/.
2. Melanie E. Brewster, "Lesbian Women and Household Labor Division: A Systematic Review of Scholarly Research from 2000 to 2015," *Journal of Lesbian Studies* 21, no. 1 (2016): 47–69, https://doi.org/10.1080/10894160.2016.1142350.
3. Abbie E. Goldberg, JuliAnna Z. Smith, and Maureen Perry-Jenkins, "The Division of Labor in Lesbian, Gay, and Heterosexual New Adoptive Parents," *Journal of Marriage and Family* 74, no. 4 (2012): 812–28, https://doi.org/10.1111/j.1741-3737.2012.00992.x.

4. Alisha Haridasani Gupta, "Why Some Women Call This Recession a 'Shecession,'" *New York Times*, May 9, 2020, https://www.nytimes.com/2020/05/09/us/unemployment-coronavirus-women.html.
5. Tim Henderson, "As Women Return to Jobs, Remote Work Could Lock in Gains," Pew Charitable Trusts, May 3, 2022, https://www.pewtrusts.org/en/research-and-analysis/blogs/stateline/2022/05/03/as-women-return-to-jobs-remote-work-could-lock-in-gains.
6. Diana Boesch and Shilpa Phadke, "When Women Lose All the Jobs: Essential Actions for a Gender-Equitable Recovery," Center for American Progress, November 9, 2021, https://www.americanprogress.org/article/women-lose-jobs-essential-actions-gender-equitable-recovery/.
7. Erin Zimmerman, "The Pandemic Has Reversed the Usual Gender Roles in My House and I Love It," HuffPost, April 23, 2020, https://www.huffpost.com/entry/coronavirus-gender-roles-parenting_n_5e9760a2c5b65eae709e50d2.
8. US Census Bureau, "FINC-05. Earnings of Wife by Earnings of Husband-Married Couple Families, by Race and Hispanic Origin of Reference Person," August 17, 2022, https://www.census.gov/data/tables/time-series/demo/income-poverty/cps-finc/finc-05.2017.html.
9. Marta Murray-Close and Misty L. Heggeness, "Manning Up and Womaning Down: How Husbands and Wives Report Their Earnings When She Earns More," US Census Bureau, Social, Economic, and Housing Statistics Division, Working Paper #2018–20, June 6, 2018, https://www.census.gov/library/working-papers/2018/demo/SEHSD-WP2018-20.html.
10. Anja Roth and Michaela Slotwinski, "Gender Norms and Income Misreporting Within Households," *SSRN Electronic Journal*, 2020, https://doi.org/10.2139/ssrn.3527342.
11. George Lowery, "Men Who Earn Less Than Their Women Are More Likely to Cheat," *Cornell Chronicle*, August 26, 2010, https://news.cornell.edu/stories/2010/08/men-more-likely-cheat-higher-earning-women.
12. Marianne Bertrand, Emir Kamenica, and Jessica Pan, "Gender Identity and Relative Income Within Households," *Quarterly Journal of Economics* 130, no. 2 (2015): 571–614, https://doi.org/10.1093/qje/qjv001.
13. Murray-Close and Heggeness, "Manning Up and Womaning Down."
14. Gaëlle Ferrant, Luca Maria Pesando, and Keiko Nowacka, "Unpaid Care Work: The Missing Link in the Analysis of Gender Gaps in Labour Outcomes," OECD Development Centre, December 2014, https://www.oecd.org/dev/development-gender/Unpaid_care_work.pdf.
15. Valerie A. Ramey, "Time Spent in Home Production in the 20th Century:

New Estimates from Old Data," National Bureau of Economic Research, Working Paper 13985, May 2008, https://doi.org/10.3386/w13985.

16. Aliya Hamid Rao, "Even Breadwinning Wives Don't Get Equality at Home," *Atlantic*, May 12, 2019, https://www.theatlantic.com/family/archive/2019/05/breadwinning-wives-gender-inequality/589237/.
17. "Chapter 6: Time in Work and Leisure, Patterns by Gender and Family Structure," Social & Demographic Trends Project, Pew Research Center, March 14, 2013, https://www.pewresearch.org/social-trends/2013/03/14/chapter-6-time-in-work-and-leisure-patterns-by-gender-and-family-structure/.
18. American Time Use Survey, US Bureau of Labor Statistics, December 2016, https://www.bls.gov/tus/charts/household.htm.
19. Megan Brenan, "Women Still Handle Main Household Tasks in U.S.," Gallup, November 20, 2021, https://news.gallup.com/poll/283979/women-handle-main-household-tasks.aspx.
20. Man Yee Kan, Oriel Sullivan, and Jonathan Gershuny, "Gender Convergence in Domestic Work: Discerning the Effects of Interactional and Institutional Barriers from Large-Scale Data," *Sociology* 45, no. 2 (2011): 234–51, https://doi.org/10.1177/0038038510394014.
21. Catherine Bolzendahl and Zoya Gubernskaya, "Racial and Ethnic Homogamy and Gendered Time on Core Housework," *Socius* 2 (2016): 237802311667627, https://doi.org/10.1177/2378023116676277.
22. Man-Yee Kan and Heather Laurie, "Who Is Doing the Housework in Multicultural Britain?" *Sociology* 52, no. 1 (2016): 55–74, https://doi.org/10.1177/0038038516674674.
23. Jessica Valenti, "The Pandemic Isn't Forcing Moms Out of the Workforce—Dads Are," Medium, July 31, 2020, https://gen.medium.com/the-pandemic-isnt-forcing-moms-out-of-the-workforce-dads-are-e0cb58e1965b.
24. Jo Augustus, "The Impact of the COVID-19 Pandemic on Women Working in Higher Education," *Frontiers in Education* 6 (2021), https://doi.org/10.3389/feduc.2021.648365.
25. Julie Kashen, Sarah Jane Glynn, and Amanda Novello, "How Covid-19 Sent Women's Workforce Progress Backward," Center for American Progress, November 9, 2021, https://www.americanprogress.org/article/covid-19-sent-womens-workforce-progress-backward/.
26. Claire Cain Miller, "Nearly Half of Men Say They Do Most of the Home Schooling. 3 Percent of Women Agree," *New York Times*, May 6, 2020, https://www.nytimes.com/2020/05/06/upshot/pandemic-chores-homeschooling-gender.html.

27. Allison Daminger, "The Cognitive Dimension of Household Labor," *American Sociological Review* 84, no. 4 (2019): 609–33, https://doi.org/10.1177/0003122419859007.
28. Arlie Russell Hochschild, "Emotion Work, Feeling Rules, and Social Structure," *American Journal of Sociology* 85, no. 3 (1979): 551–75, http://www.jstor.org/stable/2778583.
29. *You Should've Asked*, Emma, https://english.emmaclit.com/2017/05/20/you-shouldve-asked/.
30. Girls' Attitudes Survey 2015, London, Girlguiding, 2015, https://www.girlguiding.org.uk/globalassets/docs-and-resources/research-and-campaigns/girls-attitudes-survey-2015.pdf.
31. Alyssa Croft, Toni Schmader, Katharina Block, and Andrew Scott Baron, "The Second Shift Reflected in the Second Generation," *Psychological Science* 25, no. 7 (2014): 1418–28, https://doi.org/10.1177/0956797614533968.
32. Michelle J. Budig, "The Fatherhood Bonus and the Motherhood Penalty: Parenthood and the Gender Gap in Pay," Third Way, September 2, 2014, https://www.thirdway.org/report/the-fatherhood-bonus-and-the-motherhood-penalty-parenthood-and-the-gender-gap-in-pay.
33. Darcy Lockman, "What 'Good' Dads Get Away With," *New York Times*, May 4, 2019, https://www.nytimes.com/2019/05/04/opinion/sunday/men-parenting.html.
34. Olle Folke and Johanna Rickne, "All the Single Ladies: Job Promotions and the Durability of Marriage," *American Economic Journal: Applied Economics* 12, no. 1 (2020): 260–87, https://doi.org/10.1257/app.20180435.
35. Claire Cain Miller, "How Same-Sex Couples Divide Chores, and What It Reveals about Modern Parenting," *New York Times*, May 16, 2018, https://www.nytimes.com/2018/05/16/upshot/couples-divide-chores-much-more-evenly-until-they-become-parents.html.
36. Miller.
37. Luke Messac, "Outside the Economy: Women's Work and Feminist Economics in the Construction and Critique of National Income Accounting," *Journal of Imperial and Commonwealth History* 46, no. 3 (2018): 552–78, https://doi.org/10.1080/03086534.2018.1431436.
38. Silvia Federici, *Wages Against Housework* (Montpelier, Bristol, UK: Falling Wall Press, 1975).
39. Sarah Thébaud, Sabino Kornrich, and Leah Ruppanner, "Good Housekeeping, Great Expectations: Gender and Housework Norms," *Socio-*

logical Methods & Research 50, no. 3 (2019): 1186–1214, https://doi.org/10.1177/0049124119852395.

40. Cynthia Hess, Tanima Ahmed, and Jeff Hayes, "Providing Unpaid Household and Care Work in the United States: Uncovering Equality," Institute for Women's Policy Research, January 2020, https://iwpr.org/wp-content/uploads/2020/01/IWPR-Providing-Unpaid-Household-and-Care-Work-in-the-United-States-Uncovering-Inequality.pdf?linkId=88144355.
41. Matthew D. Johnson, Nancy L. Galambos, and Jared R. Anderson, "Skip the Dishes? Not So Fast! Sex and Housework Revisited," *Journal of Family Psychology* 30, no. 2 (2016): 203–13, https://doi.org/10.1037/fam0000161.
42. Claer Barrett, "Seven Things Women Need to Know About Money," *Financial Times*, March 4, 2022, https://www.ft.com/content/4bb7eb05-1bf4-4e17-841f-794d03c25178.

CHAPTER 8: MEN'S WORK

1. Daniel Kahneman and Amos Tversky, "Prospect Theory: An Analysis of Decision Under Risk," *Econometrica* 47, no. 2 (1979): 263, https://doi.org/10.2307/1914185.
2. William Samuelson and Richard Zeckhauser, "Status Quo Bias in Decision Making," *Journal of Risk and Uncertainty* 1, no. 1 (1988): 7–59, http://www.jstor.org/stable/41760530.
3. "Why Diverse Teams Are Smarter," *Harvard Business Review*, March 19, 2019, https://hbr.org/2016/11/why-diverse-teams-are-smarter.
4. Sundiatu Dixon-Fyle, Kevin Dolan, Dame Vivian Hunt, and Sara Prince, "Diversity Wins: How Inclusion Matters," McKinsey & Company, April 6, 2022, https://www.mckinsey.com/featured-insights/diversity-and-inclusion/diversity-wins-how-inclusion-matters.
5. "Can a White Man Face Workplace Discrimination for Socially Conservative Views?" Eisenberg & Baum LLP, September 13, 2018, https://www.eandblaw.com/employment-discrimination-blog/2018/09/13/workplace-discrimination-for-socially-conservative-views/.
6. Cath Everett, "Reverse Discrimination—the Other Side of the Coin for HR to Tackle," Diginomica, April 29, 2019, https://diginomica.com/reverse-discrimination-the-other-side-of-the-coin-for-hr-to-tackle.
7. Jillian Berman, "White Men Who Can't Get Jobs Say They're Being Discriminated Against," MarketWatch, April 2, 2019, https://www.marketwatch.com/story/that-google-engineer-isnt-alone-other-white-men-say-theyre-discriminated-against-2018–01–09.

8. "Raise Anatomy," Payscale, July 16, 2018, https://www.payscale.com/research-and-insights/how-to-ask-for-a-raise/.
9. Eli Landes, "Retention, Gender Gaps, and Pay Increases: New CareerArc/Harris Poll Survey," CareerArc, March 16, 2022, https://www.careerarc.com/blog/retention-harris-poll-careerarc-survey.
10. Kate A. Ratliff and Shigehiro Oishi, "Gender Differences in Implicit Self-Esteem Following a Romantic Partner's Success or Failure," *Journal of Personality and Social Psychology* 105, no. 4 (2013): 688–702, https://doi.org/10.1037/a0033769.
11. Allison J. Pugh, *The Tumbleweed Society: Working and Caring in an Age of Insecurity* (New York: Oxford University Press, 2018).
12. Stephanie Russell-Kraft, "The Danger of the Trumped-up Men's Rights Movement," *Ms.*, August 5, 2019, https://msmagazine.com/2019/08/05/the-danger-of-the-trumped-up-mens-rights-movement/.
13. Alexandra Killewald, "Money, Work, and Marital Stability," *American Sociological Review* 81, no. 4 (2016): 696–719, https://doi.org/10.1177/0003122416655340.
14. Rosie Taylor, "Number of Stay-at-Home Fathers Slumps to Its Lowest Level in Five Years," *Daily Mail*, October 19, 2018, https://www.dailymail.co.uk/news/article-6296939/Number-stay-home-fathers-slumps-lowest-level-five-years.html.
15. Briony Harris, "This Is the Only Country Where Fathers Spend More Time with Their Children," World Economic Forum, December 14, 2017, https://www.weforum.org/agenda/2017/12/finland-is-the-only-country-where-children-spend-more-time-with-their-fathers/.
16. Isabelle Roskam and Moïra Mikolajczak, "Gender Differences in the Nature, Antecedents and Consequences of Parental Burnout," *Sex Roles* 83, no. 7–8 (2020): 485–98, https://doi.org/10.1007/s11199-020-01121-5.
17. Claire Cain Miller, "Many Ways to Be a Girl, but One Way to Be a Boy: The New Gender Rules," *New York Times*, September 14, 2018, https://www.nytimes.com/2018/09/14/upshot/gender-stereotypes-survey-girls-boys.html.

CHAPTER 9: MAXIMUM IMPACT

1. Women in the Workplace 2021, McKinsey & Company, https://leanin.org/women-in-the-workplace/2021.
2. Women in the Workplace 2021.
3. Women in the Workplace 2022, McKinsey & Company, 2022, https://

leanin.org/women-in-the-workplace/2022/why-women-leaders-are-switching-jobs#!.

4. Kelly Shue, "Women Aren't Promoted Because Managers Underestimate Their Potential," Yale Insights, September 27, 2021, https://insights.som.yale.edu/insights/women-arent-promoted-because-managers-underestimate-their-potential.
5. Women in the Workplace 2022.
6. Women in the Workplace 2022, McKinsey & Company, 2022, https://www.mckinsey.com/featured-insights/diversity-and-inclusion/women-in-the-workplace.
7. Women in the Workplace 2022.
8. Women in the Workplace Study 2022, https://leanin.org/women-in-the-workplace.
9. Women in the Workplace 2022, "Flexibility and Remote and Hybrid Work," https://leanin.org/women-in-the-workplace/2022/flexibility-and-remote-and-hybrid-work.
10. Women in the Workplace 2022, "Why Women Leaders Are Switching Jobs," https://leanin.org/women-in-the-workplace/2022/why-women-leaders-are-switching-jobs.

INDEX